THE TOY & GAME INVENTOR'S GUIDE

Second Edition

Kent Press

• *Stamford, CT* •

THE TOY & GAME INVENTOR'S GUIDE
Second Edition

*by Gregory J. Battersby
and Charles W. Grimes*

Publisher's Cataloging in Publication
(Prepared by Quality Books Inc.)

Battersby, Gregory J.
The toy & game inventor's guide / by Gregory J. Battersby
and Charles W. Grimes -- 2nd ed.
p. cm.
Includes index.
ISBN No.: 1-888206-004 (hc)
ISBN No.: 1-888206-01-2 (pbk)

1. Inventions--United States--Handbooks, manuals, etc.
2. License agreements--United States. 3. Patents--United States.
4. Trademarks--United States. 5 Copyright--United States. 6.
Merchandise licensing--United States. I. Grimes, Charles W. II.
Title. III. Title: Toy and game inventor's guide.

T339.B38 1996   608-773
                                QBI95-20790

To Susan and Gwynne
without whose love, understanding
and support life would be meaningless.

About the Authors

Gregory J. Battersby holds an A.B. degree from Seton Hall University and a J.D. degree from Fordham University School of Law. He is a member of the New York and Connecticut Bars and is admitted to practice as a patent attorney before the United States Patent & Trademark Office.

Charles W. Grimes holds a B.S. degree from Pennsylvania State University and a J.D. degree from the University of Denver School of Law. He is a member of the Illinois, New York and Connecticut bars and is admitted to practice as a patent attorney before the United States Patent & Trademark Office.

Messrs. Battersby and Grimes are partners in the Stamford, Connecticut intellectual property law firm of Grimes & Battersby, 3 Landmark Square, Stamford, CT 06901 (203) 324-2828 which specializes in patents, trademarks, copyrights and licensing with a particular emphasis on the toy, game, animation and publishing industries. They have authored **The Law of Merchandise & Character Licensing, Licensing Law Handbook 1985, The Essential Guide to Merchandising Forms** and **Multimedia and Technology Licensing Law Forms Annotated.** They serve as Executive Editors of *The Licensing Journal* and *The IP Litigator* and as Editors in Chief of the *Multimedia and Technology Licensing Law Report.* They are frequent contributors to publications such as *Toy & Hobby World, The International Licensing Directory, The Trademark Reporter, The Intellectual Property Law Strategist* and other business and legal publications. They are recognized as the leading experts on the subject of merchandising law.

Mr. Battersby is the Treasurer of the New York Intellectual Property Law Association and for many years has been the editor of the *NYIPLA Bulletin*, **Greenbook** and **NYIPLA Intellectual Property Law Annual.** Mr. Grimes is an Adjunct Professor at Sacred Heart University where he teaches Intellectual Property Law and has served on the Editorial Board of *The Trademark Reporter.* They frequently lecture and author articles on a variety of intellectual property matters.

Preface

How many times have you said to yourself, "There really should be something that could do ......"? We're all inventors at heart, and anyone who has played with toys or watched his children play with toys or games is a potential toy or game inventor. (For simplicity, throughout the guide we will only refer to "toys" or "toy inventors" rather than "toys and games" or "toy and game inventors.")

The purpose of this guide is to take the toy inventor through the process of conceiving, researching, developing and eventually commercializing his idea or concept through a toy or game company. We have intentionally avoided any reference to the possibility of actually manufacturing and selling the toy. Instead, we have focused on the concept of selling or licensing the product to a major (or minor) toy company. The reason for this apparently glaring omission is simple — too few individuals have the background, experience, finances and/or desire to attempt to compete effectively with Hasbro or Mattel.

The road to putting a new toy product on the shelves at Toys 'R' Us is a long and arduous one. In the age of mega-toy companies with hundred million dollar advertising budgets, the chances of an individual attempting to compete with these large, multinational toy companies are slim. Accordingly, we have focused on commercialization through the existing toy companies.

We have similarly directed this guide toward the commercial aspects of the deal rather than the basics of toy conception and design. We chose to leave that very important topic to the individual programs, for example the Toy Design program at the Fashion Institute of Technology, which spend years in teaching students the intricacies of that very subject.

The reason for this direction is twofold. The majority of the toy company executives that we spoke to noted that there is no shortage of imaginative ideas for new products or of individuals who regularly generate these new ideas. The problem they see, is a lack of understanding on the part of these individuals about the actual mechanics of presenting and licensing new ideas to the toy companies, e.g., the commercial or business process. Based on that feedback, we conceived the idea for this guide and decided to concentrate on the business deal rather than attempt to give a course on toy design.

It has been our experience that there are certain "standards" in toy licensing that are consistent from company to company. While the words in the different agreements may change, and the personalities and people certainly do change, the underlying basis for the deal does not. In other words, a license is a license is a license.

Thus, we have attempted to take the toy inventor (both novice and professional) through the entire process of developing and licensing the next CABBAGE PATCH® doll. We have taken special care in the Appendix section to provide sample forms that toy inventors may require in practicing their trade. In addition, we have provided a directory in the Appendix that lists many of the toy (and game) companies that are currently seeking new toy ideas. The directory section not only identifies the company but provides a contact person and the type(s) of new products that company is seeking. This is intended to assist the inventor in identifying the companies to whom they should be presenting their new property or concept.

For those who would rather utilize an agent in the pursuit of their dream, we have provided a list of toy agents and brokers who would be in a position to assist inventors in commercializing their inventions. This is not, by any means, an exhaustive list of agents or brokers but instead, a list of those of whom we are aware. It should be noted that we neither endorse nor recommend any of the agents or brokers who are listed in this section. We can say, however, that we have had dealings with most of them and found them to be highly professional and quite competent. That does not mean, however, that the inventor should not independently investigate them prior to retaining their services.

The preface of any work would not be complete without expressing our appreciation for the contributions of certain special individuals who assisted us in the preparation of this guide. For starters, Charles Riotto was one of the motivating factors for this guide. Charles has worked in the toy industry for many years, formerly as Executive Director of Toy Manufacturers of

America ("TMA"). He conceived the idea of the directory listings in the Appendices which, without question, make the book a valuable reference tool for all toy and game inventors.

Similarly, Michelle Lostaglio and Catherine DeVito of our publisher, Kent Communications, were instrumental in working with us. Their contributions insured that the book not only looks good but, more importantly, reads well and is factually correct.

The forms section in the Appendices was the work product of David L. Sigalow of Grimes & Battersby. David spent many a weekend at the "office" finalizing the forms that are used in this book.

Last, but not least, are the contributions of the many professionals in the toy (and game) industry who provided invaluable information which went into the body of knowledge which is found in this guide. Included among this vast array of people are: David Berko of Tyco Toys; Chris Campbell of Tyco Toys; Dr. Richard Chase of Child Growth & Development Corp.; Larry Davis of TalkWorks (formerly of Fisher-Price Toys); Ben Kinberg of Benj. Kinberg & Associates; Dan Lauer of Lauer Toys; Steve Meyer of Meyer/Glass Design; Catherine Rondeau-Dobosz of Fun 'N Games; Mel Taft of Mel Taft & Associates; Judy Willis of Mattel; Peggy Moizel of Deloitte & Touche and a host of others whose names will, no doubt, come to us after the manuscript has been sent off for printing.

The response that we received from the inventor (and toy company) community to the original edition of this work was overwhelming. Both novice and experienced toy inventors approached us and said that they found the work invaluable. With that in mind, we set out to revise the work to bring it current. More substantivally, however, additional chapters on merchandising and international licensing have been added.

In addition, we have added new forms in the Appendix and updated the TMA statistics. Most importantly, the directory section has been updated and greatly expanded from the original edition.

We hope that readers find this Second Edition as helpful and informative as the original edition.

GJB and CWG

Table of Contents

Chapter One:
INTRODUCTION

Each February, the toy industry rolls out its new toy products at the American International Toy Fair held in New York City. Approximately twenty thousand potential retailers walk through the halls of the Toy Center Buildings at 200 Fifth Avenue and 1107 Broadway and the other toy company showrooms around New York City to view (and hopefully buy) literally thousands of new toy products. In recent years, the Toy Fair exhibits have spilled over to the Jacob K. Javits Convention Center. The Toy Fair features over 1500 exhibitors from over twenty-five countries and spans a period of eight days beginning the second Monday of February.

1.1 MEGA-HITS AND STAPLE TOY PRODUCTS

Some of the new products on display at Toy Fair are destined to become wildly successful mega-hits for a host of different reasons. Many, such as the MIGHTY MORPHIN POWER RANGER® action figures, MICKEY MOUSE® crib gym, and NASCAR® toy vehicles, attribute their fame and fortune to the famous licenses that they bear. Others, such as Playmates' WATERBABIES® doll or Parker Brothers NERF® products, are destined to succeed on the strength of their designs. Some of these new products may eventually become classics and rival such products as the BARBIE® doll or the MONOPOLY® board game. The profits from these mega-hits are so great that the inventors may never have to work again, although most do and build on their success.

These mega-hits are by far the exception. For each product that sells more than a million units a year, there are literally hundreds of other products that, with little or no fanfare, become staple, solid performers. Toy companies will sell hundreds of thousands of pieces of these staple products each and every year, resulting in hundreds of thousands of dollars of royalties for their inventors. There are many, many inventors that make a very respectable living from the royalty checks they receive based on the sale of these staple products. While some of these staple products may become household names due to promotions run by their manufacturers, the majority thrive in relative obscurity (except, of course, to the manufacturers and inventors). Each year that they remain in the toy company's line is another year of royalty income for the inventor.

1.2 ODDS ARE LONG IN LICENSING A NEW PRODUCT

This is not to imply that every new toy idea will eventually become a new product or, for that matter, that every new product introduced at Toy Fair will succeed. In fact, the chances of actually placing a new toy product with a toy company in any one year are very slim and the competition is enormous.

Each year, the toy companies review hundreds of thousands of new product ideas from which they select their new products for the following year. Some of the major toy companies even plan further ahead than that. If you were to present your new product idea to one of the major companies after June of a particular year, it would probably not be included in that company's next Toy Fair line but, instead, would only be considered for the following year's Toy Fair. That means that you would not actually see your product on the market for at least eighteen months and would not begin to receive meaningful royalty checks for almost three years.

Furthermore, the introduction of a new toy product at Toy Fair is no guarantee that the product will ever be sold. A significant number of new toy products introduced at Toy Fair every February never generate any appreciable sales. Remember, the purpose of Toy Fair is to show the retailers the new products for Christmas, i.e., offer them for sale. If the buyers find the product unattractive (or too expensive, or potentially dangerous, etc.), they will not place any orders and the product will die a quick, albeit commercially understandable, natural death.

Because of these numbers, rejection is the name of the game in the toy industry. As an inventor, you must develop a thick skin and be able to readily accept rejection. It is the rare new product idea that is licensed to the first company that sees it.

You should take some solace from the fact that virtually every major toy company rejected the CABBAGE PATCH® doll before Coleco decided to take a chance with the idea.

1.3 SO YOU STILL WANT TO BE A TOY INVENTOR?

You have heard all of the bad things about the toy industry. You know that the odds are stacked against you. You are aware that there is substantial competition from professional inventors. You recognize that the royalty stream may be years away. You know that you will be facing one rejection after another. So, why would you still want to devote the time, effort and resources to pursing a career as an inventor?

Because it is fun. Because you have the potential to make a lot of money. Because the work is gratifying. And because there is nothing more exhilarating than seeing your new product idea translated into a new toy product on the shelf of Toys 'R' Us. Second to that thrill, however, is opening the envelope from the company you've licensed which contains your first royalty check after a highly successful Christmas selling season.

Everyone is an inventor or tinkerer at heart. How many times have you had a good idea, only to forget about it as other more pressing and more seemingly important issues absorb your time? Of course, you're reminded about that earlier brainstorm when you see a product based on your idea on the shelves of your local toy store or in a television advertisement.

1.4 THE DREAMER VS. THE PROFESSIONAL

What separates the successful toy inventor from the dreamer is the ability to translate the "good idea" into a tangible product and then sell or license that product to the right toy company. The successful inventor not only possesses the imaginative genius to conceive the successful product, but also knows how to capitalize on the invention. The professional toy inventor knows exactly what steps are necessary to translate a new idea into a commercial product that can be eventually licensed to a toy company and actually generate royalty income.

Professional inventors know which companies might be interested in their products and who to contact at those companies. They understand the basics of intellectual property law and know what steps they must take in order to protect their valuable ideas. They recognize the importance of a concise and timely presentation and are prepared to respond to the types of questions they may be asked during the presentation. They know the basics of the business deals and know what they can reasonably expect to receive by way of compensation for their property. In short, they know the basics of their trade.

Doug Thompson, former Executive Director of Toy Manufacturers of America ("TMA"), said at a product development seminar held at Toy Fair a few years ago that, based on his many years with TMA and in the toy industry, he reached two conclusions with respect to the development of new toy products. He said "First, there are probably more toy inventors than there are toy customers. Second, I find that these hugely imaginative people with products quite often lack considerable imagination on how to get the product into the marketplace." He found that quite often these same inventors were quite naive on the commercial aspects of the business and did not have reasonable expectations on what to expect from the toy companies with whom they were dealing.

Mr. Thompson noted that the toy companies do not help the process. He observed that while the toy industry "thrives on new ideas and desperately needs new ideas," it "generally makes it ... quite difficult for people to present those new ideas and to get those new ideas shown." The purpose of this guide is to provide you, the toy inventor, with enough information to be able to sell or license your idea to a toy company.

1.5 A WORD OF ADVICE

Chris Campbell of Tyco Toys offered the following advice to the non-professional toy inventor: "To the non-pro, the one piece of advice I would offer is simply that the odds of placing your product with a major company are infinitesimally small. You should invent for the pleasure of inventing and the pleasure of creating, but not with a full expectation of making a profit or placing the product." These are sound words of advice. You should keep them firmly in mind to avoid developing unrealistic expectations. If you don't, you will approach the entire process of licensing unrealistically. Nothing scares toy companies more than an unrealistic inventor. Toy companies have dealt with (and have been "put through the mill" by) such unrealistic inventors enough to know they are nothing but trouble. If a toy company executive senses that there is any chance you are likely to fall into this category, he will immediately send you packing.

It is a rather amazing fact of corporate life that the toy company contact person (or "gatekeeper") you spoke to will not get into trouble for turning you down, even if your idea later becomes a mega-hit with another company. Why? First, because he won't let anyone in upper management know he did it. And second, if it does come to light that he turned you down, he's the one who will explain (and embellish to cover himself) how problematic you and your demands were.

On the other hand, the toy company gatekeeper who lets a problematic inventor in will surely find himself very quickly called on the carpet to account for the decision (and could well lose his job because of it). Bottomline — don't be unrealistic. It will make the time leading up to your success more bitter. You won't enjoy the small successes you do score. And you could destroy your chances of ever "hitting the big time."

Chapter Two:

THE TOY AND GAME INDUSTRY

2.1 THE "BIG FIVE" TOY MANUFACTURERS

Twenty years ago, the toy inventor had the world by the tail. The toy industry was composed of literally thousands of small and medium size manufacturers, all of whom were seeking ideas for new products. There were more outlets and potential markets for new toy ideas than there were ideas available. If one company wasn't interested in a new idea, there were dozens of others that might have an interest.

Times have changed. In fact, times are changing almost daily. As of the writing of this guide, there are five major toy companies. The "Big Five" is comprised of Hasbro, Mattel Toys, Tyco Toys, Lego Group and Little Tikes (a unit of Rubbermaid, Inc.). In 1994, product sales by these five companies comprised over 60 percent of the total market. Behind these Big Five companies stands a score of smaller, but nowhere near as powerful, toy manufacturers. These "second-tier" toy companies include Playmates (the marketers of the TEENAGE MUTANT NINJA TURTLES® action figures and WATERBABIES® dolls), which is followed by literally thousands of smaller entities. On the rise is Toy Biz, which is part of Ronald Perelman's Marvel Entertainment Group, Inc.

Total toy industry retail sales in 1994, according to the TMA, were an estimated $18.7 billion, up from $17.5 billion in 1993. Manufacturers' shipments were $12.63 billion in 1994 compared with $11.78 billion in 1993. The largest gains in toy sales in 1994 occurred in the male action figure, ride-on and vehicle toy areas. Complete TMA statistics are contained in the Appendices. These statistics do not include the video game market, which the authors view as a separate and distinct market. TMA has estimated that video game shipments in 1994 were $3.76 billion, which was an overall loss of 1.97 percent from the 1993 shipment totals of $3.83 billion. Retail sales of such products were estimated to be about $5 billion in 1994. Video games are sold by such companies as Nintendo, Sega and Atari, through the same channels of trade as the Big Five toy companies. In fact, Sega has begun to broaden its base outside of video games and launched a more conventional toy line at the 1994 Toy Fair.

The makeup of the Big Five has been changing dramatically over the past couple of years, as Hasbro and Mattel seem to take turns being number one in the toy industry. In late 1993, Mattel (the people who brought you the BARBIE® doll and HOT WHEELS® cars) bought Fisher-Price for $1.2 billion, quickly followed by their acquisition of Kransco (of HULA HOOPS® and FRISBEE® fame) and J.W. Spear & Sons (holder of the non-United States rights to the SCRABBLE® board game).

Hasbro was not to be outdone, buying the games division of Western Publishing for $100 million. This acquisition added the games PICTIONARY®, GIRL TALK® and OUTBURST® to Hasbro's already solid board game line, which included such games as MONOPOLY® and TRIVIAL PURSUIT®. With the Western acquisition, Hasbro clearly dominates the board game market.

The reason behind this elaborate game of Monopoly by the major toy companies is simple. According to a *Wall Street Journal* article entitled "Playing Monopoly: The Toy Industry, Too, Is Merging Like Crazy to Win Selling Power":

> Masters of the toy universe today are as pinstriped, acquisition-hungry and likely to have M.B.A. degrees as anyone else in corporate America. Bigness now seems to be well-nigh essential to success. TV tie-in shows and license deals drive the business. Just ask the Mighty Morphin Power Rangers. Clout with retailing giants like Toys 'R' Us is essential to getting shelf space. Television costs money. Getting noticed is easier if you have a slew of popular products. The fastest way to get a slew is to buy one.

"You need multimillion-dollar marketing artillery today," says Al Kahn, chairman and chief executive of Leisure Concepts, Inc., "which is one reason for the consolidation trend in the industry." (*Wall Street Journal*, October 28, 1994, 1:1)

2.2 THE TOY AND GAME RETAIL MARKET

The retail picture for toys is not much different, particularly after the bankruptcy of Child World in the early 1990's. Twenty years ago, there were literally hundreds of places where the consumer could go to buy toys. That was, of course, before Toys 'R' Us came on the scene and proved too formidable for many small toy stores. Its aggressive pricing and even more aggressive marketing and merchandising drove many small toy stores out of business. As of the writing of this guide, the "Big Five" toy retailers are: Toys 'R' Us, Wal-Mart, Kmart, Target Stores (a unit of Dayton Hudson Corp.) and Kay-Bee Toy Stores (a division of Melville Corp.). These Big Five retailers now sell approximately 60 percent of all toys sold in the United States. Of the Big Five, however, Toys 'R' Us has a market share of 20.7 percent, almost twice the share of Wal-Mart, which is its closest competitor.

Behind the Big Five retailers, the next five — J.C. Penney, Service Merchandise, Sears, Caldor and Hills — remarkably only sell about 8 percent of the total toys sold in the U.S. Thus, more than half of the toy and game products sold each year are produced by five major toy companies and sold in five retail outlets. The market has clearly shrunk over the past decade.

2.3 THE TOY INVENTOR AND THE SHRINKING MARKET

What does this shrinking market mean to the toy inventor? As stated above, the number of potential markets for a new product idea is substantially reduced from prior years. That can be both good and bad for the inventor. Unquestionably, the consolidation of toy companies affords inventors with the advantage of one-stop shopping when attempting to license their ideas. Instead of having to present product to twenty different toy companies around the country, the inventor need only present to one or two individuals at the major toy companies. Similarly, the inventor becomes the beneficiary of the increased marketing resources that a consolidated toy company can offer. As the marketing effort is increased, so are the sales volume and the attendant royalty to the inventor.

While consolidation does offer the aforementioned advantages to the toy inventor, it also offers a number of disadvantages. Consolidation dramatically decreases the marketing power or leverage of the inventor with the toy companies. Gone are the days when the inventor can become the beneficiary of a "bidding war" between rival and competing toy companies. The major toy companies know that there are fewer and fewer options for inventors and, as such, they are able to take a much harder position with inventors during negotiation, feeling relatively confident that the inventor will not be able to take the concept across the street to its competitor.

Consolidation also serves to protect the toy company from litigation by the inventor community. While it is never a good idea to sue one's customer, it is even a worse idea when there are only five potential customers. Attempting to enforce one's rights against 20 percent of the possible customer base can be quick death in the industry for an inventor, even one who truly believes that his rights have been trampled on.

2.4 FINDING THE RIGHT TOY COMPANY

Perhaps the most common mistake made by inexperienced toy inventors is attempting to sell or license their products to the wrong companies. More time is wasted by both the inventor and the company simply because the toy inventor did not do his homework and target the right company for the concept.

The successful inventors are able to quickly identify the particular companies that carry the type of product that they conceive. This is not meant to imply that companies do not expand their product lines and add categories of products that they had not previously carried. That is certainly true and frequently happens. An inventor's chances of capitalizing on that possibility, however, are remote.

As an inventor, your time is better spent concentrating on those companies that have marketed products in the product category of your idea. Thus, if you have developed an idea for a board game, the "target" licensees should be companies that have marketed games in the past. Taking a board game idea to a plush toy company is probably a waste of time for everyone involved. Similarly, if you have conceived an idea for an electronic talking doll, your target market should be companies that have previously marketed dolls.

How do you identify your target market? The directory section provided in the Appendices of this guide is a good start. It specifically identifies the companies that are actively seeking new products, provides the contact individual at each company and states the types of product ideas that they are interested in reviewing.

Another excellent reference tool is the Official Directory published annually by the Toy Manufacturers of America for each New York Toy Fair. The Directory identifies each of the exhibitors at Toy Fair and provides contact names and addresses. More importantly, however, it includes an index that lists all of the exhibitors by product category. For example, under categories such as "mechanical toys" and "dolls-talking," it lists all exhibitors who market products that fall within these categories.

A field trip to the local toy store will also produce valuable information. Walking down the board game aisle of Toys 'R' Us will permit you to quickly identify all of the major (and most of the minor) manufacturers of board games, both domestically and internationally.

Chapter Three:

DEVELOPING NEW TOYS AND GAMES

It would be presumptive of us to believe that any book can teach an individual to invent the next GIRL TALK® boardgame or WATERBABIES® doll. The vision required to create something so marvelously imaginative is not something that could ever be learned from a book on how to invent. Individuals are born creative or inventive. The ability to create or invent new products is a talent which is unique to some and foreign to many others. Most people, when looking at a situation, are able to recognize that a problem exists. The inventor or designer, however, looks at that same situation, recognizes the problem and immediately begins to think of a solution. The inventor will explore alternatives, explore "what-ifs" and before long, a new mousetrap is created. For the serious inventor, courses are offered on the topic. In fact, Fashion Institute of Technology (F.I.T.) in New York City offers a degree program in toy design. Other colleges and universities such as the Rhode Island School of Design in Providence, Rhode Island offer courses on the subject. Seminars and workshops are also offered at the New York Toy Fair each year. The inventor or would-be inventor should consider attending some of these programs to help refine creativity and inventiveness skills.

While creativity or inventiveness is a state of mind, there are certain steps that you as an inventor can take to channel your talent toward the development of new products. There are certain elements that the truly creative individual should bear in mind when embarking on a career (or serious hobby) in the toy and game design field. These elements will help you focus on the task at hand and not make the mistake of reinventing the SIMON® game. More importantly, these guidelines will assist you in creating a new product that is potentially marketable and is not destined to gather dust on your basement shelf.

3.1 RESEARCHING THE MARKET

Perhaps the most common complaint voiced by most toy company gatekeepers is that the inventor did not understand the industry. The inventor attempted to sell or license them something that the company already had in their line (or would never put in their line). Unfortunately, many would-be inventors have never been inside a toy store. Some haven't spoken with a child for years. As a toy inventor, you have to understand the industry if you want to be a player. Walk down the aisles of your local toy store. Watch what sells and what doesn't. Talk to the individuals you meet at toy stores who are buying product. Ask them why they want to buy that product and not another. Review the J.C. Penney Christmas catalog. Attend the New York Toy Fair and walk through as many showrooms as you can. Obtain copies of the catalogs of the toy companies. Understanding where the market is will help you project where it is going.

Read such industry trade publications as *Playthings* and the *Toy Book*. Try to understand licensing and its important relationship with the toy industry. Read the publications published by the Toy Manufacturers of America. Speak with as many individuals as you can who work in or are associated with the industry.

Cathy Rondeau-Dobosz, President of Fun'n Games and the inventor of the GIRL TALK and READ MY LIPS games, told the attendees at *The Licensing Journal's* 1995 toy development seminar that when she first started in the business, one of the hardest things she had to do was differentiate between the toy and gift categories. She found herself getting shunted back and forth between toy and gift companies. She counseled first time toy inventors to make regular trips to the toy stores, examining manufacturers, price points and marketing strategies of products that are already on the shelves.

Rondeau-Dobosz also recommended that first time inventors look to get connected within the industry, regardless of how much it costs. She said that the novice should, "get an agent, or if you don't want to use an agent, hire a consultant. It doesn't matter if they charge you $300/hour. It is invaluable."

Steve Meyer, president of Meyer/Glass Design offered similar advice at that same seminar. He recommended that the novice toy inventor walk through the toy stores. He indicated that this is the best way to understand the marketing strategy of a particular toy company and what it might be looking for in the future. He stressed relationships, saying that it was "amazing to him how important relationships are in this business."

3.2 REPACKAGING THE WHEEL

In the late 1800's, there was talk about closing the United States Patent and Trademark Office because some people felt that everything that could be invented had already been invented. Of course, if that had happened, we would not have seen such pioneer patents as the ones for the Model-T Ford automobile, the jet engine or the television set.

The same observation, however, may be made with respect to the toy industry. While there are some remarkably innovative inventions in the electronic game and video game markets in particular, the vast majority of toy products that you see on the market today have already been marketed in one form or another. Taking an old idea or concept and giving it a new wrinkle or package can be as important an invention as the radically new electronic speaking doll. In the days when the toy companies state that they are going back to basics, a new spin on an old idea or concept can become a very successful product.

3.3 IDENTIFYING A MARKETING NICHE

Toy companies look for marketing niches. They have targeted particular categories or market segments as areas in which they want to develop new products. As a toy inventor, you should understand what these categories or market niches are and attempt to focus your efforts in those areas. How do you find these marketing niches? Walk down the aisles of any local toy store and look for holes in a product line. When you identify these holes, work on developing product ideas that fill these gaps.

3.4 REPEAT PLAY VALUE IS CRITICAL

Developing an idea for a new product that the kids love once, enjoy the second time and are bored with the third time does not a successful product make. The name of the game for new product development is repeat play value. Children (or adults) should have as much fun playing with the toy the twentieth time as they had the very first time. This is a critical factor, and one that is often overlooked.

How do you determine whether a new product idea has repeat play value? It is simple. Make a prototype and give it to a few friends. Leave it with them for a couple of months and then call them and ask how they liked it. Ask them whether they or their children are still playing with it. If the answer is an honest yes, you have probably succeeded. If they're truthful and tell you it was neat the first time, but no one has gone back to it since, you have your answer.

3.5 DON'T FALL IN LOVE WITH YOUR IDEA

Every professional inventor offers this advice, "Don't marry your ideas." In order to be successful with a new product idea, you must remain objective. It is when an inventor starts falling in love with his idea that problems develop. You should work on creating idea after idea. Build up an inventory. The inventory will be important when making presentations to toy companies, because it will give you more than one item to present and hopefully sell or license. More importantly, however, it will assist you in making the difficult transition from someone who is obsessed with placing an idea with a toy company (and someone who will continue to badger the company night and day after they license it) to a professional inventor who works cooperatively and responsibly with the toy company and, as a result, realizes a desirable royalty stream.

3.6 GOLDEN GUIDELINES FOR SUCCESSFUL NEW PRODUCTS

At a product development seminar held in conjunction with Toy Fair a few years ago, Larry Davis, President of TalkWorks and formerly a Fisher-Price research and development director, outlined David B. Fisher's "Golden Guidelines" for successful new toy products:

- The product must be highly differentiated from existing products and must contain unique features.
- The product must communicate instantly to the consumer, who should be able to look at it and instantly know what it is.
- The product must contain important demonstrable features.
- Elements of the new product must be able to make an impact and be newsworthy.
- The product must be able to generate incremental sales for the toy company, independent of existing product sales.
- It must possess significant volume potential with the ability to sell hundreds of thousands of pieces every year.
- The product must provide both price and play value to the consumer.
- It should not be a one-shot item, but, rather, should have the ability to be extendible into a product line or product extensions.
- The product must be compatible with the image of the company.

These "golden guidelines" are quite helpful. If your new product idea achieves most of these guidelines, you probably have a potentially successful idea. If it achieves all of the guidelines, you might consider learning to play golf or sail a 60 foot ketch, since that is very likely what the future bodes for you as you begin collecting royalties.

3.7 TOY RESEARCH: MAKE IT WORK FOR YOU
by D. Lawrence Davis, President, The TalkWorks Company

You like your product idea. Your family likes it, and so does your neighbor, but will consumers like it and buy it? Research and find out. Why do research? Your motivations as an inventor probably range from the high ideals of an artist wanting to create the best toy, to the simple motivation of making money. Research is a tool to help you with your creativity and to stay in tune with the business world. Three of the most important advantages research provides are:

- Better product design — Features, size, shape, and function can all be refined based on feedback from consumers.
- Consumer satisfaction — Knowledge of what needs your consumer has and how to satisfy those needs helps create demand.
- Informed Decisions — Help avoid mistakes that can be costly in time, resources, and money.

As the inventor, your customer is actually the manufacturer who will decide if your concept or idea has market potential. Research can make a positive difference, not only in presenting a better product concept, but also in reinforcing your own marketing position as a professional inventor. In reality, these same reasons and benefits of doing research apply to the manufacturers. Their challenge is selling a product to the stores and then ultimately to consumers. Therefore by doing research, you benefit both yourself and the manufacturer.

Where do you start? One of the most efficient ways to start is to define your objectives by asking yourself a series of three simple questions:

What information do you already know? This may seem like an unimportant task, but is really very beneficial to focus your efforts on new productive questions. Avoid asking questions that consume a great deal of research time without telling you anything new. Be sure to communicate this existing information to the person conducting the research.

What information do you want to confirm? From the information you already know, decide what points need to be objectively confirmed. Be as specific as possible and allocate an appropriate but smaller amount of research time to questions that are simply verifications.

What new information do you want to find out? This is the area where you need to invest the most planning time. One suggestion is to make an outline or list of areas of useful information such as:

- key features as perceived by the consumer
- worst feature?
- age/sex appropriateness
- how would the product be used?

- where is it used?
- how does it compare with competition?
- reaction to colors?
- reactions to size?
- what's fun?
- what is unique about the product?

Move beyond "nice to know" information and concentrate on getting the responses on which you can base a decision or action. After making your outline/list, you should assign a priority of importance. An input session with your researcher will help you clarify your needs and will help design the research. This will make the most efficient use of the available time with respondents.

What is the right type of research? Once you've determined what your objectives are and given them some prioritization, you have basically three options, each with its own specific strengths and limitations:

- **Observation of Play** — This can be done through play groups, day care centers, or schools (providing that arrangements and the proper supervision of children and prototypes are agreed upon in advance.) This type of research will show you what level of interest your target end-user has in a type of play or in your specific product. It may also highlight product features that may need redesigning or emphasis. Videotaping is very helpful for comparison and analysis. Brief edited video clips may reinforce your findings for presentation to a manufacturer. It is important to remember that you need to have a model that is safe and durable enough for testing. Dialog and discussion is difficult because it interrupts natural play patterns.
- **Qualitative Interviews and Focus Groups** — These are especially helpful in identifying and exploring new areas of opportunity and the needs of consumers. This is a very effective method in the early stages when changes are easier and less costly to make. This in-depth discussion approach to research will provide general directions, but not a specific road map on your way to success. Keep in mind however, that the respondents (kids and adults alike) are not designers and will respond most strongly and effectively to visual examples. The old say-

ing applies, "a picture is worth a thousand words ... and a prototype is worth even more!" Be careful, however. There is a temptation to use feedback from a relatively small number of people as the basis for numerical projections.

• **Quantitative Questionnaires and Mall Intercept Studies** — Quantitative research methods are often used when a concept or product is very well defined. The need for statistically reliable information exists for pricing, preference, intent to buy, comparison with specific benchmarks or competitive items, etc. "Statistically reliable" means that you conduct research with a large enough sample, e.g., 100 people, so that you are confident that the answers you get from the first group will be the same as those given by another group of the same size. However, a written questionnaire does not have the flexibility to probe for additional information. The sequence and format of the questions must be carefully designed to avoid biasing responses.

Of course the best and most thorough way is to do a combination of all three types of research. Time and money may prevent this so you must evaluate your own particular needs. Observation of Play and Focus Research methods are both qualitative in nature. Qualitative research is especially useful in understanding people's motives, perceptions, reactions, reasoning, and actual use. However, it is important to remember that qualitative research should not be used as the basis for statistical/numerical projections. It is also important to remember that when using any type of research, the best decisions come from applying good business judgment to the results.

How long does research take? Often research takes longer to do than you might anticipate, so plan accordingly. There is a direct relationship between quality planning and quality results. Observation of Play research has the shortest turn around time, so plan on a few weeks. Remember, making arrangements and editing extraneous footage from your video takes time. Focus groups take longer to design, recruit, moderate, and analyze, but generally can be done in about four weeks. Quantitative studies take about six to eight weeks because of the design of the questionnaire, recruiting of a larger sample, tabulation of results, and analysis of data. Time is money so any of these lead times can be shortened, but that will increase the cost of the research.

What consumer do you talk to? As a starting point, you need to determine who your "target consumer" is. You do this by making some calculated assumptions as to who uses the product most and who makes the decision about purchasing it. Once that is determined, you develop "screening criteria" specifying the requirements your respondents should have. Criteria you may want to consider are:

- age
- income of family
- sex
- employment
- marital status
- ownership of similar products
- number of siblings

What materials are needed for research? Both children and adults respond better to visual examples. This applies even to exploratory research where you may be trying to identify areas of opportunity. Also, it is important to remember that people (young and old) respond to exactly what they see in front of them. Drawings and models need to be of professional quality. Rough prototypes of mechanisms, often referred to as "bread boards," are acceptable to demonstrate a function or action. The finished concept in drawing or model form must accompany these rough mechanisms. The use of videotaped descriptions and demonstrations are helpful in making sure all respondents see the same concept in a consistent way.

Who does the research? Experience and integrity are key factors in selecting who and how to do the research. Experience influences the design of the research, the conducting of the research itself, the analysis of the results, and the recommendations. Integrity assures you that your ideas and research findings remain yours and confidential. Unless you are experienced in toy research, you are better off getting some experienced professional help. It will pay off in the long run with better product and better decisions. Your potential customer (the manufacturer) may put you in contact with reliable sources of research for product development and marketing. Plus, TMA may have suggestions to help you.

In summary, research is important to improve your product design, satisfy consumers' needs, and make informed decisions. Choosing the right type of research increases your chances of designing a better product that catches the interest of a manufacturer, and results in both financial and artistic rewards for you the designer.

D. Lawrence Davis is President of The TalkWorks Company, a qualitative research and marketing company that builds on Larry's twenty years of experience in research, marketing, and product development with the FMC Corporation and Fisher-Price. The TalkWorks Company's client list includes Fisher-Price, Time-Life Books, Turner Home Entertainment, Hanna-Barbera, Paramount Pictures Licensing, Early Development Inc., and other children's products companies.

Chapter Four:

PROTECTING THE NEW TOY IDEA

While most industry professionals agree that new product ideas must be protected against unauthorized use, there is a great deal of disagreement over the best (and most practical) way to protect these ideas. The divergence of opinion is caused, in large measure, to the nature of the ideas and the inherent limitations of the applicable intellectual property laws, which were not drafted to protect ideas, only tangible expressions of ideas.

As a result, most inventors rely on a patchwork theory of protection to protect individual elements of their new product ideas. This patchwork theory is, however, highly dependent upon the types of ideas involved and the resources of the inventor. For example, if the cost of protection was not an issue, intellectual property attorneys could easily weave a plan of patent, trademark, copyright and trade secret protection that would protect virtually all elements of the idea. Unfortunately, that is not realistic for most inventors and, as such, cost considerations come into play.

4.1 A PATENT IS NOT A TRADEMARK IS NOT A COPYRIGHT

To say that there is some confusion among the general public between the various forms of intellectual property protection is an understatement. That confusion isn't limited to layman. There are many general business attorneys who have difficulty differentiating between patents, trademarks and copyrights. Intellectual property attorneys are frequently asked to "patent" a new product brand name. The proper request would be to "trademark" a brand name. Patent protection is available only to protect novel and utilitarian articles, processes and the like.

There are three statutory forms of intellectual property protection — patents, trademarks and copyrights. The U.S. Constitution specifically provides for patent and copyright protection, while trademark rights are based on the interstate commerce clause of the Constitution.

Set forth below is a discussion of intellectual property protection and an explanation of how it can be applied to new toy product ideas.

4.1.1 Patents

Patent protection is obtained from the United States Patent & Trademark Office in Washington, DC. In order to obtain any type of patent, an invention must be novel and unobvious over what has been invented before. There are three forms of patents: utility patents, design patents and plant patents. For obvious reasons, we will only discuss the first two.

Design patents are granted for any new, original and ornamental design for an article of manufacture. Design patents cover the aesthetic appearance of an invention. Toy inventors and toy companies have been obtaining design patents for many years covering, among other things, the aesthetic appearance of the GI JOE® action figures or the BARBIE® doll. The term of a design patent is fourteen years.

Utility patents have a term of seventeen years in the United States and cover the functional features of an invention. Utility patents are granted for any new and useful process, machine, manufacture or composition of matter or for any new and useful improvement thereof. In the toy industry, utility patents are regularly granted for functional and utilitarian features of toys; for instance, the eject mechanism in a Jack in the Box, the spinner portion of a play gym or the trigger mechanism in a water gun. In addition, a number of utility patents have been obtained on the "play" of board games. Examples of utility patents that have issued on toy products are contained in the Appendices.

The grant of a U.S. patent confers upon the inventor the exclusive right to make, use and sell his invention throughout the United States during the term of the patent. As this is an exclusive grant, any other person who makes, uses or sells any patent invention within the United States during the term of the patent is an infringer of the patent, as is anyone who actively induces infringement of the patent.

The grant of a patent gives the inventor not only the right to exclude those who may have actually copied the patented invention, but also those who, with no knowledge whatsoever of the patent, may have independently created the same invention after the original inventor had conceived his invention.

The process of obtaining a patent is, in theory, relatively simple. The inventor, normally through his patent attorney or agent, prepares a patent application which is filed with the U.S. Patent & Trademark Office, together with the requisite statutory filing fee. The filing fee for small entities (individuals and corporations with less than 500 employees) is 50 percent of the fee charged to large entities.

The utility patent application consists of a specification, a set of claims and, if necessary, drawings of the invention. In extremely rare cases, the U.S. Patent & Trademark Office may require the submission of a working model of the invention. The applicant must sign an oath or declaration stating he is the original and first inventor of the invention. There is a duty of disclosure on the part of the inventor to advise the U.S. Patent & Trademark Office of the most relevant prior art of which he is aware.

A design patent application consists of a specification and a set of drawings. The claims of a design patent application are simply claims of protection to the ornamental design as illustrated in the drawings.

Upon filing with the U.S. Patent & Trademark Office, an Examiner is assigned to the application to examine it for form and novelty. The Examiner will conduct a search of U.S. Patent & Trademark Office records to determine the novelty of the invention. The initial examination process typically takes between four and twelve months. At this time, the Examiner will issue an Office Action that either allows or rejects the application. If the Examiner rejects the application, the Office Action will give the reasons for the rejection and list any prior patents found by the Examiner in the course of the search.

The inventor then has an opportunity to file a response with the Examiner and amend the application in response to the Office Action. Typically, such an amendment must be filed within six months from the issuance of the Office Action, although a fee will be charged if filed more than three months after the issuance of the Office Action.

After the filing of this response or amendment, the Examiner will again examine the amended application and eventually issue a second Office Action which, again, will either allow or reject the application. Typically, if the second Office Action is a rejection, it will be made "final" which limits the applicant's options. Upon the issuance of this final rejection, the applicant must either place the case in condition for allowance upon the filing of a second response, abandon the application, take an appeal to the U.S. Patent & Trademark Office Board of Appeals or re-file the application as a continuation application.

Assuming that the application is allowed, the U.S. Patent & Trademark Office requires the payment of an issue fee and, upon payment of that fee, a formal patent will be issued. The inventor must anticipate that the entire process, from start to finish, will take between one and three years at a cost of between $3,000 and $10,000 depending upon the complexity of the invention and the difficulty experienced in prosecution.

Patent protection is governed exclusively by the scope of the claims of the issued patent. If the claim does not cover an allegedly infringing device, a court will not enforce the patent against the product. Similarly, patent protection is only effective upon the issuance of a patent and only in the country in which the patent has issued. Accordingly, no protection is obtained during the "patent pending" period. A United States patent will not prevent a company in the U.K. from manufacturing and selling a product in a country outside the United States; which would otherwise be an infringement if sold in the United States.

4.1.2 Trademarks

A trademark is "... any word, name, symbol or device, or any combination thereof used ... to identify and distinguish one's goods, including a unique product, from those manufactured or sold by others and to indicate the source of the goods, even if that source is unknown."

Most people understand that brand names such as HASBRO and MATTEL are trademarks for a line of toys. Similarly, product names such as GI JOE® or BARBIE® are also trademarks of their respective owners to identify a particular product or line of products. What may be more difficult to appreciate, however, is that slogans such as "Where's the Beef?" and product configurations, such as book style package designs, can also qualify as trademarks.

Service marks are little more than trademarks that are used in association with services rather than products. For example, when the mark MCDONALD's appears on the outside of the MCDONALD's chain of restaurants, it is functioning as a service mark identifying the restaurant services being provided. When, however, it appears on a line of toy trucks or on hamburger packages, it is being used as a trademark.

Trademark rights in the United States are based on use of the mark, not registration. Accordingly, common law rights accrue from the date the mark is first used to identify the goods or services and not upon registration with the U.S. Patent & Trademark Office or with a state trademark office. However, the U.S. Trademark Law was amended several years ago to permit the filing of "intent to use" applications. Intent to use applications accord applicants protective rights as of the filing date of their applications, the equivalent of a "constructive use" date — so long as the applicants do in fact commence use and thereby obtain a registration. The owner of an unregistered trademark has the right to sue third parties who may adopt and use marks that are confusingly similar to the mark in question.

Unlike patents, which only protect the underlying invention for a finite period of time, trademark protection exists as long as the owner of the mark continues to use that mark. Thus, trademark protection can exist for literally hundreds of years.

While registration of a trademark or service mark is not a prerequisite to establishing trademark protection for a mark, registration does offer the trademark owner substantial procedural advantages when suing an infringer. Accordingly, registration of a trademark is strongly advised.

A trademark may be federally registered with the U.S. Patent & Trademark Office by the filing of an application to register the mark and paying the statutory filing fee. The typical cost (including attorney's fees and government filing fees) of obtaining a federal trademark registration for one class is approximately $1,000. The mark may be registered in additional classes for approximately $400/class. The application may be based on actual use of the mark in interstate commerce or on a bona fide intention to use the mark. If based on such an intent to use, actual use must be effected before registration of the mark will be permitted.

The U.S. Patent & Trademark Office, like most trademark offices around the world, has classified all of the potential goods and services into a series of classes. The trademark application must designate the class or classes for which registration is sought. Separate fees must be paid for each of the classes for which registration is being sought.

As is the case with patent applications, the trademark application is assigned to a Trademark Examining Attorney who will examine the application for form and conduct a trademark search to see whether the mark is confusingly similar to any existing registration or prior pending application. The Examining Attorney will thereupon issue an Office Action either allowing the application or rejecting it for a stated reason. The applicant then has the right to amend the application to overcome the rejection.

Assuming that the Examining Attorney finds that the mark is not confusingly similar to any previously registered or pending mark, the application will be allowed and published for opposition in the Official Gazette of the U.S. Patent & Trademark Office. Any firm or individual with a valid basis may oppose registration of such mark by filing a Notice of Opposition within 30 days of publication in the Official Gazette.

If no opposition is filed, the mark becomes registered on the Principal Register of the U.S. Patent & Trademark Office, which is presumptive notice to all of the existence of these trademark rights. It takes a minimum of one year to obtain a federal trademark registration and potentially longer if difficulties are encountered during prosecution.

All registrants must file a declaration alleging use of the mark during the sixth year of registration to maintain the registration. Thereafter, applications for renewal of the registration must be filed every ten years from the date of registration. Actual evidence of use must accompany all such filings.

State trademark registrations are easier (and cheaper) to obtain, although they are often of little value and do not offer the protection that a federal registration does. There are some notable exceptions, however. A number of states, most notably California, have strong laws prohibiting the counterfeiting of state registered trademarks. Thus, the obtaining of state trademark registrations in such states will enable trademark owners to bring state actions against knock-off artists who infringe their marks.

Trademark rights exist on a country-by-country basis. The fact that an inventor may have common law trademark rights in the U.S., or may have even acquired a trademark registration in the U.S., is absolutely meaningless outside the United States. Someone in Canada, or the U.K., or any other foreign country, can infringe the inventor's trademark with impunity if the inventor has not also established trademark protection in the particular foreign country where the infringer is active. As a result, the inventor must also consider obtaining foreign trademark protection in two types of countries: those where commercial opportunities exist (where the product might be sold), and those where infringing products may be manufactured.

Unfortunately, most foreign countries do not have common law trademark rights. Rights can only be established by registration, and registering in all the relevant foreign countries can be a very expensive proposition. Consequently, inventors with some resources try to come up with one composite that combines all the potential trademark components of their idea and register that as a "single" mark. Generally speaking, most inventors cannot afford even that, and decide to keep their ideas confidential until a toy company is licensed which assumes the cost of trademark protection.

4.1.3 Copyrights

Copyright protection is provided for original works of authorship fixed in a tangible medium of expression. That means one cannot copyright an idea, only the expression of the idea. The various categories of copyrightable works include:

- literary works;
- musical works, including accompanying words;
- dramatic works, including accompanying music;
- pantomimes and choreographic works;

- pictorial, graphic and sculptural works;
- motion pictures and other audiovisual works; and
- sound recordings.

Copyright rights are limited in duration to a term of life of the author plus 50 years for individuals, and a term of 75 years from the first publication or 100 years from creation (whichever expires first) for works made for hire by employees.

Copyright rights commence upon the creation of the underlying work, and registration is not absolutely required. Until 1989, a copyright owner was required to include a copyright notice on all product embodying the copyrighted work. Failure to include such a notice could have resulted in loss of copyright rights. That requirement was eliminated when the United States became a signatory to the Berne Convention.

Registration of the copyright claim with the U.S. Copyright Office is a prerequisite for commencing an action for copyright infringement. If completed before infringement occurred, or within three months of first publication of the mark by the copyright owner, registration establishes a right to recover statutory damages and attorneys' fees against an infringer.

Copyright applications are frequently filed without the services of an attorney and are the biggest bargain in the intellectual property field. The current copyright filing fee is $20 per application, and it typically takes about six weeks for the Copyright Office to process the application and issue a registration. No separate foreign filing is required. The U.S. filing achieves rights in all countries adhering to the Universal Copyright Convention or Berne Convention.

All toy inventors should learn how to prepare a copyright application and should be seeking copyright protection for their designs, artwork and eventual products. A sample copyright registration form is included in the Appendices.

4.2 COMMON LAW RIGHTS OF PROTECTION

Common law forms of protection are available for protecting ideas. These non-statutory rights find their basis in the English common law and include common law trademark protection, unfair competition, palming off and the right of publicity.

Whenever possible, however, these common law forms of protection should be viewed as an adjunct to — not a substitute for — statutory protection. There are a number of disadvantages in relying on common law protection over statutory protection. Inventors who opt only for common law protection rather than statutory protection may be held to a higher standard of proof than are those who also obtain statutory protection.

4.3 INTERACTION BETWEEN FORMS OF PROTECTION

The fact that patents, trademarks and copyrights are separate and distinct forms of federal statutory protection does not preclude protection of an idea under several of these forms of protection. In the toy industry, all three forms of protection are often combined to provide the strongest possible protection. The most common areas of overlap are between copyrights and trademarks, between design patents and trademarks and between copyrights and design patents. The courts have long recognized that there is an overlap between the various forms of statutory protection under the intellectual property laws.

It is not uncommon to obtain both trademark and copyright protection for the same artwork, with the copyright protecting its creative or artistic aspect and the trademark protecting it as an indicator of source, origin or sponsorship for the product to which it is applied. By way of example, consider the artistic rendering of SNOOPY® sitting on his doghouse basking in the noonday sun. Such an artistic rendering is generally protectable under the copyright laws. When that same rendering is used as the basis of a plush toy, it is protectable as a trademark since it serves as an indicator of source, origin or sponsorship of that plush toy by United Feature Syndicate, the owner of the licensing and merchandising rights to the SNOOPY® property.

The courts have also held that trademark and design patent protection can coexist. Moreover, the courts have held that reliance on trademark protection after patent protection has expired is perfectly acceptable since the two forms of protection exist independently and the termination of either has no legal effect on the continuance of the other.

4.4 WEAVING TOGETHER A PATCHWORK QUILT

The problem facing the toy inventor is that all too often a product concept does not fall neatly into one of the above forms of intellectual property protection. Frequently, two or more forms of protection are required to fully cover the concept.

Let's consider for a moment how one would go about protecting an articulated three-dimensional action figure called SAMSON. The novel and unique mechanism which the inventor has come up with to achieve the articulation feature of the figure could be the subject of a utility patent. A design patent could be sought for the aesthetic appearance of the figure. The underlying artwork on which the figure was based could be protected under the copyright laws. If the figure became tremendously popular and the appearance of the figure becomes associated exclusively with the manufacturer, such appearance could also potentially be protected as a trademark. The name SAMSON could be subject to trademark protection for action figures. If the product spawned a line of trading cards or a Saturday morning cartoon show, the SAMSON name could also be protected for such uses. The packaging in which the action figure is sold could be subject to protection under the copyright laws, as could the advertising copy for the product. Similarly, all promotional pieces accompanying the product are potentially copyrightable.

4.5 CONSIDERATIONS AFFECTING PROTECTION

The cost of fully protecting a new product idea can be extremely high. As a result, in virtually all instances, there must be a judicious trade-off between the amount of protection thought to be needed and the cost of obtaining such protection.

In determining the protection to be secured, the first consideration must be the nature of the particular idea involved. In other words, the inventor must first identify what the unique element of the idea is. Is it the word SAMSON? Is it the appearance of the figure? Is it the mechanism that accomplishes the articulation of the figure?

The reason for this exercise is to determine what aspects of the idea should be protected and in what order. For the well-funded, professional toy inventor, the best approach to protecting a new product idea is to seek across-the-board protection, combining as many of the various forms of statutory and common law protection as possible. The inventor who is not well capitalized, however, must be more judicious in attempting to protect the new product idea.

The results of this exercise should be shared with the inventor's intellectual property attorney who will recommend a course of action within the inventor's budget. Seeking wide scale protection of the new toy idea is the ideal situation, although it is more important to protect the elements that need to be protected and save the remaining resources for marketing the idea.

In developing a plan for protection, there is one word of caution that must be considered. Trademark rights are based on use, not registration. Copyright rights are obtained on creation not registration. Thus, delaying the filing of either of these forms of protection is *not fatal*. Failure to file a patent application before or within a limited time (a one-year grace period) after the date of the first public use of the invention or commercial sale, however, is *absolutely fatal*. The patent laws provide that if an inventor waits to file his patent application more than one year after either of these events, he has dedicated his invention to the public, and anyone is free to use his invention. Such an inventor who failed to timely file his patent application is precluded from ever obtaining patent protection for such invention.

Another issue that the inventor should consider is that, as discussed above, patent and trademark protection is granted on a country-by-country basis. A patent obtained in the United States will not stop someone in Japan from practicing the same invention. A trademark registered in the U.S. does not prevent infringement in Japan. Separate patents and trademark registrations must be obtained in each country.

Certain foreign countries are absolute novelty countries and require that the U.S. patent application be filed before any commercial use or sale of the invention. In other words, these countries do not recognize the one-year grace period for filing the patent application after public use or sale. If the inventor intends to seek patent protection in these countries, his U.S. application or his application in the particular foreign country must have been filed prior to such commercialization, otherwise foreign rights will be prejudiced.

4.6 LEGAL MARKING

The use of appropriate legal notices is very important. Valuable property rights and the ability to collect damages may be lost as a result of failure to comply with the requisite statutory notice provisions. The basic legal notices inventors should be aware of are the two trademark notices, the copyright notice and the patent notice.

The ® symbol is used to designate a federally registered trademark. Some trademark owners prefer to use the designations "Registered in the U.S. Patent and Trademark Office" or "Reg. U.S. Pat. & TM Off." This is a matter of choice, but most copywriters and advertising personnel prefer the ® symbol simply because it is easier to place. The tag line "Registered Trademark" is not a statutory notice and may actually be misleading because it does not indicate where the mark was registered.

The U.S. Trademark Laws provide that if a trademark owner commences suit against an infringer, if the owner had not indicated that his mark was registered, the owner is precluded from recovering profits and damages unless it can be established that the defendant had actual notice of the registration. Many countries, including Canada, require products to bear a notice identifying the owner of the licensed mark and stating that the product is being manufactured by the licensee under license from the owner.

The formal copyright notice requires the word "Copyright," the abbreviation "Copr.," or a ©, followed by the name of the copyright owner and the year of the work's first publication. The legend "All Rights Reserved" should follow the standard copyright notice when distribution is contemplated in South America. While the application of a copyright notice is no longer required to obtain copyright rights, the use of such a notice is still recommended because of benefits afforded by the statute where proper notice has been used.

Goods that are covered by a pending patent application should be marked "Patent Pending." Upon issuance of a patent, the "Patent Pending" notice should be replaced with a notice identifying the actual patent number, for example, "Patent No. 1,234,567." Failure to mark a product or its appropriate packaging with proper patent notices may result in an inability to recover damages against an infringer, absent proof that the patent owner had actually notified the infringer of such infringement and the infringer continued to infringe thereafter. Thus, failure to mark such a product or its appropriate packaging can result in the loss of all damages against an infringer who immediately ceased selling the infringing products upon notification from the patent owner.

While the patent laws afford specific advantages to patent owners who place patent notices on their products, there are no such advantages offered to individuals who indicate that their products are covered by a pending patent application. Nevertheless, many people believe that there is a commercial advantage to be gained by warning a competitor that the product is the subject of a patent application. The belief is that a competitor, who might otherwise be inclined to copy or knock-off the product, might be reluctant to copy a product which may be patented in the future. The hope is that the competitor will reason: "Why make a major investment in tooling and promotion, only to be enjoined from selling the product when the patent issues?"

The ™ designation is used to designate a property that is considered a trademark by the owner but is not federally registered. Similarly, the designation ℠ indicates that the word, symbol or logo is considered by its owner to be a service mark. There is no particular legal necessity for inclusion of the ™ designation with the mark other than to indicate to the public at large that the user considers the particular mark to be his mark. The inclusion of this designation can be quite helpful in convincing a judge that the particular mark should be protected.

Chapter Five:

SHOULD YOU DO IT YOURSELF?

5.1 WILL THE TOY AND GAME COMPANIES DEAL WITH YOU?

The question of whether to use an agent is a question that every first-time toy inventor asks at some point in time. In some instances, the inventor will find that there is no choice in the matter. Some of the major toy companies prefer not to deal with first-time inventors unless they are represented by agents. These companies will return submissions by first-time inventors, typically with a letter advising the inventor that the company only considers new product ideas submitted by professional design firms (i.e., firms with established track records) or, alternatively, by professional agents or brokers. Some toy companies will even provide the inventor with a list of agents that represent independent inventors. Where the toy company refuses to deal with the independent inventor, the choices are simple. Either retain the services of one of the agents recommended by the toy company, find another toy company to whom to submit your idea or find another occupation.

A number of the major toy companies have adopted this policy to avoid having to deal with the tens of thousands of submissions that they receive annually, the vast majority of which simply do not pertain to the business in which they are operating. Few will argue that it is a total waste of everyone's time for a board game company to have to consider a submission for a baby bib. Using the agent as a "middle man" insulates the toy or game company from having to take the time to log in and respond to such a submission.

Remember the earlier discussion about how toy companies dislike dealing with unrealistic inventors? This practice of making first-time inventors go through someone else is the toy company's "first line of defense." The agents first-time inventors must "go through" understand that they cannot risk their relationship with the toy companies by assisting a problematic inventor in getting access to the toy companies. They, in essence, become the toy company's unpaid screening agencies.

There is still another reason why many of the major toy companies refer first-time inventors to agents and refuse to consider their submissions. The answer is liability. Chris Campbell, now VP Marketing, Tyco Toys, explained the rationale for such a policy in an interview that he had given for *The Licensing Journal* (February 1991, at 4.) while at Parker Brothers, explaining:

> Almost all companies have listings of agents that they refer people to. We get about 4500 requests each year to review concepts from non-pros, and we can not look at any of those for two main reasons: one is legal liability and the other is simply the time element associated with properly reviewing items. What we do for those people is we send them back a letter that says, "Thank you for submitting the concept but we deal principally with a closed list of inventors and utilize our own internal groups and that we don't accept unsolicited ideas." We give them a listing of the names, addresses, phone numbers etc., of about six different agents in the U.S. and also internationally that they can choose from.
>
> I think the difficulty is that individuals believe that certain elements of their concept are proprietary. That may be the theme or certain mechanical elements. One thing that we try to avoid is a situation where the inventor believes that we have in some way misappropriated some element of their concept and incorporated it into another item without compensating them. The difficulty really is that individuals who are non-pros can be much more fanatical than the professional inventors about their belief that their idea was misappropriated. The pros clearly understand that we have been in business for many, many years and that we're a publicly traded Fortune 500 company and that we rely heavily on outside concepts for our products. Our lifeblood is from the outside and we don't misappropriate ideas. But that doesn't stop the uneducated from believing that we have in some way misappropriated some element of it.

5.2 THE AGENT BUSINESS

In those instances where the toy company will consider re-viewing products submitted by independent first-time inven-tors, the inventor has an extremely important decision to make. Do you go it alone and attempt to present the idea to the com-pany, or do you retain the services of an agent or broker to rep-resent you and your idea? This is frequently a difficult decision for many inventors due, in large measure, to the seemingly high commissions that most agents or brokers require.

Let's take a moment and discuss the agent community to assist the first-time inventor in making an informed decision. Most toy agents or brokers are highly experienced individuals who have worked in the toy industry for many years. Some are former toy company R&D executives. Mel Taft of Mel Taft As-sociates is one such individual, setting up his company after many years as head of R&D for Milton Bradley. Other agents are former (and still current) inventors who take on the proper-ties of other inventors to round out and supplement their own line. An example of one such individual is Dan Lauer of Lauer Toys, the inventor of the WATERBABIES® doll marketed by Playmates Toys.

The one thing that all toy agents or brokers have in com-mon is that they have the ability to get in the door of the toy companies and get the inventor's new product idea seriously considered by the appropriate person at that company. That ability is not to be taken lightly.

Most toy agents or brokers work on a commission arrange-ment, similar to a lawyer's contingent fee arrangement or a real estate broker's commission. The commissions charged by agents range between 25 and 60 percent of the gross sums received by the inventor, although commissions vary widely depending upon the agent, the idea and the anticipated difficulty in selling or licensing the idea. Since the fee is typically a straight com-mission arrangement, agents only get paid if they are success-ful in licensing the new product idea and the inventor receives money. That gives the agent a tremendous incentive to do a good job for the inventor.

It should be noted that most agents work only on an exclu-sive basis. That means that the inventor will be contractually tied to that agent for a period of time during which the inventor cannot directly approach a toy company and also cannot utilize the services of another agent to approach such companies on his behalf. The reason for this is simple. The agent wants to control the idea and not have all his work destroyed when another agent (or the inventor) happens to get in the door of the toy company a week prior to his own presentation. The agent also realizes the obvious drawbacks of giving an interested toy company the opportunity to play the numbers they are receiving from the inventor against those being negotiated by the agent.

Most agents will want exclusive rights for an extended period of time, recognizing that the selling cycle is relatively long. Thus, most will want a minimum period of at least a year and, oftentimes, as long as two years. The term of their retention is a function of the idea and how long it will take to be sold or licensed.

5.3 THE DECISION

You now understand who agents are and how they work. Assuming that the toy company will agree to deal directly with you, the inventor (and the vast majority of toy companies will), the question presented is, "Should you do it alone and keep 100% of the royalties or use an agent and pay them as much as 50% of the money?"

This is not an easy question. The answer depends in large measure on your background and personality. If you are a corporate marketing manager, are familiar (and comfortable) with the art of persuasion and salesmanship and have the time and desire to try to market the idea, it makes perfect sense for you to at least try and sell the product yourself. If, however, you feel uncomfortable with business and marketing issues and lack the time or desire to embark on a selling program, it certainly makes sense to retain the services of a professional toy agent who will gladly take on the assignment and perform in a professional and competent manner. The expression, "50 percent of something is better than 100% of nothing" is appropriate in this instance.

The inventor who knows that he wants to go it alone and present his ideas to toy companies on his own should STOP

READING THIS CHAPTER and immediately go to the next chapter. If, however, you're not positive as to how to proceed, or know that you need the services of a good toy agent or broker, read on.

5.4 IDENTIFYING POTENTIAL AGENTS

One chooses a toy agent or broker the same way one chooses any professional. The first step is to identify all possible agents. Research the industry to find the names of the prominent agents. Speak with some of the toy companies. Call the Toy Manufacturers of America. Ask friends and colleagues for recommendations.

A list of agents with whom we have had dealings over the years is provided in the Appendices. This is, by no means, an exhaustive list nor does it constitute a recommendation on our part. All we can say about each of the agents listed is that they are highly professional and have extensive experience in the toy industry. The final decision on who to initially contact and eventually retain is a personal one, which should be made carefully, particularly after communicating with the potential agent. Through such communication, you can find out about the agent's past and current activities (to see if he is active in the area of your idea), and you can determine if you will be able to establish a collaborative rapport with the agent. Any agent who doesn't give you the "time of day" at this juncture, or with whom you have trouble carrying on a conversation, isn't going to be any better once you've retained him.

It should be noted that when we speak about toy agents or brokers, we are not referring to general invention development firms. In the 1970's, a rash of invention development firms sprang up around the country on the premise that they would receive ideas from individuals which they would patent and try to license to Fortune 100 companies. These firms charged naive inventors many thousands of dollars to procure meaningless patents and send computer-generated form letters to large corporations addressed merely to "Director of New Product Development." It should come as no surprise that such letters quickly ended up in the trash, and few (if any) inventors' ideas were ever commercialized. After hundreds of complaints were filed with the various State Attorney General's Offices, at least two of the major firms were driven out of business. Since then, the government has attempted to carefully control such invention development firms, although every year or so there are a number of reported horror stories concerning them. In 1994, there was even a Congressional inquiry into the entire industry.

We are not suggesting that all general invention development firms are non-productive. All we are saying is that if you want to use the services of such a firm, you should be careful. We believe that there isn't any need for the services of such a firm to commercialize an idea for the toy industry. As evidenced by the list of agents provided in the Appendices, there are a number of reputable agents available who specialize in the toy industry and who will do more than take the inventor's hard earned money and send out some meaningless form letters.

In contrast to the real estate agents who stress the importance of "location, location, location," toy agents rely on many different factors when selling ideas to toy companies. While the location of the agent and proximity to the inventor or a toy company or companies is a factor the toy inventor should consider, it should not be the major consideration. We live in the days of telecommunications and overnight package delivery services. Eliminating an agent who would clearly appear to be the best fit for your idea simply because the agent is located in New York City and you are in South Dakota is not a good idea. If the agent is the best qualified to represent your idea to the targeted toy company and you can work with him, carefully examine whether the geographical remoteness really will be a problem. In actual fact, you will probably find that there is little need to actually meet with the agent on an regular basis and that most of your communications can easily be handled by telephone, telefax and overnight delivery.

5.5 SELECTING THE RIGHT AGENT FOR YOU

After identifying potential agents, the next task is to contact each of them, show them your idea and discuss with them the possibility of their representing you and your idea.

The agent will undoubtedly want to see the concept or idea before agreeing to represent you. You should not be surprised by this request or, for that matter, be afraid to show the new product idea to the agent, provided that you have taken the appropriate steps to protect you new product idea (as explained in the prior chapter) and you get the agent to sign a confidential disclosure agreement. Requesting the agent to sign a confidential disclosure agreement is entirely appropriate, and the agent should not have any difficulty with the request. If he does, don't tell him your idea and don't use his services.

This is not to imply that agents are unscrupulous and, absent a confidential disclosure agreement, would steal your idea. In virtually all instances, nothing could be farther from the truth. The purpose of having the agent sign such an agreement, however, is to protect you from that small percentage of agents who might consider "taking" your idea.

A common concern of many agents who are reluctant to sign confidential disclosure agreements is that they might be either working on a similar idea themselves or, alternatively, have another client who is working on a similar idea. In such instance, the negotiation of the confidential disclosure agreement might become a two-step process. The inventor would disclose to the agent, on a non-confidential basis, a broad, general description of what he has invented. (i.e., "I've invented a new form of articulation for action figures." This tells the agent the subject matter *but not* the "gee whiz.") This would permit the agent to determine whether he has any potential conflict. Assuming there is none, the agent should then have no difficulty signing the confidential disclosure agreement, after which the inventor can fully disclose the idea. If there is a conflict, the agent will so indicate based on the broad, general description, and the inventor will seek out another agent to represent the idea.

You should ask each potential agent to provide you with a description of his background and a list of references. You should explore in detail the agent's specific experience with respect to the type of idea that you will be asking him to market. While the toy industry is not terribly large, it is highly segmented. (i.e., board game, plush doll, electronic learning aid, etc.). Certain agents have better contacts and working relationships with particular toy companies or market segments than with others. For example, there are agents who specialize in board games, due to their background, experience and contacts. Retaining such an agent to license a new electronic game to the pre-school market may prove frustrating for both the inventor and agent. You should be satisfied that the agent you retain has the requisite contacts with the specific companies most likely to buy or license your idea.

Once you are satisfied that the agent has the requisite experience in the particular area of interest, the question of compensation should be discussed and resolved. This is an essential element of the relationship and should not be avoided.

As stated above, most agents are paid a commission based on the monies that they bring in through the sale or licensing of the idea. Commissions vary widely, although they tend to range between 25 and 60 percent, depending on the amount of work that the agent is expected to perform and whether the agent is being called upon to do more than merely sell the concept. Where the agent makes a creative contribution to the idea and/or actually manufactures prototypes and the like, the arrangement tends to become more of a joint venture with the agent rightfully seeking a higher percentage of the eventual income. Where, however, the agent is merely a marketing representative for the inventor and the inventor's fully-developed and prototyped idea, there is a justification for the agent receiving a lower rate. Nevertheless, the majority of agents receive a commission in the 40 to 50 percent range.

Some agents will seek an up-front and/or ongoing monthly or quarterly fee or retainer in addition to the percentage commission. This will normally result in the agent accepting a lower commission. Thus, in situations where the agent is to receive a monthly retainer of $2,500 per month, for example, the commission rate will decrease to between 10 and 25 percent. Typically, this retainer or fee is only paid during the first year or so of the relationship and terminates upon execution of an agreement with a toy or game company to commercialize the idea. If, after careful deliberation, you decide to agree to retain an agent who you will pay a fee, make sure you get a written agreement which states what the agent has promised to do for you in exchange for such payment. If the agent is merely going to act as a marketing representative selling your idea (i.e., and won't be further developing it or preparing presentation materials, etc.), no retainer or fee should be necessary.

The arrangement between inventor and agent should also determine who will be responsible for costs associated with the agent's duties. Normally, they are the agent's responsibilities, although in some cases they are borne by the inventor. Similarly, in cases where the inventor is to pay the agent a monthly retainer, it should be clear whether that retainer is either independent of the commission or, alternatively, is recoupable as a credit against the agent's commission. In the first instance, the agent might receive a non-refundable retainer fee of $2,500 per month for one year plus 25 percent of the gross income received from the toy company. In the latter instance, the agent would receive a retainer of $2,500 per month for one year and 25 percent of the gross income received from the toy company after deduction of any retainer fees paid by the inventor to the agent. Like most things in the toy industry, the compensation structure for the agent is negotiable, and the inventor should not be afraid to explore alternative forms of compensation. In no event, however, should these issues be left to chance or later resolution.

As an inventor, perhaps the most important factor in deciding whether or not to retain an agent is the "chemistry" that exists between the inventor and the agent. After all, the agent will not only be representing your idea, but you as an inventor. It is, therefore, important that there be a certain *simpatico* between you and your agent. You should be able to trust that the agent not only can, but will, represent your best interests. Check the agent's references. Speak with other inventors represented by the agent. Ask them how it worked out, whether they were satisfied with the agent's performance. While the agent will probably only provide the names of satisfied clients, what these satisfied clients have to say could be telling. Perhaps the most important question to ask each of these clients is, "Did the agent do everything for you that he said he would do before you retained him?" If the answer is consistent with your expectations, you have probably found the right agent.

5.6 THE AGENT AGREEMENT

You have finally selected the right agent to represent you and your idea. What's next? Entering into a written agreement is an imperative first step to insuring that your inventor-agent relationship will succeed. Nothing should be left to chance with something as important as the relationship between you and the agent representing you.

Most agents have what they will refer to as their standard agreement. You should recognize that this "standard" agreement is typically anything but that. In fact, the agent may actually have a number of "standard" agreements to fit different circumstances. You must appreciate that this "standard" agreement was, no doubt, drafted by the agent's attorney pursuant to the following instructions, "Draft an agreement for me that is totally in my favor. Leave out any provisions that could potentially burn me. We can always put them in if the inventor asks for them." For example, an agent agreement drafted by an agent's attorney might run three pages. That same attorney, however, might draft a twelve-page agreement when representing the inventor. Thus, you should be prepared to carefully review and negotiate the terms of this "standard" agreement. If you are in doubt, ask an attorney that has experience in the toy industry to review the agreement on your behalf and provide you with appropriate comments or suggestions.

At the very least, a well-drafted agent agreement from the inventor's perspective should address the following issues:

- whether the agent is to represent all of the inventor's ideas and concepts for all markets or merely one specific idea for a particular market;
- whether the relationship is exclusive or non-exclusive;
- the territory in which the agent will operate;
- the term (or length) of the relationship;
- the obligations and responsibilities of the agent (e.g., what he has promised to do to sell the inventor's idea and what he has promised to take care of, such as, presentation of the idea, negotiation of the license, collection of royalties, etc.);
- financial items (e.g., how monies are to be received and disbursed, what the agent will receive as compensation for his services, who is responsible for any expenses that may be incurred);
- how and when the agreement may be terminated early;

- whether the agent will continue to receive monies after expiration and/or early termination and, if so, how much; and
- last (but by no means least), the confidentiality obligations of the agent.

5.6.1 Extent of Representation

The scope or extent of the representation by the agent must be clearly defined to avoid any problems in the future. Agreements may be structured wherein the agent is to represent all of the ideas or concepts of a particular inventor or merely one or more concepts. In the former case, the agent is, in essence, the agent for the inventor. That means if you should develop a new product idea after retaining the agent and during the term of your agreement, you must advise the agent accordingly and give the agent the opportunity to present that new product idea to a toy company. In the latter case, the agent is simply the agent for a specific new product idea. Accordingly, as an inventor, you would be free to attempt to sell or license other ideas or concepts during the life of the agreement either directly or through the use of another agent.

It is possible to have an agent agreement that is exclusive to a particular toy company. For example, an agent may have a special relationship with a company like Hasbro. The inventor may want to use that agent solely to present the property to Hasbro and reserve the right to directly approach other companies or to use other agents for those other companies.

5.6.2 Exclusive vs. Non-exclusive

There are two types of relationships in which agents will work, i.e., exclusive and non-exclusive. An exclusive arrangement means that the agent will be the only person or firm that can represent the inventor during the term of the agreement. In a non-exclusive arrangement, the inventor is free to independently attempt to sell or license the idea himself or to retain the services of other non-exclusive agents to perform this task. The agreement should clearly define whether exclusive means to the exclusion of the inventor. There have been instances in "exclusive" agent relationships where the inventor retains the right to independently attempt to sell or license the concept or idea himself. In that context, "exclusive" only means to the exclusion of another agent. Most agents will want to include a provision in an exclusive agreement that requires the inventor to refer any inquiries that the inventor may receive from toy companies directly to the agent. Such a provision is obviously intended to protect the agent from direct inquiries to the inventor. It also insures that the agent is fully aware of the knowledge and reaction(s) of the marketplace to the idea.

In most instances, you will want to grant an agent an exclusive license. You have to assume that you have selected the best possible agent. The next object is to make sure the agent has the desire to sell the idea. Nothing disincentivizes an agent quicker than the knowledge that whatever hard work he puts into presenting and selling an idea may be for nothing if the inventor has only given him a non-exclusive agency and someone else needs the idea. It is for this reason that most agents will only take on ideas they represent exclusively. If they do take on an idea on a non-exclusive basis, they will normally just add the idea to their "line," and put absolutely no effort or resources into selling it beyond taking it out of their bag at a toy company meeting with a "what do you think?" attitude.

5.6.3 Territory

The agent grant should specifically define the territory in which the agent is empowered to act on behalf of the inventor. The territory of the agent grant is similar to the licensed territory of the eventual toy license agreement — e.g., United States, North America, Japan, worldwide, etc.

Before granting worldwide representation rights, you should be completely satisfied that the agent has worldwide contacts. If not, the agent grant should be modified accordingly. For example, the territory could be the U.S. with a proviso that broader rights will be given *if* the agent interests a toy company in the territory with distribution capabilities outside the territory. In such case, the agent grant will be "expanded" to be commensurate with the ultimate license that is entered into.

5.6.4 Term of the Agreement

The "term" of the agent agreement refers to its length, i.e., the time period during which the agent will be representing the idea or the inventor. From the inventor's perspective, the term of the agreement should be short, e.g., between six months and a year. If the agent has not sold the product to a toy company within that time period, the agent's right to represent the idea or the inventor should expire. In the toy industry, time is important. A new product idea may be timely one year, but stale the next. A short term in the agent agreement serves, in essence, as a "try out" for the agent and does not bind the inventor to a non-performing agent for a prolonged period of time. The longer that a non-performing, exclusive agent retains rights to a particular idea, the more difficult it will be for you to either license that idea yourself or, alternatively, find a new agent that would be interested in taking on the project.

Most agents will seek a longer term, e.g., two or more years. They will argue that the selling cycle for a new product idea is long, and it will frequently take that period of time to effect commercialization. A frequently used compromise in such negotiations is to set a longer term for the relationship, i.e., two or more years, and include performance milestones that must be met by the agent in order for him to continue to retain rights during that longer term. Typical milestones include the requirement to contact a minimum number of companies, generate a minimum compensation, etc. These minimums vary widely and depend, in large measure, upon the type of idea and the territory involved. Performance is the name of the game in agency relationships. If the agent is performing and meets these milestones, the agent should retain the rights for the longer period. If, however, the agent is not performing and fails to meet these milestones, then the agreement should give the inventor the right to terminate the relationship during the term.

This is not to imply that you should deny the agent a solid and reasonable chance to attempt to sell or license a new product idea. Both parties must recognize that the commercialization of new toy ideas does take a certain amount of time, and the agent should be given a fair opportunity to accomplish the task.

An alternative approach is to provide for a shorter term and build in a series of options which may be independently exercised by the agent provided that the agent meets certain requirements. The most frequently used requirement for exercising an option is minimum compensation generated on behalf of the inventor. In such a situation, an agent may be granted a two-year term with the unilateral right to renew the agreement for additional two-year extended terms provided that during the then in-effect term, the agent generates at least $X of compensation (after deduction of the agent commissions) for the inventor.

A typical provision relative to such an option would be the following:

If the agent fully performs according to all terms and conditions hereof during the initial term and, during that initial term, produces gross compensation for the inventor (after deduction of the agent's fees and expenses) of at least ONE HUNDRED THOUSAND DOLLARS ($100,000), the term of this Agreement shall automatically be extended for an additional term of two (2) years commencing immediately upon expiration of the preceding term. The Agreement may, thereafter, be extended for further extended terms of two (2) years per extended term, provided that the agent continues to fully perform in accordance with all terms and conditions of the agreement and, further, produced gross compensation for the inventor (after deduction of the agent's fees and expenses) during the preceding term of at least ONE HUNDRED FIFTY THOUSAND DOLLARS ($150,000). In the event that the agent does not fully perform in accordance with all terms and conditions of this Agreement and/or does not achieve the enumerated minimum gross compensation for the inventor, this Agreement shall terminate on the normal termination date.

5.6.5 Obligations/Responsibilities of the Agent

It should be appreciated that most toy agents are not "agents" in the classic legal sense, since they generally lack the ability to legally or contractually bind the inventor. More often than not, these "agents" are little more than sales representatives for the inventor with the obligation to seek out and bring back for consideration and execution by the inventor the most favorable deals.

There are, however, situations in which the agent will request and be granted the power to bind the inventor. There are even situations in which the agent not only has the power and authority to bind the inventor, but is also named as a party to the eventual contract with the toy company. In some situations, the inventor's name does not even appear on the agreement with the toy company. Such a situation should be clearly avoided, if at all possible. This type of relationship is replete with potential problems, particularly in the event that the inventor seeks to terminate the agent. Untangling the ties that bind in such a situation is quite difficult.

The contract with the toy company should always be between the inventor and the company directly, not between the agent and the company. The inventor has the greatest interest in maintaining the property and, as such, should have the ultimate control in any given situation.

It is recommended that the agent's responsibilities be limited to negotiating the terms and conditions of a proposed agreement with a toy company and then presenting the proposed license agreement to the inventor for approval and execution. The inventor should always reserve the unconditional right of final approval over such agreements.

Defining the obligations and responsibilities of the agent is, perhaps, one of the most important elements in any agent agreement and one that is frequently omitted. The inventor should insist that the representations made by the agent during the "honeymoon" period be incorporated into the agent agreement. This will insure that there will be no misunderstanding as to exactly what the agent will do on behalf of the inventor and avoid potential problems down the road.

The following is a list of certain duties which are often expected of the agent:

- assist the inventor in refining the new product idea so that it is marketable;

- develop marketing and presentation materials for use in presenting the new product idea to toy companies;
- identify a list of toy companies most likely to be interested in the new product idea;
- present the new product idea to those toy and game companies most likely to be interested in the property;
- negotiate the terms of an agreement between the inventor and the company;
- administer the licensing program with the toy manufacturer to insure that the inventor's royalties, guaranteed minimum royalty payments and sales reports are promptly submitted;
- periodically review each of the licensed products produced by the toy manufacturer as well as all associated advertising, packaging and promotional materials to insure that the quality control provisions of the agreement are being met;
- wherever necessary, personally inspect the toy company's manufacturing facilities to insure that the quality control provisions are being complied with; and
- collect all advances, guaranteed minimum royalty payments and actual royalty payments from the toy company which are due under the agreement and, after deduction of the agent's commission and allowed expenses, if any, transmit the remainder to the inventor.

In short, the outside agent should be doing everything that is done by a vigilant inventor.

5.6.6 Financial Issues

In most instances, the agent is compensated on a commission basis, i.e., paid out of the royalty income received from those toy companies within the agent's territory for which the agent has concluded business deals. Typical commissions for agents vary widely. Commissions can range between 25 and 60 percent, although most are typically between 35 to 50 percent of the gross revenue received from toy companies. "Gross revenues" mean *all* monies received by the inventor and are not limited solely to monies based on the product the toy company makes incorporating the product idea. Gross revenues typically also include any monies derived from ancillary product licensing or entertainment sublicensing. For example, the CABBAGE PATCH® doll spawned an active third party ancillary licensing program and TEENAGE MUTANT NINJA TURTLES® characters appeared in a television series and in a motion picture. Any monies derived from such venues would be included in the agent's commission base.

As indicated earlier, most agent agreements are "negotiable," and the most frequently negotiated provision of any agreement is the compensation provision. There probably are as many ways to compensate agents as there are agents in existence today. One avenue to explore is a "declining scale" formula wherein the agent's commission will decrease as a function of gross compensation received. For example, an agent may receive a 50 percent commission on the first $1,000,000 in gross compensation, 40 percent on the next million and 30 percent thereafter. This is one way to compensate the agent for his initial up-front investment of time and resources yet not make the agent wildly rich should the idea develop into the next Saturday morning cartoon blockbuster.

As indicated earlier, some agents will seek a monthly (or quarterly) retainer fee which may (or may not) be creditable against their commission. This should be negotiated and memorialized in the agreement to avoid any potential confusion in the future.

Most agents are reimbursed for any actual out-of-pocket expenses which they may incur in connection with their obligations under the agreement. Such expenses may include, for example, advertising costs, promotional costs and legal fees. The reimbursement of such expenses is normally predicated on their prior approval by the inventor.

The mechanics of actually getting paid is always one of considerable negotiation. Most agents will want to directly receive the gross monies from the toy company, have the ability to deduct their commission and remit the balance (within a specified period of time) to the inventor. Conversely, most inventors will want to receive the monies themselves and perform the function of dividing up the money. The manner in which this issue gets resolved is a function of the parties.

Permitting a long-established agency to collect and distribute the money should not pose any problem to most inventors. In fact, it relieves the inventor of the hassle of handling the accounting. In such instances, the inventor may want the agent to segregate the funds received from the toy companies from the agent's own funds and from the funds of other inventors for whom the agent is working. Many inventors require that an agent maintain a special account in the name of the inventor for receipt and deposit of such royalty payments. The agent is given access to such special account during the term of the agreement.

The inventor may not, however, have the same comfort level with a one person agency firm that has only been in business for a short period of time. In such instances, the inventor should insist that all monies from third parties be paid directly to the inventor, who will assume responsibility for compensating the agent. The inventor who elects this alternative must be prepared to handle the accounting which it entails.

One compromise, when all else fails, is to have royalty income from the toy company paid to an escrow agent (e.g., a bank, an accounting firm, etc.) that is authorized, pursuant to an escrow agreement, to collect and distribute monies to the respective parties in accordance with the agreement.

5.6.7 Termination Rights

There may, unfortunately, come a time during the course of the agency relationship when the inventor will become dissatisfied with the agent and want to terminate the agent agreement. There should be a termination provision in the agreement setting forth the mechanism for such early termination. Some agreements spell out a whole list of reasons why an agent may be terminated. Normally, it all boils down to one reason: the inventor wants to terminate the agent because the agent is not doing what he promised to do. As such, if the obligations/responsibilities provision of the agreement is well-drafted, all that is required in the termination provision is an ability on the part of the inventor to terminate the agent for failure to fulfill his obligations/responsibilities. At most, the agent should be given thirty days' notice of termination, during which time the agent can cure the failing and avoid termination.

5.6.8 Post Expiration or Early Termination Compensation

One of the most hotly debated provisions in negotiation of an agent agreement typically is whether the agent will receive compensation after expiration or early termination, and if so, how much and for how long. Many agents want to receive their full commission for as long as deals they put together continue paying royalties to the inventor. Some agents will also seek their full commission from particular toy companies if they made the introduction of the inventor to the companies, regardless of what idea is ultimately licensed, whether they ultimately put the deal together or when the agreement went into effect. The inventor would thus be obligated to pay the agent his full commission for *any* new product idea that the inventor might sell or license to XYZ Toy Company at any time, on the theory that the inventor never would have been able to make the deal absent the agent's assistance.

The logic for this request is that most agents believe that the most difficult task in representing an inventor is to get the inventor's first product idea sold or licensed to a particular company. The sale or licensing of subsequent ideas, particularly to that company, becomes much easier. The agent reasons that had it not been his efforts, the inventor would never have gotten into that company. As such, the agent should be paid his full commission for life, or at least a relatively long period of time.

At the other end of the spectrum, there are many inventors who adamantly refuse to pay the agent anything whatsoever after termination or expiration of the agent agreement. They believe that once an agent is terminated and ceases to work on their behalf, the agent forfeits his entitlement to any further compensation. They also recognize that they will have to retain a new licensing agent or, alternatively, assume that obligation themselves and, as such, incur additional expense. The prospect of paying two agents full commission is deemed unacceptable by the inventor and may leave the inventor, after paying both commissions, with very little left over.

This is a very real question and must be considered by the parties prior to entering into any agent agreement. This is one issue that should never be left for resolution at the conclusion of the agency relationship. From a negotiation strategy standpoint, it will be far easier to reach an amicable resolution during the "honeymoon" period when everyone is looking to work together forever, than later when the inventor has terminated the services of the agent for whatever reason.

One possible compromise frequently used in resolving post-termination or expiration compensation problems is for the inventor to agree to continue to pay the agent after termination or expiration of the agent agreement a reduced commission on any income received by the inventor as a result of agreements negotiated or secured by the agent during the term of the agency relationship or within six months thereafter. The latter requirement, frequently called a "trailer," protects the agent from the situation in which he presents and negotiates an agreement on behalf of the inventor with a particular toy company, only to have the inventor delay signing the agreement until after termination or expiration of the agency relationship. This approach reflects the fact that the agent is entitled to receive some compensation for having negotiated the license in the first instance but recognizes that the agent will no longer be working for the inventor after termination or expiration.

The actual declining scale is, of course, a matter of negotiation between the parties, as is the question of whether it will merely cover existing licenses or any agreements at all with a particular company. Final resolution of these questions should reflect the realities of the marketplace.

A typical provision regarding post-termination or expiration compensation is as follows:

> After expiration or termination of this agreement, the agent shall be entitled to an ongoing commission based on contracts or agreements with licensees in the territory secured by the agent which were entered into during the term of this agreement or for a period of six months thereafter for which the agent would have received a commission had the agreement not expired or been terminated. In such event, however, the agent's commission relative to such licensees shall be proportionally reduced after expiration or termination in accordance with the following schedule:

Calendar Year Following Expiration or Termination	Percentage of Gross Compensation
1	50%
2	40%
3	30%
4th and subsequent years	20%

5.6.9 Confidentiality

Since the inventor will be disclosing his ideas to the agent, the agent agreement should include a confidential disclosure provision, whereby the agent promises to hold such ideas in confidence. The confidential provision is often reciprocal, to protect the agent's confidential contact information, as well as confidential details of the agent's operations.

Normally, prior to discussing details of a new product idea with a prospective agent, an inventor will have entered into a confidential disclosure agreement. Nevertheless, since the agent agreement normally will include an integration clause (that says there are no other agreements between the parties except those expressly contained in the agent agreement), it is a good idea to include a confidentiality provision in the agent agreement.

5.6.10 Warranties and Indemnification

Most agents will require that inventors represent and warrant that they are the owners of the new product ideas and have the rights to license and sell such ideas. In addition, many agents further require that inventors agree to defend, indemnify and hold the agent harmless against any and all claims made by third parties in connection with that warranty. This warranty is generally non-negotiable from the agent's perspective.

5.7 TIP ON MAKING THE ARRANGEMENT WORK

Particular care should be taken with respect to defining the obligations and responsibilities of the agent. Experience has shown that more often than not, the problems which are encountered between the inventor and agent are due to a misunderstanding of exactly what the agent is supposed to do for the inventor. Many of these misunderstandings can be eliminated by a well-drafted and definitive agent agreement which identifies what the agent will and will not do for the inventor.

Chapter Six:

PRESENTING THE IDEA

6.1 PREPARING THE "VICTIMS LIST"

You've elected to "go it alone" without the services of an agent. The first order of business is to identify the particular toy companies ("victims") most likely to be interested in your new idea. Where do you start?

You should carefully review the directory provided in the Appendices of this guide as a start. Next, you should go on a field trip to the local Toys 'R' Us and walk down the aisles, identifying the manufacturers of other products in the same product category as your new product idea. By product category, we mean such broad product categories as board games, water guns, action figures and the like. Write down the names (and addresses, if available) of these manufacturers. They are all potential "victims."

You should also consult as many mail order catalogs as are available with the same goal in mind, i.e., identifying the manufacturers of products in the same product category. Walk through the showrooms and exhibit booths at the next Toy Fair and, again, see which companies already manufacture and market the products in the product category into which the idea that you have invented falls.

These field trips will accomplish a number of things. Not only will it help you identify potential licensees, it will also confirm that your new product idea is just that — new. Moreover, it will provide you with invaluable insight into the market and the potential competition that will be faced when a company introduces a product incorporating your idea. This information will assist you in presenting the new idea to toy companies, since one of the questions they will undoubtedly ask you is, "What is the competition?"

You should not limit your list to strictly the companies that already market products of a similar type. There are many toy companies that would love to expand their product line into other product categories if they had the right product. Your idea for a new product could be just the impetus they need.

The following experience is a case in point. Parker Brothers had been one of the leading board game companies in the world with games such as MONOPOLY® and others. Although primarily a board game manufacturer, Parker Brothers decided to take a chance and broaden its basic product line around the NERF® line of products. These products clearly are not board games, but they have produced hundreds of millions of dollars in additional revenue for that company.

For the most part, however, you should limit your "victims" list to those companies already in the product category, because these companies already possess the desired focus. It is difficult enough to convince a product manager to include your product in his company's new line and pay you money to acquire the rights to the idea. It is substantially more difficult to convince him that, in addition to the foregoing, he should consider introducing a new product line around your idea.

After creating this so-called "victims list," you should prioritize the list in the order that you want to contact and make presentations. Theoretically, it is preferable to contact one of the major manufacturers first, since their sales volume can be expected to generate greater royalties.

6.2 GETTING IN THE DOOR

On paper, the process of selling or licensing a new product idea to a toy company is relatively straightforward. You identify the potential companies, call each one of the so-called "victims" to arrange to present the idea, make a presentation of the new idea to a decision-maker at each of the companies, and then conclude a business arrangement with the first company to express an interest in the new product idea. It is a simple process, until the first-time the inventor tries it and quickly finds that the process is anything but simple. In fact, it can be downright frightening and frustrating.

Getting in the door of a major toy company can be difficult. Most major toy companies (and even some second and third tier companies) designate a specific individual with the responsibility for the initial evaluation of new product ideas from outside the company. That individual may have a variety of different titles, although they are often colloquially referred to as "gatekeepers."

Getting to the gatekeeper is often not easy, particularly for the uninitiated. While the gatekeeper of at least one toy company stated at a Toy Fair seminar that he works hard at maintaining an ongoing dialogue with the inventor community, the opposite is often the case. If you are a first-time inventor, obtaining an appointment with a toy company gatekeeper can be more difficult than getting an evening dinner reservation at an expensive New York City restaurant on New Year's Eve.

As an independent inventor, you need a game plan to establish contact with the gatekeeper at the company or companies with whom you want to do business. The game plan should not be to blindly send out a detailed description (or worse yet, drawings) of the new idea to a hundred different toy companies with the hope that one or two will bear fruit. Instead, the objective should be to arrange for personal presentation of the new toy idea to the decision-makers at these companies.

The shotgun approach of sending descriptions of your new product idea to hundreds of different toy companies is doomed to failure from the outset. Most companies will not consider the submission absent a written agreement concerning confidentiality. Many companies will simply return the submission with a form letter explaining the company's policy for considering new ideas submitted by outside inventors. More importantly, such letters are clearly non-confidential, and if they mistakenly describe the idea, they serve to do little more than to publish the new idea to all potential competitors.

A more focused approach toward commercializing the new product idea is preferred. Working with the prioritized "victims list," the inventor should proceed down the list with three objectives:

- identify the individual(s) at the particular company who has the responsibility for reviewing outside submissions;
- obtain the written policies of the companies relative to the submission of new product ideas; and
- make appointments with the designated gatekeepers at

these companies to personally present the new product idea.

The first objective is partially accomplished by referring to the directory section in the Appendices to this book. Gatekeepers frequently change, however, and the individuals that we designated in 1995 may be long gone in 1996. Thus, you should make contact with each company of interest to specifically identify the contact individual.

The second objective is to determine whether the toy company has a policy concerning the submission of new product ideas and, if so, obtain a copy of that policy and any standard agreements that the company may require prior to their consideration of any new idea. All of the major toy companies and most of the second tier companies have standard corporate policies (with forms that they require signed) governing the submission and consideration of new product ideas from the outside. These policies are designed to protect the company from possible litigation in the event that the company should eventually market a product similar in appearance to what had been presented to them on an unsolicited basis.

The third and last objective is to obtain an appointment to personally present and explain the new idea. The first two objectives are relatively easy to achieve. Obtaining an appointment to present the new idea, however, is much more difficult.

There have been stories of inventors dressing up as nuns and waiting in the reception area of a toy company to get an appointment with the head of new product development. Other inventors have sent stacks of one reminder letter stapled to all previous reminder letters to toy company executives to get this all important appointment.

Then, of course, there is the old boy's network. When all else fails, knowing someone in charge will always work. Many first-time inventors have gotten through the doors of toy company gatekeepers because their brother's college roommate was the cousin of the chairman of the board. Bottomline, you will need an ample amount of perseverance coupled with a healthy dose of ingenuity to yield the opportunity to make your presentation to the desired companies. When you succeed and get the opportunity to make a presentation, make the most of it!

David Berko, Vice-President for Business Development at Tyco Toys, gave the following bad news to novice inventors at the 1995 *Licensing Journal* seminar on toy development. He stated that most major toy companies have adopted a policy that restricts outside submissions. He indicated that it was a numbers game and that the numbers were stacked against the novice inventor. At Tyco, he has personally reviewed over 5000 products. Of those 5000 products, Tyco paid money on about 40, and of those, only 20 actually made it to Toy Fair. Of those 20, between 5 and 6 got to the marketplace.

Berko stated that most toy companies work with a group of approximately 200 professional toy invention firms. He noted that some of these firms have staffs of 25 or more designers. That's the competition for the first time inventor. His advice to novice inventors was "It's a difficult job. Make sure you're having fun and have enough to eat. Don't quit your day job."

6.3 TIMING OF THE PRESENTATION

It is worthy to note that some inventors use the New York Toy Fair as an opportunity to make the rounds of the toy companies. The thought is that these companies are all in one location, and this permits the inventor to make a number of different presentations to a number of different toy companies without having to travel from city to city.

While this approach has certain advantages, it also has some significant disadvantages. The purpose of Toy Fair is for the toy companies to roll out their new products and sell them to buyers for the upcoming Christmas season. It is undoubtedly one of the most hectic times of the year for toy company executives. Thus, while the company may take time to see inventors with new product ideas, they will not have a tremendous amount of time to fully consider such presentations. At the very least, the gatekeeper will be distracted and may not be in the proper frame of mind to openly consider your new idea.

If the only time you can show your new products is at Toy Fair, then you should try to schedule your appointments during that busy period. If, however, you are able to present your ideas at a more sane time and at the headquarters (or New York showroom) of the company, that is a preferred approach.

Another timing issue relates to the product schedule of most of the toy companies. Since most companies look toward Toy Fair in February (or private shows in December and the foreign shows in January) as the time when they will be introducing their new lines, in order to meet this introduction date, most will have closed down their line in June of the year before. That means that if you want to see your new idea at next year's Toy Fair, you will have to have presented and concluded a deal with the toy company by the summer before. This schedule, of course, is not cast in concrete. Some products that require intricate tooling or molds may require longer lead times. Other products that are more paper and ink or that capture the imagination and excitement of a toy company's upper management may require less time or be given a "special push."

The ideal time to be making presentations to toy companies is in late winter (after Toy Fair and the vacations that follow) and early spring (i.e., March or April). That will give the new product personnel time to consider and test the new idea and the legal department the time to negotiate the final agreement.

6.4 CONFIDENTIAL DISCLOSURE AGREEMENTS

If you do get the opportunity to make a presentation directly to the toy company, you are quickly faced with the issue of confidentiality. You have, no doubt, been instructed by your intellectual property attorney that you should only show your new product idea to someone who first signs a confidential disclosure agreement. But what if the company won't sign, or sends back their form?

Briefly stated, a confidential disclosure agreement (also called a non-disclosure agreement) provides that the receiving party (i.e., the toy company) will hold the idea in confidence and will not use or disclose such idea to any third party for a defined period of time without the prior express written consent of the inventor. A sample confidential disclosure agreement is included in the Appendices.

Thus, prior to any presentation, many inventors attempt to have the toy company sign a confidential disclosure agreement. Some companies will agree. Others, however, will not, particularly with first-time inventors. Instead, the toy company will insist that its standard "waiver agreement," which provides that no confidential relationship is being established between the inventor and the toy company and that the company is not assuming any duty to preserve the confidentiality of the disclosure, be signed by the inventor. The company will typically agree to honor any valid intellectual property rights that the inventor may have or ultimately obtain in the idea. Alternatively, the toy company may include the waiver in their standard product disclosure form. A sample waiver agreement and product disclosure form are included in the Appendices.

There is a rational basis for the toy company's position. The last thing that a toy company wants is to find itself embroiled in a battle with an inventor who may have submitted an idea to them that is similar to one they had been working on for many years and in which they had invested millions of dollars. The easiest and safest way for the toy company to avoid (or at least reduce the likelihood of) litigation is by not entering into confidential relationships with inventors but instead, having them waive any claim which they might otherwise have against the company.

The inventor may seek to engage the toy company in a "battle of the forms." In the end, however, most toy companies will insist that the inventor sign their agreement, whatever it might be, as a pre-condition for the company to review the inventor's proposed submission.

In the unlikely event that you are able to make a presentation without either a confidential disclosure agreement or a waiver agreement having been signed, you must appreciate that there is no confidential relationship between the parties. Thus, the company has no obligation to preserve the confidentiality of your submission. Therefore, you are taking a chance in presenting your idea and leaving documentation of your idea with the toy company without some written agreement. The bottomline is that, at some point in time, you will surely be faced with the question of whether to make a presentation to a company that is willing to consider your idea, but which refuses to establish a confidential relationship, or to take the idea elsewhere. You must make the decision whether it is worth disclosing the idea on a non-confidential basis or taking your idea and going home.

In the end, most first-time inventors acquiesce to the desires of the toy company and waive any confidential relationship. While their intellectual property attorneys will not be happy, they have made the business decision that it is worth taking a chance when the alternative may be not having the idea considered at all.

The decision to proceed without a confidential disclosure relationship is not entirely unjustified. More often than not, the toy company will not copy an independent inventor's brilliant ideas. All toy companies depend, to a large extent, on the inventor community to bring them the newest and brightest ideas. If a company gets a reputation for copying ideas from the inventors who present to them, the company would quickly develop a bad reputation in the inventor community, and the lifeblood of new ideas would be shut off. One of the best things that inventors can do is to rely upon the reputations of the companies they present to and upon their own gut instincts about the integrity of the individual to whom they are showing the idea. This is not fool proof, but is not foolhardy either.

This doesn't mean that you should not develop a paper trail documenting the submission of your idea to the toy company. A letter should be sent to the toy company executive you are meeting with to confirm the date of the meeting and that at this meeting, you will be presenting a new toy product idea. Once the meeting takes place, you should send another letter, confirming the meeting and documenting what was shown. If at all possible, a signed record of the meeting should be prepared identifying who was in attendance and what was shown. If any documentation or materials are left with the company, obtain a receipt from the company. In other words, you should attempt to develop a clear record demonstrating what was presented to the company, when it was presented and to whom it was presented.

6.5 MAKING THE PRESENTATION

Once you get the chance to make a presentation to a toy company, you make the most of the opportunity. The presentation will probably be made in the office of the toy company gatekeeper, although it could be made at the company's showroom, in a hotel room or in your own offices. The toy company may be represented solely by the gatekeeper, or a conference room full of toy company personnel may be present.

One word of advice for the inventor — try to have more than one new product idea ready for the presentation. The gatekeeper is looking for something that his company can buy. Coming in with a single new product idea can result in a very short meeting. The ideal number of new ideas for a presentation is between three and six. That substantially increases the odds for the inventor. Presenting more than six ideas at a meeting may be counterproductive, since the gatekeeper may subconsciously keep moving to the next idea and not give enough thought to any one idea.

While the circumstances may change, there are two things that will not change: (1) you will have a relatively short period of time in which to convince the toy company executive(s) in attendance to invest millions of dollars into making your idea the next blockbuster product; and (2) you had better be prepared to convince the company executive(s) of the potential of your idea in the short period of time you will be allowed.

There are as many approaches to making these presentations as there are people presenting new ideas. Many inventors expend vast sums of money in making working prototypes or producing videotapes of children playing with a prototype toy or game. Other very successful inventors can convince the toy company to license their ideas from sketches or drawings. Sketches or drawings, however, have severe limitations and should only be used for discussion purposes or to determine whether the company has any interest in the idea and if it is worth pursuing further.

The approach which you finally take is highly dependent on the idea or product involved. In many cases, it is advisable to prepare a working prototype, so that the toy company gatekeeper can see exactly what is involved and what type of play pattern is involved. The toy must be demonstrable to the gatekeeper. That's the only way anyone can make a decision.

That doesn't mean that the prototype has to have all of the features of the final product. For example, if the item is a board game with thousands of cards, it is usually sufficient to have a few cards to be able to demonstrate the concept. Similarly, you do not usually have to worry about the packaging or how the item will translate into ancillary product merchandising, e.g., T-shirts, trading cards and the like. No matter what you use, however, you must be able to convey to the gatekeeper "the flavor" of the item and the play value. A prototype is often the best way to accomplish that task.

Many inventors have begun to use videos to demonstrate their new ideas and, more importantly, the play value of such ideas. The advantage of a video is that it can show how children play with a prototype product. It also offers the advantage that it can be left with the gatekeeper so that he can show it to others involved in the idea evaluation process. It is often problematic for an inventor to leave behind his only working prototype. Leaving behind a video of the idea, however, is a less expensive way of accomplishing the same objective.

Ben Kinberg, a toy designer for more than three decades, told attendees at *The Licensing Journal*'s 1995 toy development seminar that inventors can no longer rely on rough prototypes of toys during presentations. He indicated that most manufacturers will want to look at something that they can evaluate very quickly. As a result, the final model should be as finished as time and money will allow. The inventor may want to consider hiring an outside model maker, particularly one with a toy background, to make the final prototype.

It is sometimes advisable for the first-time inventor to retain an experienced toy agent as a consultant before making the first presentation to the toy company. The toy agent should be able to advise the first-time inventor on the likely reception his presentation will receive from the toy company, affording him the opportunity to adjust the presentation before it is made.

Chris Campbell of Tyco Toys, in an interview that he gave for *The Licensing Journal* when he had been at Parker Brothers, offered the following advice to toy and game inventors concerning the all-important presentation:

> The key, if they get an audience, is that (1), they need to have a working prototype and (2) they need to be able to explain to the basic audience for the game the thematic element — why the theme is important and how it is integrated into the game. What age group is most ap-

propriate for the game? What is unique about the item? Why is the item a mass-market item and not just a niche item? What are the principle promotional features of the item? And lastly, why do they believe that it is a product capable of supporting a million dollars or more of television promotion? They need to be able to explain these basic elements of the game as well as the game-play and the game experience in a fairly short period of time.

It is a common mistake, I think, for many inventors to get into a great deal of minutia about the instructions and who goes first and what happens next and so on, without really getting down to the meat and potatoes of the game. One thing that I tell inventors is that when we present a product at Toy Fair or otherwise to a toy buyer, our experience is that literally within about 30 to 60 seconds, that toy buyer has made up his or her mind as to whether or not something is really liked or not liked. In addition to that, we find from consumer dynamics, that when a consumer goes into a store and picks up an item off the shelf, that consumer has generally made his or her purchase decision within ten seconds after picking it up.

So the point I'm trying to make is that the more succinct the inventors are and the better ability they have to define the parameters of their game or toy in a quick summary-type fashion, the better they are going to be at holding the attention of the person reviewing it. (February 1991, at 4-5.)

Cathy Rondeau-Dobosz, the inventor of the GIRL TALK® game, told this story of her first presentation to a toy company at a Toy Fair seminar on new product development:

I had done this doll that I thought was the best. I made up this presentation. I did poster boards, sound tracks, music — the whole works. I had a pointer in my briefcase. It was wonderful. I got there and they brought me into a shoebox of a room. They told me I had nine minutes. I sat there across from two toy industry executives who had dead panned expressions. Straight out of the casket, no breath, dead. I brought out my first product and explained why they should love it. One of the guys goes "Blah." I got out my next one and before I started they both went, "Blah."

Then I said, "Look, I've never done this before. I don't know what I'm doing. I really like this business. Be a nice guy. Give me a break. Let me tell you about another idea. Totally seat of the pants, no non-disclosure agreement, no nothing."

The toy executive said, "I love it. I want to see it."

Two weeks later, I had an option agreement on the product for which I had no prototype, no artwork.

I don't recommend this. It's not the way to go. But that's what this business is. Seat of the pants. You've got to go in there and wing it. You're going to have people ask you questions about issues you don't have the foggiest idea about. When you don't know something, be honest. Be yourself and don't take yourself too seriously.

David Berko of Tyco Toys told prospective toy inventors at *The Licensing Journal*'s 1995 toy development seminar that they should not try to sell their products, but simply present them. If the product doesn't sell itself, the inventor will not be able to sell it. Rejection should be a way of life for the toy inventor. He noted that most inventors present several products. That way, when one gets rejected, the inventor can move on to the next one.

6.6 SUBMISSIONS BY PARCEL POST

Not every inventor will have the opportunity to make a formal presentation to the toy company gatekeeper. Some will choose to simply send their ideas into the toy company with a product submission form and hope that the new product idea and the explanatory material associated with it will sell the idea.

Clearly, "submissions by parcel post" are not the ideal way to make new product presentations, although there are times when the inventor has no other choice. Some inventors simply lack the financial resources to make the trips necessary for face-to-face presentations. Other inventors cannot afford the time necessary to make such presentations. If you have no other choice but to present your new product idea in this manner, the only suggestion we can offer is to make the submission as complete as possible. Provide as much detailed material as possible to accompany the prototype to assist the gatekeeper in evaluating the submission. A short video explaining the item and its features might be a good substitute for a face-to-face meeting. Clearly label everything — the video, the prototype and its component parts and the accompanying materials — with your name.

6.7 THE EVALUATION PROCESS

The gatekeeper sometimes advises the inventor at the presentation that the inventor's idea does not fit into the company's future plans. In which case, the gatekeeper and the inventor part as friends and the inventor then moves down to the next company on the victim's list. If, however, the gatekeeper likes the idea, he will typically ask the inventor for time to show it to others at the company and to further evaluate the idea, during which the inventor will be asked not to show the idea to any other company.

Typically, the gatekeeper will want this first evaluation period to be a freebie. As an inventor, you should anticipate that the company will need time to properly consider and evaluate the property. As such, you should be prepared to allow the company to conduct this evaluation for a reasonable period of time, i.e., two or three weeks. During this time, it is reasonable for the company to expect that you will not continue to show the idea to other companies, even though there is no contractual obligation on your part to refrain from continuing to market the idea. It is a good policy to reach an understanding with the gatekeeper as to whether the idea will continue to be shown or presented and how long this freebie evaluation period will last.

Most toy companies have product review committees to which the inventor's new idea must be presented. The product review committee is normally composed of product development, marketing and management personnel. If the gatekeeper believes that the idea has merit, he will arrange to have the new idea submitted to the product review committee for their consideration. The gatekeeper has to champion the new product idea before this committee. Therefore, the inventor needs to give the gatekeeper the tools to help him to champion the idea through the system. A great idea is important. Support from the gatekeeper for the great idea can be just as important when the idea is presented to the product review committee.

Obviously, the evaluation of the idea by the toy company takes time. The company will examine such factors as how much it will cost to manufacture the finished toy product, where it fits into the company's product line and whether or not it is legally protectable. At this point, the company may also run studies to measure the toy's play value and even talk to retailers about the idea (assuming they are permitted to by the terms of any confidential disclosure agreement). Many of the major toy companies have play labs in which they field test new product ideas. These new toys are played with by children while company executives observe them in action.

Most toy companies will advise inventors within two to three weeks after the presentation whether the company has any interest in the new idea. Those items that are rejected are usually returned with a personal letter explaining why they were rejected. Unfortunately, a relatively high percentage of new ideas that are taken for purposes of evaluation are never ultimately licensed.

In the event that the toy company believes that the new idea has promise, one of two things will happen. The company may contact the inventor and indicate that it would like to enter into an agreement and turn the matter over to their attorney or legal department. Alternatively, the company may require further time to evaluate the new idea to see whether it fits within their future plans. Perhaps, they believe that additional costing is required or that testing in a play lab would be helpful. They may even want to speak with prospective buyers at retail outlets to determine what the potential market for the product is. Whatever the reason may be for delaying the final decision, what the company needs is additional time. In such case, they will go back to the inventor and ask for that time. Sometimes the additional time may be a matter of a week or two. There are other occasions where the additional time needed is four or eight weeks.

6.8 FOLLOW-UP

Follow-up is perhaps the most often overlooked area in the selling process. You have spent hundreds or even thousands of hours in the conception and development of the new product idea, invested many thousands of dollars in the creation of a working prototype and expended time and energy in making the rounds of the toy companies to convince them to license your product ideas only to have a company take your new idea for evaluation. It is at this point, that cold feet normally develop.

Weeks go by and neither a letter nor a telephone call has come from the gatekeeper. You are, of course, afraid to call for fear that the call will offend the gatekeeper and destroy any chances you might have to sell the product idea. Weeks go into months and still there is no communication from the gatekeeper. During this period you have taken the idea off the market and potentially passed up a number of possible selling opportunities.

Finally, you call the gatekeeper and ask whether the company has made a decision. The gatekeeper apologizes and offers some reason for the delay. More often than not, the pressures of time and other matters have caused the gatekeeper to "sit on" the idea. A couple of days later, a letter arrives either accepting or rejecting the idea.

If the letter indicates that the company has decided to license the new product idea, all is forgiven. If, however, the new product idea is rejected (as are most submissions), you have lost weeks or months in the selling season.

Toy companies should not be offended by inquiries by inventors as to the status of ideas under evaluation. That does not mean that you should become a nuisance and start calling every other day. It does mean, however, that you should ask the gatekeeper when the gatekeeper first informs you that the company wants to keep the idea for evaluation when you might expect a decision by the company. When that date comes, if you have not received an answer, it is totally proper and prudent for you to follow up on the submission with a call to the gatekeeper. Thereafter, regular inquiries should be made until a decision (one way or the other) is finally made by the company.

6.9 THE OPTION AGREEMENT

If, at the end of this initial evaluation period, the decision-makers at the toy company believe there is some merit to the new idea, but they have not concluded the evaluation process, they may ask you for an option to enter into a license agreement. For a fixed sum of money, an amount negotiated between the parties, the company buys time from the inventor for purposes of further evaluation. The option payment should be a non-refundable, non-recoupable payment. It is analogous to the company renting the idea for a fixed period of time. Pursuant to most option agreements, the inventor agrees that he will not show the new idea to any other company during the option period.

Most option payments are between $500 and $25,000, depending on the quality of the idea and the amount of time that the toy company needs to evaluate the idea. Most option periods are between thirty and sixty days, although some may run as long as six months.

If the toy company's product review committee has not done so already, it will typically conduct extensive market studies on the idea during the option period. The cost of introducing a new toy product is quite high and most toy companies will not commit themselves to a new product without first conducting extensive market studies. These studies will consist of one or more focus groups where prototypes of the product are given to children to play with. In addition, they will fully study the cost of manufacturing the product.

Getting the toy company to take an option on a new product idea is, unfortunately, merely the first step. Not all the properties which go to option are ultimately licensed. At the end of the option period, the company will either return the idea or, alternatively, exercise the option and begin to discuss a license agreement. If the toy company decides against licensing the product, the inventor is free to present the new product idea to other companies and to enter into agreements with those companies. Any monies that were paid for the option are retained by the inventor since such payments were non-refundable.

Assuming that the toy company elects to proceed with a license agreement, one of the first issues raised will be how to handle the option payment. Some companies ask the inventor to treat the option payment as an advance against eventual earned royalties when they begin to market product. Others honor the original deal — the money is a non-recoupable option payment and should be retained by the inventor and not treated as an advance.

There have been instances where at least one toy company has asked the inventor of a new product idea that they optioned and rejected to rebate a portion of the option monies in the event that the inventor was ever able to license the idea to another company. That is a bit overreaching and typically finds no basis in the contractual documents. The toy company's arm-twisting "logic," however, is "If you want to continue to do business with us, ..." Inventors should not feel obligated to comply with such requests.

One thing which the inventor should bear in mind when entering into an option agreement with a toy company is timing. Most major toy companies introduce their new products every year at the Toy Fair in New York City in February. The product line for each of these companies is often closed during the previous spring. That means that if the idea is not licensed by June, the chances of getting any other toy company to pick up the idea for introduction the following year is quite slim. Thus, if a toy company wants an option from April until July, you need to recognize that if the company does not exercise its option at the end of the option period and take a license, you have effectively lost a year for the idea. Thus, the value of an option for such a three month period should be much greater than an option for a shorter period of time or during the fall months. A sample option agreement is included in the Appendices.

First and foremost, the option agreement must define specifically and precisely which idea or ideas are being optioned. The specifics as to how to identify each of the optioned ideas will vary, depending upon the particular idea and ultimate product. A detailed description of each idea is the minimum that should be included. Photographs or drawings may be attached. The goal is to include sufficient specificity to permit an impartial party years later to read the option agreement and understand exactly what was to be covered.

Second, the duration of the option agreement must be clearly specified. No specific guidelines can be provided for deciding what the duration should be, as it will vary depending upon the complexity of the idea and the amount of testing or evaluation required. The time frame should, however, only be long enough to permit the company to fully evaluate the idea.

The option agreement should also provide that in the event that the company exercises the option, the parties will enter into a written agreement within a specified period of time (e.g., thirty days). This protects the inventor from having the company drag its feet in the negotiation of the eventual license agreement. It is also not a bad idea to include some of the more salient provisions of the eventual license agreement in the option agreement, including the royalty rate, the advance, the product introduction date and any guarantees.

The option agreement should also provide how the option fee is to be treated in the event that the company exercises the option, e.g., either the option fee is a non-refundable, non-recoupable payment or the option fee will be treated as a recoupable advance against royalties which the company will owe the inventor under the license.

Finally, as in a confidential disclosure agreement, the option agreement should specify that, in the event that the toy company chooses not to exercise the option, it will return to the inventor all materials relating to the idea and will neither use the idea itself nor disclose it to third parties.

6.10 HANDLING REJECTION

All inventors, no matter how successful they may have been over their lifetime, will experience rejection when attempting to license. The reason is simple — the invention industry as it relates to new toy products is a numbers game and, unfortunately, the numbers work against the inventor. For every new product idea that a toy company licenses each year, they have probably seen a thousand submissions, all of which were rejected in favor of the one that they eventually licensed. Thus, the odds are clearly stacked against the inventor. The inventor must understand that there are many reasons why a toy or game company will turn down a brilliant idea. These reasons include:

- **Bad timing.** The line for the next Toy Fair may have already closed, and the company may not want to begin considering ideas for new products for the following year.
- **The product "fit" is wrong**. The company may believe that its future direction is with girl's games and the rejected idea is for a new boy's action figure that simply does not form part of their short or long term marketing plans.
- **Previous bad experience.** The company may have had a bad experience with similar products in the past and is reluctant to try again.
- **Other similar ideas already in-house**. The company may already be developing a similar product idea in-house, or may have received one from another inventor. Alternatively, the company's next line may contain a number of similarly positioned products, and the company knows that they will not be able to convince a retailer to take more than a certain number of the same type products at the same time from them.
- **Too expensive.** The company may believe that it would cost more to manufacture the product that it could reasonably be sold for.
- **The idea stinks.** As difficult as this might be to imagine, some new product ideas are just lousy. The company representative may simply not like the idea or, more importantly, may believe that the consuming public will not like it.

In an ideal world, the toy company representative will tell the inventor the real reason or reasons why he has elected to pass on the new product idea. Unfortunately, however, we don't live in an ideal world. Most companies are reluctant to tell an inventor that his idea is bad or unworkable. To do that would offend the inventor and effectively close the door in the future when he brings in the next CABBAGE PATCH® doll. Instead, most toy companies will try to let the inventor down gently (but firmly).

The toy inventor should not be discouraged. Toy executives are not infallible. The CABBAGE PATCH® doll was passed on by virtually every toy company in the world until Coleco finally took the chance and made it a tremendous success. One former game company executive stated that he was lucky that he was not shown the TRIVIAL PURSUIT® game. He stated that he would have rejected the idea believing that the market wasn't ready for a question and answer game that sold for $40, when the market was reluctant to pay more than $15 for similar games.

Dan Lauer, President of Lauer Toys and the inventor of the WATERBABIES doll, revealed his success story at *The Licensing Journal*'s 1995 toy development seminar. He said that he got the idea for his product, a doll that you fill with water to make it feel like a real baby, from his sisters. They used to make dolls out of water balloons. His first prototype was made from a balloon and four condoms. Four years later, it was the top selling doll in the country.

He indicated that the licensing process was a "roller coaster ride with a lot of peaks and valleys." Lauer initially committed 10 hours and a $100 per week to the project. He was very aggressive in trying to find a toy company that would take on the project and contacted the presidents of the major toy companies, only to learn that they were too busy to return his calls. He was initially rejected by all the major toy companies. They didn't have a problem with the concept, but with the execution. He went through 35 prototype stages, later admitting that each was needed. Every failure in the process was a learning experience.

Finally, after manufacturing and selling a limited number of products, he achieved success. Many of his retail accounts recommended him to several major toy companies and the rest is history. Perseverance finally paid off.

The inventor should take solace in the words of Mel Taft, former head of product development for Milton Bradley who stated that, "Any inventor or member of management who tells you that he's a genius in looking at an idea and can tell you whether it's good or not is full of baloney."

Chapter Seven:
NEGOTIATING THE DEAL

At long last, the telephone call comes from the toy company advising you that their testing of your idea was positive, and they want to license your idea and introduce the resulting product at next year's Toy Fair. You are told that you will be hearing from the company's attorney in the near future and will receive a copy of the company's standard inventor license agreement. The fun has only just begun.

7.1 TO USE A LAWYER OR NOT?

The first question you should consider is whether to negotiate the agreement yourself or to turn it over to your attorney. A number of professional toy design firms regularly negotiate their own agreements, believing that they have probably seen more license agreements than the average lawyer. In contrast, there are a number of other professional toy invention firms that regularly rely on counsel to review each of their agreements, believing that their forte is creation, while the attorney's strength is negotiating the best deal for them and, more importantly, protecting them.

There are pros and cons to both approaches, particularly when using a general attorney who is not familiar with the toy industry. Inventors should understand that the toy company will be represented by an attorney who has drafted and negotiated hundreds of similar contracts. Thus, if you have any hesitation about the structure or terms of the agreement, you are probably well-advised to seek counsel.

Counsel can be used in a number of different ways. You can use an attorney simply to review the agreement, providing comments but allowing you to negotiate the terms with the toy company. In such a scenario, the attorney works behind the scenes. Alternatively, you can turn the entire matter over to the lawyer who will represent you in the negotiation. Both ways work. The only question is how comfortable you feel in actually negotiating on your own behalf.

If you decide to utilize an attorney in either capacity, you should make sure that the attorney has had experience in the toy industry. There are certain "standard" provisions in toy inventor license agreements which are necessitated by the nature of the toy industry. The negotiations will proceed must faster and with less acrimony where the attorney understands the toy industry, the standard clauses in toy industry agreements and the process toy companies typically follow in negotiations. As an inventor, you do not want to be in the position of having to pay to educate an inexperienced attorney on the toy industry.

7.2 THE INITIAL NEGOTIATION

The structure of an inventor license agreement in the toy industry is not dissimilar to the structure of most intellectual property license agreements. It should be understood, however, that the respective negotiating positions of the parties are vastly different than in a typical licensor-licensee setting. While toy companies will regularly say that they need the inventor community, their attorneys often act in a manner that conveys just the opposite. Inventor attorneys will frequently hear the dreaded statement, "This issue is non-negotiable. If your client won't accept it, we'll return the idea." Translated, that means "Take it or leave it." Both you and your attorney must understand that while the company may be very interested in the particular new product idea, there are literally thousands of other concepts that "almost" made the company's product line. If you become overly difficult in negotiations or ask for the moon, the company's attorney will quickly tell the company's business people that you are unreasonable and that a deal cannot be structured.

Thus, the role of the negotiator (you or your attorney) is to get the best deal from the company's lawyer without ruining the underlying business deal. That makes toy license agreement negotiations very difficult. Your attorney must understand what issues he can press and what issues must be dropped; when you can successfully "go over the toy company attorney's head" to the business people you had originally spoken to, and when the business people are powerless because it is the attorney's "call." For toy inventors and their lawyers, it is perhaps the most challenging negotiation that they may ever experience.

7.3 THE LETTER OF INTENT

One of the most effective ways to insure that oral negotiations between the inventor and the toy company business people ultimately result in a formal license agreement is through the use of a letter of intent. At the conclusion of the negotiation of the salient business terms (e.g., royalty rate, advances, product introduction date), the parties both sign a simple letter agreement that should reflect these negotiations, with the understanding that each would then turn the matter over to their respective attorneys for negotiation of the formal license agreement.

The letter of intent is simply a one- or two-page letter from the inventor to the toy company (generally prepared in advance by the inventor's attorney), which outlines the salient business considerations of the ultimate arrangement. When the inventor's attorney prepares such a letter, the specific business terms are left blank with the understanding that it will serve as an outline for the negotiation. At the conclusion of the negotiations, the parties insert the appropriate numbers agreed upon during the negotiations and then sign the letter. The letter of intent should address the following essential elements of the arrangement:

- the nature of the grant, i.e., exclusive vs. non-exclusive;
- an identification of the new product idea to be covered by the license;
- the licensed territory;
- the term of the agreement;
- the royalty rate, advances and guaranteed minimum royalties;
- the extent of quality control procedures to be followed by the company;
- the product introduction date both domestically and internationally;
- the amount of product liability insurance required; and
- the date by which all negotiations must be concluded and the license signed.

The letter of intent is intended to serve as a preliminary document to bind the parties for a limited period of time to particular terms and conditions. It is subject to the parties' entering into a formal license agreement within that period of time. Failure to conclude such a formal license agreement will result in expiration of the letter of intent.

Letters of intent are frequently used for "hot" ideas, i.e., where the company executives are afraid that they may lose the new product idea while their legal department undertakes drafting and negotiating the final agreement. In such cases, the letter of intent serves to bind the deal. Frequently, part or all of the advance will be paid by the company upon execution of the letter of intent. The advantage of the letter of intent is that it helps the attorneys draft the agreement, since the relevant business terms have already been included.

Letters of intent are particularly effective in avoiding endless hassling between the attorneys over legal issues. As the letter of intent will generally include a time period within which a formal definitive license agreement must be concluded, the attorneys are presented with an agreed-upon outline of business terms and a deadline when a formal agreement must be completed.

If either side's attorney knit-picks over minor legal issues, he runs the risk of killing the deal — a deal which his client considers a *faitaccompli.* Attorneys know they better have a good reason for killing such a deal. When negotiating an agreement, attorneys often need an impetus to proceed in an expeditious fashion. A deadline within which an agreement must be worked out is an excellent impetus.

7.4 THE AGREEMENT

When the company finally decides to proceed with a new product idea, it will transmit to the inventor its "standard form" agreement. Types of arrangements between inventors and toy companies include:

- assignment of the new product idea from the inventor to the company solely for use in connection with products manufactured by the company;

- assignment of the new product idea from the inventor to the company for use in connection with products manufactured by the company and/or others;
- non-exclusive license from the inventor to the company solely for use of the new product idea in connection with the company's products;
- exclusive license from the inventor to the company solely for use of the new product idea in connection with the company's products; and
- exclusive license from the inventor to the company for use of the new product idea in connection with the company's products with the right to grant sublicenses to others to use the idea.

Under the license arrangements, the inventor retains all rights in the new product idea and simply grants a "license" to the company to use such rights. In the event that the license agreement should terminate for any reason, the right to use the idea is terminated, and the rights revert back to the inventor.

In contrast, an assignment means that the inventor has assigned or otherwise conveyed his rights in his idea to the toy company which will retain such rights forever. Upon expiration or termination of the agreement, there may (or may not) be a provision in the agreement assigning back the rights in the invention to the inventor.

In either case, the inventor is paid a royalty or a percentage of the company's sales of products based on the new product idea. By and large, most toy companies prefer to license ideas rather than to take assignments of them. From the perspective of the inventor, this is preferable as well.

7.4.1 Battle of Forms

Most toy companies have their own standard agreements that they send to the inventor for review and, hopefully, signature. Similarly, most professional design firms have their own standard agreements that they are comfortable with and prefer to use. Each of these standard agreements were obviously drafted to protect the interests of their clients. In other words, each agreement favors the party drafting the agreement.

You are always better off using your own agreement and negotiating off the provisions contained therein. There are toy companies that will not object to this practice. The major toy companies, however, will insist that you work from the company's form agreement. In the final analysis, however, there is really little difference whose form is used. The obvious objective is to conclude a deal that both parties can live with.

7.4.2 Terminology

The terminology used in most license agreements varies greatly and is almost always a function of the attorney drafting the agreement. In license agreements, the parties are typically referred to as "Licensor" (the inventor) and "Licensee" (the company) although terminology varies greatly. In assignment agreements, the parties may be referred to by their respective names or, alternatively, as "Inventor" or "Designer" and the "Company" or "Manufacturer."

The new product idea may be called the "Property," "Licensed Property," "Concept," "Item," "Work" or any other word or phrase the parties may choose and define in the agreement. The actual words or phrases chosen are irrelevant, provided that a definition for each word is provided in the agreement. For purposes of this chapter, we will use the term "Property" to refer to the new product idea that is to be the subject of the agreement and any patents, trademarks, copyrights or other intellectual property rights relating thereto. Exhibits to the agreement which provide a detailed description of the Property, as well as photographs or drawings of the Property, are strongly advised.

The product in connection with which the Property is used is usually called the "Licensed Product," the "Product" or the "Article." For purposes of this chapter, we will refer to the goods in connection with which the Property is being used as the "Products." Another term used in such agreements is the "Territory," which refers to the geographical area in which the Licensee may make, use and sell Products.

7.4.3 Grant of Rights

The essential element of any agreement is the grant of rights.

In a license agreement, the grant will be an authorization to use the invention. In an assignment agreement, the grant will be a conveyance or transfer of all property rights in the invention.

In the context of a license agreement, there are two essential types of grants, i.e., exclusive and non-exclusive. An exclusive license agreement is where the company is the only entity that can use the Property with respect to the Products in the Territory. Note that the grant is restricted by Property, Product and Territory. Thus, the inventor can grant other exclusive (or non-exclusive) agreements to third parties for items other than the Property or for products other than the Product or outside the Territory.

In a non-exclusive relationship, the company is simply one of potentially many who may use the Property. Most toy companies are reluctant to enter into non-exclusive arrangements. In the toy industry, non-exclusive arrangements are used mainly to settle disputes between parties, typically after a claim of infringement has been made.

7.4.4 Term of the Agreement

Perhaps the most significant difference between inventor agreements and traditional intellectual property license agreements is the term. Most intellectual property license agreements are for a fixed term, e.g., two years, five years, life of the patent, etc. In stark contrast, most toy inventor agreements are for an indeterminate length, e.g., "for so long as the Company or its sublicensees continue to use the Property."

Toy companies generally do not want to assume all of the risks associated with a new, undeveloped product idea without knowing that they can control rights to it for its entire commercial life. The last thing they want to do is find themselves in a bidding war with their competitors for the very idea that they spent millions of dollars in developing, promoting and making a commercial success.

In those instances where a new product idea is licensed for a fixed period of time, the companies may request options to renew the agreement for defined terms, the only qualification being that they must meet certain threshold sales levels to exercise the renewal options. For example, the term of the agreement may be three years, with the company being given the option of renewing the agreement for additional three-year terms, provided that it generates at least $100,000 in royalty income for the inventor during each of the then in-effect terms.

7.4.5 Compensation

The manner in which the inventor is compensated for the use of the Property by a toy company and any sublicensees can vary widely. Possible options include:

- one-time lump sum payment to the inventor;
- ongoing royalty to the inventor, based solely on sales of Product by the company, and not on sales by third parties under sublicense from the company, with no advance or guaranteed minimum payment;
- ongoing royalty or commission to the inventor based on both sales of Product by the company and royalty income derived from third parties, with no advance or guaranteed minimum payment; and
- either of paragraphs 2 or 3 above except that the inventor is paid an advance and/or a guaranteed minimum royalty payment.

Toy companies typically pay inventors a royalty of between one and ten percent of their net domestic sales of Products, although typically the rate is between five and six percent of such net sales. Many companies sell on an F.O.B. or Letter of Credit (L.C.) basis, where the retailer will assume possession of the Products at an off-shore factory at a substantially lower price. It is not uncommon for the F.O.B. rate to retailers to be as much as thirty percent lower than the domestic selling price. One reason for this lower rate is that the retailer is absorbing the shipping costs. In order to protect the inventor's royalty rate in such instances, most toy companies will agree to pay royalties to the inventor at two different rates, e.g., on domestic sales and on F.O.B. sales. The difference between the royalty rate for domestic sales and the one for F.O.B. sales is typically between two and four percentage points. Thus, if the royalty rate for domestic sales is five percent, the F.O.B. rate may be eight percent.

Character licensing is a way of doing business in the toy industry. Incorporating, for example, the SESAME STREET or the DISNEY name and characters on a pre-school toy product will assuredly enhance the sales of such product. The right to use famous characters, however, costs the toy company money. Typical royalty rates for licensing such famous characters are usually between six and ten percent of the company's net sales of the licensed products. If the product is one brought in from the outside, the toy company is facing a double royalty situation, e.g., ten percent to DISNEY and five percent to the inventor. In such double royalty situations, the company will look to the inventor to reduce his royalty rate. For example, the company may want the inventor to reduce his domestic rate from five to twenty-five percent where the Product is to be marketed in conjunction with a licensed character.

While reducing his royalty rate because of the toy company's decision to license and use a famous character in connection with the Product may at first seem unpalatable to the inventor, the ultimate outcome for the inventor may actually be very positive. Clearly, the incorporation of a MICKEY MOUSE® or a BIG BIRD® character on the Product will increase the sales of the Product, as well as justify an increased selling price. The combination of the two will, hopefully, not only make up for the reduced royalty rate applied against sales, but actually result in greater total royalties.

One word of caution. The use of a "famous" licensed character will, undoubtedly, increase sales. The use of an unknown character, however, will not. The inventor should have some control over the types of characters that may be used which will trigger a reduced royalty rate.

Most toy companies will agree to pay the inventor an advance against royalties, typically in a range between $2000 and $50,000, depending on the Property involved, the toy company and the track record of the inventor. There have, of course, been much higher advances paid and, likewise, there have been instances where no advances were paid at all.

The need for an advance is quite important in the toy industry for two reasons. The first is because of the inventor's financial situation. Major toy companies regularly work at least one year ahead of product introduction dates. That means if a product is to be introduced at Toy Fair 1995, the toy company will undoubtedly have entered into an agreement with the inventor sometime before summer 1994. Assuming that the Product was introduced in February, 1995, first shipments of the Product would normally not begin until the summer of 1995 for the Christmas season. It is possible that actual earned royalties won't start to accrue on such shipments until the fourth quarter of 1995, and royalty payments of any consequence won't be made until January 30, 1996. Thus, without an advance, the inventor could go more than eighteen months before he begins to see any money from the Property.

The second reason an advance is important is that it tends to push the toy company to introduce a product idea rather than let it drop. The greater the toy company's investment in a Product, the more likely it is that the Product will be launched and supported with advertising and promotion. Sometimes, the company has licensed more ideas than it can actually commercialize and, as a result, the company decides to reduce the number of new products being introduced. If this occurs, the company is much more likely to drop those in connection with which it has little or nothing invested. If the toy company won't agree to pay an advance, "all is not lost" — at the very least, get the toy company to agree to spend an equivalent amount on advertising and promotional support for the Property (admittedly a different form of "investment" but nevertheless, one which still results in the same beneficial self-motivated commitment).

The inventor should explore the possibility of receiving a guaranteed minimum royalty from the toy company. A guaranteed minimum royalty means that the toy company guarantees the inventor that it will pay him a minimum of $X per year or $Y over the term of the agreement, regardless of the actual sales of the Product. Thus, if the Product is a flop, the inventor knows that he will receive at least the minimum guaranteed amount. The obvious purpose of a guaranteed minimum royalty is to protect the inventor from the failed or marginally successful product. While guaranteed minimum royalties are commonplace in the merchandising and entertainment areas, they are not in the toy industry, except for really hot properties.

Many toy companies will, however, agree to a non-guaranteed minimum royalty that must be met to maintain rights under the agreement. That means that should the earned royalty fall below that minimum royalty during any calendar year, and should the toy company elect not to supplement the actual earned royalty payments to meet the minimum royalty amount, the inventor will have the right to terminate the agreement. For example, the parties may agree that the inventor will receive a minimum royalty of $25,000 per year. In the event that the company fails to meet the $25,000 minimum royalty obligation for any one year, and in the event the toy company elects not to supplement the earned royalty payments to achieve the $25,000 minimum royalty, the inventor would have the right to terminate the agreement.

7.4.6 Sublicensing and Ancillary Rights Provisions

Most companies are incapable of fully commercializing an idea in all possible toy forms in all countries in the Territory of the agreement. In many instances, toy companies will grant sublicenses to unrelated third parties or work through foreign affiliates or distributors to commercialize the invention in all possible toy forms in all possible countries. Accordingly, most toy companies will want to obtain from the inventor the unilateral right to grant sublicenses to third parties to commercialize the invention.

We live at a time when ancillary product licensing encompasses every imaginable industry. We are surrounded by SNOOPY® sweatshirts, LOS ANGELES DODGERS® baseball caps, CABBAGE PATCH® trading cards, BATMAN® costumes, and the list goes on and on. Ancillary product licensing is a very lucrative field. The toy companies are very much aware of this fact and seek at every opportunity to capitalize on ancillary licensing. Accordingly, most companies will seek to acquire (either by license or assignment) all ancillary product licensing or merchandising rights associated with the Property.

Toy companies also realize the tremendous licensing opportunities in the entertainment field and will want the entertainment rights associated with the Property. This is particularly important with respect to action figures that readily translate into animation productions, and games which often translate easily into electronic video games and television game shows.

Where the toy company intends to acquire sublicensing rights or ancillary or entertainment rights, the agreement should so provide. The inventor should have the right to approve all sublicenses, although this may be a right that is difficult to obtain. The toy company usually will argue it is sufficient if the inventor receives compensation from such activities. At the very least, the toy company should be obligated to advise the inventor of any sublicenses that it grants.

The critical point of negotiation usually is how the inventor and the company are to share any income derived from the sublicensing or ancillary or entertainment licensing programs. While most companies agree that the inventor should share in revenues received from such activities, the question always presented is: to what extent?

A fifty-fifty split of net income (gross income less the cost of conducting the program or an agent's commission if an outside agent is used) between the inventor and the toy company is ostensibly fair. Such a formula gives the company the ability to deduct its costs of conducting the program against such income prior to an equitable distribution of the remainder to the inventor.

Most toy companies, however, are not so benevolent. Typically, the first offer to the inventor is either no sharing of income at all or an 85/15 split of net income in favor of the toy company. Companies making such offers believe that they should be entitled to the entire proceeds or this larger share because, if it hadn't been for their efforts, no one would have been interested in taking a sublicense or an ancillary or entertainment license.

The entire question of division of these types of revenues is a matter of negotiation between the parties. The ultimate goal is to achieve an equitable sharing. In no event should the inventor ever be lulled into merely having such income added to the toy company's net sales, such that all the inventor gets is an amount equal to the royalty rate times the income the toy company receives, i.e., a 5 percent royalty on the 5 percent sub-licensing royalty paid to the toy company from the sublicensee. In such circumstances, what the inventor is getting is tantamount to zero.

Perhaps a simpler approach to the entire matter is to base the split on gross income rather than on net income, with the recognition that the toy company will assume the financial responsibility for conducting the sublicensing or merchandising program. Thus, the inventor might receive 30 percent of the gross sublicensing and merchandising income. This is the financial equivalent of a 50/50 split of net income after the deduction of a 40 percent commission for the licensing agent (which is a fairly typical commission in merchandising). This eliminates any future arguments between the parties over what is (or is not) an allocable expense. For example, was the ten-day trip the toy company's vice-president took with his wife to Switzerland during the ski season really necessary, even though he talked with two potential sublicensees?

One word of caution on the issue of sublicensing is needed. The inventor should not permit the toy company to sublicense the Product in the major market areas, e.g., the United States, etc., as this can substantially reduce the inventor's ultimate income. Assume that the parties negotiate a royalty rate of five percent. The inventor therefore receives $5 for every $100 worth of Products that are sold. If, however, the company sublicensed these rights to a third party for a 5 percent royalty and if the parties had agreed to share equally the gross sublicensing income, the inventor's effective royalty rate would be 2.5 percent. If the parties agreed to base the sharing on a net rather than gross basis, it could be even less than that.

Ultimately, the reason the inventor chose the particular toy company was because of its ability to market the Product in a particular area. The inventor should insist that the company market the Product itself in that area, and not attempt to sublicense these rights. An alternative approach that would protect the inventor in such a situation would be to base the inventor's share of sublicensing income on the higher of 50 percent of the sublicensing income or 5 percent of the sublicensee's net sales.

7.4.7 Accounting Provisions

One of the most important considerations in any license agreement is the definition of "net sales," since this is the basis for the calculation of the company's royalty payment to the inventor. In general terms, "net sales" are normally defined as the gross sales of a particular product less shipping costs, taxes, credits and discounts and returns. Some companies prefer to negotiate a flat percentage for such deductions, rather than attempting to individually itemize each one. Such percentages normally range from between five and ten percent of gross sales.

Royalty accounting for most toy companies is provided on a quarterly calendar basis, with statements and payments due within thirty days after the conclusion of the previous quarter. Thus, the companies will report and pay royalties by January 30th, April 30th, July 30th and October 30th of each year. The agreement should clearly spell out the types of statements that the company is obligated to provide the inventor. A sample statement may actually be appended to the agreement.

The inventor should have the right to audit the company's books to verify the accuracy of the company's accounting. The inventor is required to give reasonable notice to the toy company, and the inspection should be at the company's place of business during reasonable business hours. The inventor should have the right to make copies of what he is shown during the course of the audit. The agreement should further provide that in the event that the audit reveals an underpayment of at least a certain amount, the toy company will pay for the reasonable cost of the audit as well as paying the underpayment with interest. A normal threshold figure is $5,000, although it could be a percentage of the sums actually paid, e.g., three percent.

The agreement should also provide that the toy company will pay interest on any late payments made to the inventor. It is a good idea to establish the index for such interest payments, e.g., at the rate of one percent per month from the date the payment was originally due.

7.4.8 Additional Design Work

Almost invariably, a new product idea presented to a toy company by an outside inventor will require further development work prior to introduction. In most inventor/company relationships, a question arises as to who is responsible for the effort and expenses of such additional development work. Most toy companies will undertake this further development effort, although some do require the inventor to take care of it. In either event, however, the parties should reach some agreement as to what additional development work, if any, is required, and who will undertake such development work at whose expense.

In certain instances, toy companies will retain the services of the inventor as an independent contractor on a per diem or flat fee basis to continue the development work on the item. Whether those sums are treated as non-refundable or, alternatively, as an advance against royalties, is a matter of negotiation between the inventor and the company to be memorialized in the agreement.

The inventor may be required to travel in furtherance of the development work or commercialization of the idea, and the parties again must determine to what extent the inventor can be required to do this, on how much notice and who will be financially responsible for the costs associated with such travel.

7.4.9 Product Introduction Dates

One of the essential elements of any toy agreement is when the company will first introduce the new product. It is important because the introduction date will determine when the earned royalty stream will begin. It will also light a fire under the toy company, because it will be tied to a termination provision that will allow the inventor to terminate the toy company and move on to another company if the original company doesn't actually commercialize the idea when promised.

Almost all toy agreements will include at least a product introduction date, i.e., the company agrees to introduce the product on or before the 1995 New York Toy Fair, and should the company fail to meet such date, the inventor shall have the right to terminate the agreement.

Product introduction dates are wonderful, but they do not trigger a royalty obligation. Sales trigger royalty obligations. Thus, in addition to the product introduction date, there should be a first shipment date, e.g., the date the company agrees to begin shipment of the product in commercially reasonable quantities. Typically, the first shipment date is a few months after the product introduction date.

If the agreement is a worldwide agreement, a time requirement must be given for introduction outside the United States. Typically, the company is given one year from the introduction in the United States to introduce and begin shipping product abroad. Consideration may also be given to handling this on a country-by-country basis. For example, if the company has not begun shipping product in a particular country by a particular date, the inventor has the right to sever that country from the license grant.

7.4.10 Quality Control Provisions

Where a trademark forms part of the Property being licensed, there has to be a quality control provision in the agreement. The licensing of trademarks without the monitoring of the quality of the licensed products is "naked licensing," which can result in a loss of the underlying trademark rights.

Most inventors will want to monitor the quality of the licensed products even if trademarks are not included. Every toy license agreement should provide for the submission of samples of the products to the inventor for review and approval. Preliminary and final artwork might also be required and to be submitted for approval. In addition, the agreement should obligate the company to continue to provide the inventor with samples of the product after manufacturing has begun. This insures that the quality levels are being maintained.

A word of caution is appropriate here. Most toy companies are more than capable of producing toy products without any help from the inventor. The professional inventor is supportive of the company and does not use the approval rights in the agreement to obtain artistic control. Reviewing products for trademark and marking requirements is different from reviewing products to insure that the color blue is the proper hue and that the nose should be moved a quarter inch to the right. If the toy company gets the sense that an inventor will allow ridiculously minute artistic matters to get in the way of commercialization, they will not take a license under the inventor's idea.

7.4.11 Representations and Warranties

Every inventor will be asked to make certain representations and warranties to the toy or game company. Generally, these include reps and warranties that:

- the inventor has the right to enter into the agreement and there are no agreements in conflict with the agreement;
- the inventor is the sole and exclusive owner of the Property; and
- the Property does not infringe upon the rights of any third party.

The first two of the reps and warranties are relatively easy and straightforward. The last, however, is replete with problems. This last rep and warranty is basically a guarantee of non-infringement. By such representation and warranty, the inventor is guaranteeing that the Property does not infringe upon anyone else's patent, trademark or copyright rights. That is a very serious guarantee and one that most inventors are simply not able to make. Such a guarantee requires the inventor to conduct extensive patent, trademark and copyright searches.

What the inventor should do is attempt to limit this last rep and warranty to one based on the inventor's "knowledge and belief." This limits the resulting guarantee to intellectual property rights of which the inventor may be aware. If the inventor is aware of any prior patent, copyright or trademark rights, he has an obligation to tell the toy company. If a patent, copyright or trademark exists which covers the Property but the inventor has no knowledge of it, such fact is not a breach of this representation and warranty. From the inventor's perspective, this is an essential restriction to include in the agreement. At most, the inventor might give in to a refusal by the company to permit this restriction to apply to copyrights. After all, the company will argue, while patents and trademarks can be infringed unknowingly, copyright infringement can only result from willful copying. The inventor surely should be able to represent and warrant that he did not copy anyone else's work!

The inventor should request that the company represent and warrant that it will use its best efforts in advertising, promoting and marketing the product.

7.4.12 Indemnification and Insurance

Indemnification means that in the event that a claim is made or a law suit is filed against one of the parties, there may be circumstances where the other party is obligated to assume the legal defense of the action and even pay any costs or judgments against that party. In most toy license agreements, there are two standard indemnities that are typically provided. These are:

- the inventor will defend and indemnify the company against claims for infringement made by third parties; and
- the company will defend and indemnify the inventor against product liability claims made by third parties based on the manufacture of the product.

The first indemnification involving claims for infringement by third parties is always the most hotly negotiated provision in any toy agreement. Many companies will seek an absolute indemnity from the inventor in the event that they are sued for infringement by a third party based on the licensed property.

For most toy companies, this is one of the most onerous provisions in any such agreements since most inventors are small entities and cannot reasonably be expected to defend and indemnify companies with the resources of a Hasbro or Mattel. From the inventor's perspective, however, it can be life or death. In the event that a third party should sue the company for infringement, the inventor could be looking at hundreds of thousands of dollars in legal fees and a million dollar judgment. Thus, an inventor who agrees to such an open-ended indemnity is literally betting the ranch on the fact that the Property does not infringe anyone else's.

The inventor should attempt to limit this open-ended indemnity as much as possible. One way is to restrict the indemnity only to breaches of the "best of knowledge and belief" warranty previously discussed. Thus, the indemnity only applies to intellectual property rights of which the inventor was aware. If he was not aware of the existence of the intellectual property right, there would be no indemnity obligation.

Similarly, the inventor should attempt to cap the indemnity obligation at the total amount of royalty income received by the inventor during the term of the agreement. In such instance, all the inventor need worry about is giving back to the company what the company had already paid to him.

One further limitation is to predicate the indemnity obligation to only cases where a court has found that the inventor has breached his indemnity obligation. This protects the inventor from frivolous lawsuits, and from lawsuits that might be brought by someone who would never have sued the inventor, but who is angry at the company for a reason that may have nothing to do with the inventor, e.g., maybe he thinks he showed the company a similar idea. In order for the indemnity obligation to apply, the court must have found that the inventor was aware of the existence of the intellectual property right.

The toy companies will not sit idly by, however, when the inventor is seeking to limit this indemnity obligation. Some companies will agree to place a cap on the indemnity obligation, but will want to escrow ongoing royalties to the inventor during the pendency of the claim, and then be able to use the monies in the escrow account to pay the company's legal fees as well as any settlement or judgment. The company will typically want to control the litigation, as they undoubtedly have the most to lose. The issuance of an injunction during the Christmas selling season, for example, can cost the company millions of dollars.

It cannot be emphasized enough that this is a critical provision in any toy agreement and should be carefully and thoroughly considered before any inventor signs the agreement.

The inventor should expect an indemnity back from the toy company should a third party sue both the toy company and the inventor for a claim based on product liability. Product liability claims are those claims based on injury or death to a third party caused by a product that failed. For example, if a child lost his sight because a cap pistol exploded prematurely, that child has a cause of action against the company that manufactured the pistol. They might also have a cause of action against the inventor or designer of the pistol. The purpose of this indemnity is to protect the inventor from such third party causes of action. The inventor should request that the toy company defend and indemnify him against any and all such product liability claims.

Virtually all toy companies carry product liability insurance protecting them against such claims. The inventor should request that the company add the inventor to the company's insurance policy as a named insured. This insurance provision is intended to stand behind the company's indemnity obligation. Limits of product liability insurance should be considered. The minimum acceptable product liability limit is $1,000,000 per occurrence, although a more reasonable limit is $5,000,000 per occurrence. By being included as a named insured on the company's product liability insurance policy, the inventor is protected against such claims in the unlikely event that they are separately named in the lawsuit.

7.4.13 Termination Provisions

The termination provision of any license agreement is perhaps the most important provision. If the relationship between the parties proceeded in the manner both parties expected at the time they entered into the agreement, the parties might never have an occasion to again review the license agreement. When, however, a problem develops in the underlying relationship between the parties, the first thing that one of parties considers is termination of the agreement. It is at that time that they review the legal document to see how they can extricate themselves from what has become a bad relationship. The provision that the parties will review in such cases is the termination provision. In all too many agreements, this provision is either inadequate or totally missing.

A well-drafted termination provision should give the inventor the right to terminate the relationship at various steps of the relationship. For example, the inventor should have the absolute and immediate right to terminate the agreement upon any of the following events:

- the company fails to introduce product prior to the product introduction date;
- the company fails to meet the initial shipment date;
- the company fails to maintain product liability insurance;
- the company fails to make the minimum royalty payments;
- the company fails to continuously sell or market products;
- the Consumer Product Safety Commission recalls the product;

- the company fails to continue to conduct business; and
- the company repeatedly (i.e., two or more times in any one year time period) fails to timely pay royalties when they come due.

In addition, both parties should have the right to terminate the agreement on notice (usually 30 days) in the event of a breach of a material provision of the agreement by the other party and the failure to cure that breach within the notice period.

7.4.14 Post Termination Provisions

In the event of expiration or termination of the agreement, the company will typically want time to sell-off the existing inventory of the Product. Such a request is reasonable, provided that the basis for termination was *not* a failure on the part of the toy company to meet the requisite quality standards or to utilize proper legal notices. In such event, the company should not be able to dispose of existing inventory.

Where the basis for termination is another reason, the company should be permitted to sell off existing inventory for a reasonable period of time. Most companies would like a sell-off period of at least one year. Most inventors want to limit the period to thirty days. The typical compromise is between three and six months. It should be understood, of course, that all such sales are subject to the payment of a royalty to the inventor.

7.4.15 Boilerplate Provisions

We hesitate to use the term "boilerplate" because it implies that these provisions are blindly included in every agreement with no thought or consideration. Nothing can be further from the truth. These provisions are important, and consideration should be given to their inclusion since they are intended to govern the conduct of the parties and control how certain events will be treated, for example:

- who is responsible for obtaining/maintaining intellectual property protection, both in the U.S. and internationally;

- who is responsible for pursuing infringers and how any recovery will be divided;
- in what manner notices are to be given under the agreement;
- in what manner disputes are to be resolved and what law will control; and
- under what conditions the parties may assign the agreement and its rights and obligations.

Last, but not least, the agreement should include an integration clause which provides that the license agreement is the final and *entire understanding* between the parties, incorporates all prior written or oral agreements between the parties (including the option agreement and/or letter of intent) and may not be changed or modified except by written agreement signed by all parties. The purpose of this provision is to put both parties on notice that, if a promise or statement isn't written in the agreement, it doesn't exist. In essence, it negates either party's ability to rely on a prior oral representation.

Chapter Eight:

MERCHANDISING AND THE
TOY INDUSTRY

While the thrust of this book is directed to the relationship between the inventor and the toy company for the development of new toy products, the impact of merchandising on new toy product development cannot be overlooked. By merchandising, we are not referring to a retailing procedure or technique but, instead, to the concept of incorporating a highly recognizable name or character image on a product to enhance its marketability. Typically, these names or images emanate from the entertainment industry, and their use is pursuant to a license from the entertainment company. Some call it "soft" licensing since it generally does not involve an actual product *per se*, but, rather, the application of a name or character image to an existing product to give the product instant consumer recognition in the marketplace.

Examples of toy products that depend on the strength of their merchandise licenses include the WINNIE THE POOH and BARNEY plush dolls, the MIGHTY MORPHIN POWER RANGER action figures and playsets and the BATMAN "Batmobile" toy vehicles. There are also lines of articulated action figures made under licenses from the National Football League and Major League Baseball and their various players and teams.

8.1 THE HISTORY OF MERCHANDISING

Merchandising actually began as far back as the 1770's, when two enterprising ladies of British nobility permitted their names to be used in association with a line of facial cosmetics in return for a royalty based on the sale of those cosmetics. The first modern instance of merchandising, however, was in 1904 when the BUSTER BROWN mark was licensed for a variety of unrelated children's products. Merchandising became a real business in the 1930's due, in large measure, to the foresight of Disney's Kay Kamen who recognized the potential of MICKEY MOUSE as a merchandising property. In the 1950's, HOWDY DOODY, ZORRO and DAVY CROCKETT became household words based on their highly successful television shows. The success of these shows was quickly translated into lines of related clothing and toys.

In the early years of merchandising, the Walt Disney Company was, far and away, the moving force in the field. It has been estimated that the MICKEY MOUSE character has found its way onto over 50,000 different licensed products. Even today, more than 200 manufacturers produce licensed MICKEY MOUSE products for sale throughout the world.

While Disney may have been the major player in merchandising in the early years, the other Hollywood studios jumped on the bandwagon in the 1970's. Lucasfilms, Paramount Pictures and Warner Bros. quickly recognized the substantial revenues that could be generated from licensing the STAR WARS, STAR TREK and LOONY TUNES marks for apparel and toy products. They were quickly joined by the comic strip syndicate, United Media, with their SNOOPY and GARFIELD characters.

Today, merchandising is truly big business. *The Licensing Letter*, a licensing trade publication, estimates that over $70 billion worth of licensed products were sold in 1994. That is up from $9.9 billion in 1980 (a 600% increase!!). A significant portion of these sales involved licensed toy products.

8.2 SOURCE OF MERCHANDISING PROPERTIES

Where do most merchandising properties come from? Without question, the entertainment industry is the principal source for most of the highly successful merchandising properties. The trend that started in the 1970's with the STAR WARS and STAR TREK motion pictures was continued through the 1980's and 1990's with such movies as SATURDAY NIGHT FEVER, TOP GUN, URBAN COWBOY, E.T.—THE EXTRATERRESTRIAL, SUPERMAN, WHO FRAMED ROGER RABBIT, DICK TRACY, THE FLINTSTONES, JURASSIC PARK and other less notable (from a merchandising point of view) films. Disney remained a major player with such motion pictures as THE LITTLE MERMAID, BEAUTY AND THE BEAST, ALADDIN and THE LION KING.

While most of these motion pictures translated well into merchandising, THE LION KING was in a class by itself. *The Wall Street Journal*, in an article entitled "Toy Sellers Wish that Pocahontas Were a Lion," reported that Disney took in $310 million at U.S. box offices for THE LION KING motion picture, while THE LION KING toy licensees (led by Mattel) received $162 million in the sale of THE LION KING licensed toys.

Another recent motion picture that spawned a particularly successful line of licensed toys was BATMAN FOREVER (as well as the earlier Batman movies). Individuals in the licensing industry often refer to the Batman toy licensing program as a franchise, due in large part to its success over a relatively long period of time. In addition to a series of hit motion pictures to support the license, there is a regular television show, strip syndication and the presence of the property in a variety of media formats. This keeps the characters, plots and storylines at the forefront of consumers' imaginations. As of this writing, more than $1.5 billion of Batman licensed products have been sold at retail.

In addition to the silver screen, television has contributed its share of merchandising properties, particularly shows that have been aired on the Public Broadcasting Stations ("PBS"). The pioneer in that market was Children's Television Workshop with its award winning SESAME STREET show featuring characters such as Big Bird and Oscar the Grouch. Other television shows that have proven to be strong merchandising properties over the years include the DUKES OF HAZZARD, MORK & MINDY, M*A*S*H, BARNEY and BEVERLY HILLS 90210.

As of this writing, two television shows which appear to have the strongest merchandising potential are MAGIC SCHOOL BUS and PUZZLE PLACE, both aired on PBS. From commercial television come such properties as SEINFELD, JAG, and a host of Saturday morning cartoons. The merchandising potential for children's television shows is so great that the producers find themselves negotiating master license agreements months before finalizing their own network deals.

Comic book characters such as SPIDERMAN, X-MAN and the HULK also translate well into licensed products. In fact, the extension is so logical that Ron Perelman, who owns Marvel Comics, purchased a toy company, Toy Biz, to produce licensed Marvel products. The company, headed by noted toy inventor Avi Arad, has stated that in addition to the Marvel licenses, it will also seek merchandise licenses from other property owners. One such license obtained by Toy Biz was the toy license for the FLIPPER motion picture.

The new venture DreamWorks SKG founded by Hollywood heavyweights Steven Spielberg, Jeffrey Katzenberg and David Geffen hired Bruce Stein, a former executive with Kenner Toys and Mattel, to consider the toy connection. Warner Bros. created its own toy division to produce toys based on its motion pictures and television characters. DC Comics and Archie Comics also license their characters into the toy industry. The syndicated comics SNOOPY and GARFIELD have historically translated well in related toy and game products, including classic plush products, playgyms, action figures, manipulative toys and others.

Merchandising is not all character licensing. Over the years, well-known properties from many fields have entered the merchandising arena. For example, designers such as BILL BLASS, CHRISTIAN DIOR, GLORIA VANDERBILT and CALVIN KLEIN have recognized the power of licensing. While their basic designer lines continue to prosper, they found that they could dramatically increase their revenues by licensing their names for lines of consumer-oriented clothing and accessories.

The professional sports leagues and colleges jumped on the bandwagon in the 1980's. Each of the major sports leagues formed licensing divisions which took responsibility for licensing team names and logos. Merchandising in this area has not been limited to the leagues. The various players' associations also began capitalizing on the popularity of licensing, particularly where a group of players was included in a particular promotion.

Over the years, colleges and universities such as NOTRE DAME, FLORIDA STATE, DUKE and UCLA have found that there is a tremendous demand for products bearing the university name and/or mascot, particularly after a highly successful football or basketball season. Athletic success is not a prerequisite for success in merchandising, however, as HARVARD and YALE learned. Both have experienced a strong demand for their licensed products. Surprisingly, many colleges have found that the market is not limited to the geographical region in which they are located but extends nationwide and even worldwide.

Corporations have also seen a market for ancillary products bearing their names and marks. For example, automotive companies license their names and model names for such accessory products as key chains, T-shirts, models and replica toy vehicles. Consumer product companies also recognized early on that there was a market not only for their primary product, but for a line of accessory products as well. For example, Winnebago (which markets recreational vehicles) found a host of licensees interested in selling WINNEBAGO camping products such as sleeping bags and tents.

Breweries such as Coors and Anheuser-Busch quickly recognized the value of licensing, not only for the royalty income it generates but as a way to advertise their products without running into the limitations imposed on the advertising of alcoholic products. Licensees appreciate the value that the marks COORS or THIS BUD'S FOR YOU bring to coolers and baseball caps. Merchandising has become a win-win situation for all involved.

Not-for-profit entities have also seen the value of merchandising as a fund raiser for their programs. The last few Olympic Games staged in this country have been supported in large measure by corporate sponsors and licensees who pay the Olympic Committee a royalty for the use of the OLYMPIC name and symbol. Congress recognized this when it enacted special legislation protecting the Olympic name and symbol. The first Dream Team of Olympic basketball athletes generated millions of dollars for the United States Olympic Committee in royalties from the sale of related products which were used to help support and underwrite amateur athletics. Museums such as the SMITHSONIAN and the WINTERTHUR have long-standing licensing programs based on their names and items that appear in their hallowed halls.

Events such as the Bicentennial, the NCAA FINAL FOUR, the ROSE BOWL and even the Pope's visit to America have formed the basis of licensing programs. While such properties have spawned broad-based licensing programs, the nature of such properties is particularly suited to gift and novelty items rather than staple toy products.

8.3 MERCHANDISING MEETS THE TOY INDUSTRY

Merchandising typically lends itself to mass market, consumer-oriented products. Such products are relatively low priced, impulse-type items where the strength of the license is the motivating force which makes the consumer want to purchase the licensed product. As such, toys are a logical choice for merchandising. Other significant licensed products include clothing, such as T-shirts and sweatclothes; paper products, such as posters, books, notebooks, etc.; tote bags and badges and buttons.

Clearly, plush dolls and action figures are two of the most frequently licensed toy products because of the ease of translating characters to such products. Other licensed toy and game products include playsets, activity sets, juvenile furniture, board games and puzzles, ride-on toys and infant and pre-school toys. Even electronic toys and learning aids are being marketed under merchandise licenses.

The special relationship between merchandising and the toy industry began in the late 1970's when Kenner Products (now a division of Hasbro) obtained the master STAR WARS toy license from Lucasfilms and parlayed that license into the sale of hundreds of millions of dollars worth of toy products based on the STAR WARS trilogy of motion pictures. The relationship was not a one way street. In addition to the millions of dollars received in royalties, Lucasfilms also received an untold amount of publicity and promotion for its motion pictures. While it may not have been a marriage made in heaven, it was certainly one made in outer space.

Following the STAR WARS success, every major toy company (and some minor ones) began looking at merchandising as a way to sell their products. Partnerships were formed between toy companies and motion picture and television studios in the form of "master licenses." For example, Mattel is Disney's master toy licensee for such properties as MICKEY MOUSE, WINNIE THE POOH, THE LION KING and POCAHONTAS.

Fisher-Price is Lancit's master toy licensee for PUZZLE PLACE and Tyco is the Children Television Workshop's licensee for a line of SESAME STREET toys. These licenses have become win-win relationships for all involved.

The toy companies view merchandising as a way to take a ride on the enormous advertising and promotional budgets of the motion picture and television production companies. For example, Paramount Pictures was expected to spend almost $100 million on promoting its CONGO motion picture and News Corp.'s Fox Films Entertainment intended to generate $200 million in advertising outlays for the MIGHTY MORPHIN POWER RANGERS movie. Clearly, the toy and game companies view merchandising as a way to tie themselves into that promotion and advertising for a relatively modest sum in the form of a percentage of their sales.

Toy lines built on merchandising licenses have begun to dominate the toy and game market. For example, in 1994, nearly half of the $17 billion in retail toy sales came from licensed goods based on motion pictures and television shows. In 1995, toy companies expected $300 million in sales tied to THE MIGHTY MORPHIN POWER RANGERS, plus $130 million from BATMAN gear and $100 million from merchandise linked to POCAHONTAS. In contrast, Sky Dancer, a new flying doll from Lewis Galoob Toys, expected to achieve only $50 million in sales from this unlicensed toy product, which was recognized as the year's big non-licensed hit. In 1995, four of the five toy lines from Playmates Toys were based on a merchandise license while six of the seven new product lines from Kenner Toys were licensed products.

8.4 IMPACT OF MERCHANDISING ON TOY PRODUCT DEVELOPMENT

Merchandising has begun to dictate the types of products that a toy or game company will offer to the trade each year. In the "old days," the toy company would take an existing toy product and apply a character name or image to that product and introduce it to the market. Merchandising had been viewed merely as a way to enhance product development and sales. That is changing.

Merchandising now drives new toy product development. Toy products are developed from the board up with a character license in mind. No longer are the toy and game companies simply recycling existing inventory by the application of a licensed name or character. Instead, new products are being designed around a particular merchandised character.

Toy companies are now taking pro-active roles in the development of the underlying entertainment properties to ensure that they will translate easily into successful toy lines. Studios are even soliciting suggestions from their master toy licensees early on to enhance the merchandising potential of the motion picture or show. Accessory items and props that will eventually translate into licensed toys are now regularly included in the movie or show for the sole purpose of supporting the merchandising program.

It was recently reported in the article "Toy Makers' Addition to Hollywood Figures Reshapes Kids' Play," *Wall Street Journal*, July 13, 1995, that a Disney animator had claimed that at least one scene in Disney's motion picture POCAHONTAS — the one in which the raccoon Meeko briefly braids the star's hair — was created based on a suggestion from Mattel which wanted to make Braided Beauty Pocahontas dolls. The same article reported that Kenner convinced Warner Bros. to clothe the Riddler character in BATMAN FOREVER in tights, because baggy pants did not translate well in action figures.

Suggestions by toy companies to incorporate potentially licensable toy products into the script are not new. What is new, however, is the fact that the studios are now listening and actually adopting some of these suggestions. This is a clear recognition of the power of merchandising.

The impact of merchandising on toy product development is significant. Many toy companies are now hesitant to undertake the risk of developing a new product unless it can be incorporated into a licensed line. *The Wall Street Journal* indicated that many leading toy makers have shelved much of their own research and development and changed the way new toys are created. Robert Solomon, chairman of Dakin, Inc., was quoted as saying that Hollywood-related toys sell so well that they would be foolish to invest heavily in the risky business of creating the next FRISBEE or ETCH-A-SKETCH.

8.5 MERCHANDISING "OUT" BY THE TOY COMPANIES

Understanding that merchandising can be a two-way street, many toy companies have recognized that there is merchandising value to some of their own brand names. These toy and game companies have started merchandising programs around their own popular and well-known marks.

This trend was, no doubt, started by Bally-Midway shortly after it introduced its PAC-MAN video game in the early 1980's. Recognizing that there was a demand for PAC-MAN products, Bally undertook a massive merchandising program for a wide variety of licensed products that had nothing to do with the video game market. Sega Enterprises followed with a merchandising program built around its SONIC property.

Two of the strongest brand names in the pure toy market are the BARBIE line by Mattel and G.I. JOE by Hasbro. Over the years, these two companies have invested billions of dollars in promoting these two important brand lines. As such, it should come as no surprise that there are scores of companies who are willing to produce their own BARBIE or G.I. JOE products under license from Mattel or Hasbro. Other toy and game properties that have resulted in licensing programs include the GIRL TALK line of games originally marketed by Western Publishing (now Milton Bradley), the game UNO by Mattel and CABBAGE PATCH (originally by Coleco, now Hasbro). In the case of GIRL TALK, a line of accessories for teenage girls was a logical product extension. The success of CABBAGE PATCH as a merchandising property is a legend in the licensing industry.

8.6 MERCHANDISING AND THE TOY INVENTOR

What does merchandising mean to the toy inventor? From a product development point of view, it may actually dictate the type of products that a toy company will consider. For example, if a major portion of a particular company's product line is built around a BATMAN license, that company will clearly be more receptive to new product concepts that can be marketed under that license than products which will be marketed generically.

As such, when making a presentation to a toy company, the inventor must be sensitive to the toy company's current licensing arrangements. It would be to the inventor's advantage to "pitch" a new product concept based on a merchandising property to an existing licensee of that property, since that company will obviously be looking for a product that can fall under that merchandise license. That could be the difference between whether a toy company will accept or reject a new product.

The inventor should also know how attaching a merchandising property to a concept will affect the economics of the toy license agreement. Merchandise licenses are not inexpensive. Most entertainment companies regularly charge toy companies a royalty between eight and twelve percent for the right to use their properties on a line of toy and game products. In view of this royalty, most toy companies try, wherever possible, to use their own in-house designers to develop the toy products that will be sold under the merchandise license. That, of course, is not always possible.

Where a toy company elects to market a toy concept developed by an outside inventor under a merchandise license, it faces the prospects of a double royalty for that product, i.e., a royalty to the entertainment company for the right to use the character or name *and* a royalty to the inventor for the right to manufacture and sell the product. That can result in a total royalty obligation that is as high as eighteen percent.

In most instances, the merchandise license royalty is not negotiable. Seeking to reduce their total royalty obligation, many toy companies will attempt to cut the inventor royalty, thereby lowering their royalty payments and, hopefully, increasing their profit margins. For example, a toy company may ask an inventor to reduce a five percent domestic royalty rate to three percent (or lower) where the item is sold under a merchandise license. If the item is sold on an F.O.B. basis, the F.O.B. royalty rate might be reduced from seven to five percent for the same item.

An obvious outgrowth of this trend concerns the royalty rate that a toy company will offer the inventor where the item is to be included in a "branded" line. In this situation, the toy company might well ask the toy inventor to take a lower royalty. For example, Mattel might offer a toy inventor a royalty rate that is between one and three percent when the item is to be included in the BARBIE line. Mattel would argue that it has invested billions of dollars in developing the BARBIE brand, and as a result, the item will sell in far grater quantities due to that brand recognition. In essence, the toy companies are applying the same logic as if a third party merchandise license was involved.

At the end of the day, the inventor may actually make more money in royalties due to the fact that, historically, licensed or branded products sell in greater quantities than non-licensed products. Moreover, the merchandise license royalty will increase the item's net selling price (due, if nothing else to the inclusion of the merchandise license royalty) thereby increasing the basis on which the inventor's royalty will be calculated.

Despite this logic, many inventors seriously question why they should be the source of relief to the toy company and refuse to consent to a reduction in royalty rate. They question why two multinational companies with annual sales in the billions of dollars must seek relief from an individual inventor. There is, of course, a certain logic to that question. Nevertheless, that is the way the game is played, and if the inventor wants to play the game, he must follow the rules.

Chapter Nine:

SPECIAL CONSIDERATIONS IN INTERNATIONAL LICENSING

9.1 THERE IS A WORLD OUTSIDE THE UNITED STATES

Contrary to what some toy and game inventors may believe, there is a market for new toy concepts outside of Hasbro, Mattel and Tyco. In fact, there is even a market for new concepts with toy companies located outside the United States.

A toy inventor who is considering the question of whether to license a new concept to a non-United States-based company typically has two major concerns: (1) how does one penetrate the international market; and (2) what special provisions should be included in an international license agreement?

For the American toy inventor, there are essentially three ways to penetrate the international market:

- contact the international division of a major U.S.-based toy company;
- contact non-U.S.-based toy companies directly; or
- use an agent who specializes in the licensing of new toy concepts to contact non-U.S.-based toy companies.

9.2 DEALING WITH INTERNATIONAL DIVISIONS OF U.S. COMPANIES

Most of the major United States-based toy companies have international divisions which are constantly looking for new toy concepts to sell into markets outside the United States. While the international division for each of these companies is typically charged with the responsibility for internationally marketing those items that the company is selling in the United States, there are many instances where the international division will take on a new toy product exclusively for international distribution. It may be a product which another toy company is currently marketing exclusively in the United States but who lacks an international sales force or, alternatively, a product which has not been introduced in the United States.

The inventor should contact the international divisions of these major toy companies to determine whether they have any interest in a new toy concept for international sales. By and large, the agreements reached with these international divisions are similar to the agreements entered into on the domestic side.

One specific consideration that is frequently raised in international agreements involves the ability of the toy company to sublicense its rights in certain countries. The toy inventor must be prepared to permit the toy company to enter into sublicense arrangements with local toy companies to manufacture and/or market the item in those countries. While this concept should be acceptable in theory to all, the question typically presented is how to split the income received from the sublicensees.

Many inventors will initially seek a 50/50 split of gross sublicensing revenue with a particular floor, e.g., a royalty no less than four percent. In contrast, most toy companies will initially offer the inventor a small percentage of such sublicensing revenue, e.g., fifteen percent of the net income after the deduction of any agent commissions. Clearly, the final split is negotiable. Equity suggests that the final resolution should be fair to both parties, e.g., a 50/50 or 60/40 split of sublicensing income after deduction of the agent's commission, if any. If the toy company is also acting in an agent capacity, it might be entitled to receive a higher percentage of the gross revenues to compensate for the time and money it will have to expend to conduct the program.

9.3 DEALING DIRECTLY WITH NON-UNITED STATES TOY COMPANIES

In considering the international market, the toy inventor must appreciate that there are literally thousands of toy and game companies outside the United States. While many of these companies are regional in nature (as are many of the United States companies), there are some international giants including, for example, Early Learning Centre in England, Tomy in

Japan and Estrela in Brazil. Though they may be located in different countries, manufacture and sell different types of products and even correspond in different languages, they have one thing in common — they are all seeking new product concepts.

This is not meant to imply that there is a shortage of new product concepts from the countries in which they are based. United States inventors do not have a lock on good ideas. What it means, however, is that they are as interested in new toy concepts as their sister companies in United States. Thus, the toy inventor should not overlook these companies in preparing their "victims list."

How does the toy inventor find out about these companies? The easiest way is to study the directory provided to attendees of the American International Toy Fair, held every February in New York City. Many of these companies exhibit at the show, and the toy inventor can quickly generate a list of international companies who produce and market similar types of products. The International Toy Fair in New York might even be an appropriate time to try to contact some of these companies and present a product concept, thereby saving the expense of foreign travel.

By and large, the inventor will find that the non-U.S.-based toy companies will be more receptive to new product presentations and will be less formal in their dealings with the inventor, particularly with respect to such things as confidential disclosure agreements. United States toy companies have been sued so often for misappropriation and breach of confidential relationships that they are reluctant to enter into any sort of a confidential disclosure agreement with an inventor. That may not be the case with many of the international toy companies.

While some of these companies attend and exhibit at the International Toy Fair in New York, many do not. The toy inventor may want to attend some of the international toy fairs held each January and February in foreign countries. For example, international toy fairs are held every January in London, England; Toronto, Canada; North Yorkshire, England; Hong Kong; Paris, France and Milan, Italy. The Nuremberg Toy Fair is held every February in Nuremberg, Germany.

These international toy fairs present the toy inventor with a wonderful opportunity to not only learn what is being developed and sold outside the United States, but also to meet the major players in the international market. They might even give the inventor the opportunity to present one or more concepts to these companies.

9.4 DEALING WITH NON-UNITED STATES TOY COMPANIES THROUGH AGENTS

The toy inventor should be aware that there are toy agents who actually specialize in placing new concepts with international toy companies. Some of these agents may have worked directly for these international toy companies in an earlier life. Others may have worked for the international divisions of the major United States toy companies where they acquired a particular expertise in the international markets. By and large, they are all based in the United States although, obviously, their contacts are far reaching.

Whatever their background, these agents offer the toy inventor the opportunity to place new toy products with non-United States-based toy companies. Generally speaking, these agents work in much the same manner as United States agents, i.e., should they succeed in placing the product, they receive a percentage of the royalties otherwise payable to the inventor. It has been our experience that their commission rates are comparable to those charged by agents who specialize in dealing with domestic companies.

9.5 CONSIDERATIONS IN DRAFTING INTERNATIONAL LICENSE AGREEMENTS

Toy inventors (and their attorneys) will find that international toy license agreements do not radically differ from domestic agreements. This is particularly true when dealing with an international division of a United States-based toy company that has the same in-house attorneys drafting agreements for both the domestic subsidiary and the international division.

When dealing with non-United States-based toy companies on a direct basis, however, the inventor may find some provisions that he had not previously seen in domestic agreements. In some instances, these provisions are diametrically opposite to companion provisions contained in domestic agreements. There are some fundamental differences between domestic license agreements and international transactions.

Generally speaking, most non-U.S. toy companies structure the main clauses of their agreements in a similar fashion to domestic companies. That means simply that the agreement will be a "license" agreement in which the company is permitted to use the new toy concept for a period of time. In exchange, the toy company will pay the inventor a royalty based on its sales of licensed products. Most international toy companies will agree to pay an advance against royalties upon signing the agreement and some will even agree to minimum guaranteed royalty provisions. Typically, these companies will pay similar royalty rates as domestic toy companies, i.e., between four and six percent.

The following are some of the notable provisions found in the international agreement that are either absent from domestic agreements or are radically different:

- Governing Language
- Value Added and Withholding Taxes
- Blocked Currency Provisions
- Intellectual Property Protection
- Exclusivity vs. Non-Exclusivity
- Insurance Requirements
- Governing Law and Disputes Provisions

9.5.1 Governing Language

The toy inventor must appreciate that frequently English is not the native language for the toy company. As such, while the inventor may be negotiating the English language version of the agreement, the toy company executive may be considering the French or Spanish language version. Some agreements even present the different language versions in a two column format, i.e., the English provision in the left column and the foreign provision in the right column. While translations are typically very accurate, errors do occur. As such, it is important that the agreement include a provision indicating which version will govern in the event that two provisions are inconsistent.

9.5.2 Value Added and Withholding Taxes

Contrary to domestic practice, many countries provide for a Value Added Tax ("V.A.T.") which is applied to the payment of royalties. In many instances, the V.A.T. is deducted from gross sales prior to the calculation of the royalty obligation due the inventor. Some toy inventors will not permit the licensee to deduct the V.A.T. from its gross sales, although it will frequently depend upon the item involved and how badly the toy company wants to make a deal.

Some countries also impose withholding taxes against U.S.-based licensors. The inventor should appreciate that foreign taxes can be credited against U.S. tax liability, provided that appropriate documentation is provided to the IRS. Thus, the inventor may require the licensee's assistance in obtaining the necessary documentation.

9.5.3 Blocked Currency Provisions

There are certain foreign countries where governmental action will "block" or otherwise prevent the removal of currency from a country. Since the toy company will incur a royalty obligation for sales of the licensed products within the country, its inability to remove currency and pay the inventor in the United States would automatically place the company in breach of the agreement. Most toy companies will want to avoid that possibility. Similarly, most inventors are concerned with getting their full royalties from sales within that country. To avoid such situations, most agreements contain provisions requiring the toy company to deposit the blocked monies into local bank accounts or pay them to individuals within the country as directed by the inventor. Brazil, India and some of the former Eastern Block countries have, historically, had problems exporting monies from the countries. At least one Brazilian company has employed the services of a bank located in another South American country as a conduit for moving funds from Brazil to U.S.-based licensors. This is a very practical approach to the problem of overcoming blocked currency problems.

9.5.4 Intellectual Property Protection

Another issue in international agreements relates to intellectual property protection and rights. It should be appreciated that patent and trademark protection is territorial. That means that a United States patent or trademark will only protect property rights in the United States and will not extend to other countries. Separate patents and/or trademarks must be obtained on a country-by-country basis to protect those rights outside the United States. While we are moving closer to regional patent and trademark protection, the day of a true international patent or trademark is a long way off. On the other hand, copyright rights are generally international in scope.

As such, most international agreements, by necessity, address the question of how a particular property will be protected in the applicable countries. More importantly, it will address who is to be responsible for the payment of the fees associated with such protection. In many instances, the international toy company might assist the inventor in obtaining such protection, although it will frequently seek some offset or credit against its royalty obligations.

9.5.5 Exclusivity vs. Non-Exclusivity

The question of exclusivity of a license agreement may present certain problems outside the United States. Regional laws may restrict a toy inventor/licensor from guaranteeing exclusivity in a particular country since there is no way to limit parallel goods from being shipped into that country from surrounding countries outside the territory. All exclusivity provisions need to be appropriately worded to indicate that such grants may be limited to local law or regulation.

9.5.6 Insurance Requirements

By and large, the product liability concerns in the United States are not universally shared around the world. As such, while product liability insurance provisions are contained in most domestic license agreements, they are rarely included in international agreements. Many non-U.S.- based toy companies who do not ship product into the United States may not carry product liability insurance. As such, the toy inventor will be hard pressed to require that such companies obtain and maintain such insurance.

9.5.7 Governing Law and Dispute Provisions

Where will disputes be resolved and what law will apply? While there may be some difference between the common law of New York versus the common law of California, generally speaking the same legal principles will apply. This may not be the case when comparing the law of two countries, e.g., the United States and France. The United States law is derived from the English common law while French law finds its roots in the Napoleonic Code. There are fundamental differences between the laws of these countries. Thus, the toy inventor should pay careful attention to the governing law provisions of any agreement to determine whether the laws of such country favor or limit the licensor's rights.

Similarly, the question of where disputes will be resolved is another significant issue. Apart from the cost of having to litigate disputes in another country halfway around the world in a foreign language, the inventor should have a real concern about his status as a foreign litigant against a national company. One possible compromise is to agree to international arbitration at the Hague.

Chapter Ten:

ACCOUNTABILITY OF TOY COMPANIES AND TAX PLANNING

At least one professional toy inventor (who wishes to remain anonymous) has proclaimed to us that his number one rule of operation is guided by the belief that, "Every licensee cheats."

That belief is clearly an overstatement and is, no doubt, based more on instinct than on actual facts. Most toy companies are honest. Most toy companies regularly pay the inventors they work with their proper royalty every quarter. Most toy companies have never contemplated the idea of trying to cheat their inventors. In actual fact, there are relatively few instances of companies intentionally failing to pay inventors their rightful share.

Nevertheless, however, toy companies have been known to make unintentional accounting errors. Toy companies have been known to have taken improper credits in determining the royalty base. Toy companies have mistakenly failed to include certain sales in calculating the royalty base. In short, errors do happen and there are instances where inventors have not received their proper royalty income.

10.1 DETERMINING WHETHER A PROBLEM EXISTS

Most inventors trust the toy companies with whom they are dealing and as well they should. Every quarter they receive a royalty statement and a royalty check based on that statement and, on its face, the numbers appear quite correct. Or, at least, the inventor believes that they appear correct.

There are times, however, when an inventor may begin questioning the correctness of the statements. For example, the inventor may know of sales of the product in retail markets that do not appear on the royalty statement. Similarly, the inventor may be aware of substantial sales in a particular country that do not appear on the statement. An inventor may believe that a particular item sold well during a particular season, only to find that the sales are reported as being lower than in the previous quarter. All of these circumstances make an inventor begin to question whether or not the company is accurately reporting the royalty income. Some inventors are simply skeptics by nature. They immediately question whether the toy company is really paying them their fair share.

What should an inventor do in these situations? The answer is to speak with an accounting firm or a professional royalty auditor. These professionals can help an inventor determine whether a problem truly exists or whether the inventor's paranoia has begun to run rampant.

10.2 ROYALTY AUDITS EXPLAINED

Most Certified Public Accountant firms do not like to use the term "audit" in conjunction with an examination of a company's books and records to determine whether it has fully paid the inventor. Instead, the phrase "royalty investigation" is typically used. Others have referred to the exercise as an "on-site compliance review." Regardless of how the professionals refer to the exercise, most laymen and attorneys still call it an audit.

There are a number of excellent accounting firms that have departments that specialize in royalty audits. Similarly, there are a number of smaller, regional firms that specialize in royalty audits and will do an excellent job for the inventor. Some of these firms represent a number of different inventors in the toy industry. In fact, they frequently will perform a royalty audit of a particular manufacturer on behalf of a number of different clients at the same time. This obviously results in lower rates for the inventors since the cost of the audit is borne by all of the participants.

While most accounting firms will only work on an hourly billing rate, there are a handful of independent accountants that will perform royalty audits on a contingency fee arrangement, i.e., where they will only receive payment if they are successful in recovering monies for the inventor.

One word of caution is necessary. Royalty audits can become quite expensive. The inventor should understand the potential expense prior to embarking on such an audit. More importantly, however, the inventor should be reasonably sure that there are substantial sums of money at issue prior to undertaking an audit that may cost tens of thousands of dollars.

Prior to retaining any accounting firm to perform a royalty audit, the inventor should insure that the agreement with the toy company affords him the right to conduct such audit. While this right is a standard provision in most toy agreements, it is not universally granted.

Most audit provisions include the following elements:

- the inventor is given the right to conduct the audit on reasonable notice with the right to make copies;
- in the event of an underpayment, the toy company is required to pay the underpayment plus interest, as well as pay for the cost of the audit if the underpayment is greater than a threshold amount;
- the company is required to maintain relevant records for a minimum period of time; and
- the inventor is required to preserve the confidentiality of any business information to which he may be exposed.

A typical "audit" provision reads as follows:

(a) Licensor shall have the right, upon at least five (5) days written notice and no more than once per calendar year, to inspect Licensee's books and records and all other documents and materials in the possession of or under the control of Licensee with respect to the subject matter of this Agreement at the place or places where such records are normally retained by Licensee. Licensor shall have free and full access thereto for such purpose and shall be permitted to be able to make copies thereof and extracts therefrom.

(b) In the event that such inspection reveals a discrepancy in the amount of Royalty owed Licensor from what was actually paid, Licensee shall pay such discrepancy, plus interest, calculated at the rate of One Percent (1%) per month. In the event that such discrepancy is in excess of Three Thousand United States Dollars ($3,000.00),

Licensee shall also reimburse Licensor for the cost of such inspection including reasonable attorneys' fees incurred in connection therewith.

(c) All books and records relative to Licensee's obligations hereunder shall be maintained and kept accessible and available to Licensor for inspection for at least three (3) years after termination of this Agreement.

(d) In the event that an audit of Licensee's books and records is made, certain confidential and proprietary business information of Licensee may necessarily be made available to the person or persons conducting such audit. It is agreed that such confidential and proprietary information shall be retained in confidence by Licensor and shall not be used by Licensor or disclosed to any third party without the prior express written permission of Licensee, unless required by law or in connection with any proceeding based on Licensee's failure to pay its actual Royalty obligation.

In preparation for the first meeting with the accountants, the inventor should compile all of the royalty statements rendered to him by the toy company since commencement of sales. Similarly, the inventor should attempt to document all potential inconsistencies of which he may be aware. As noted earlier, these inconsistencies can be reflected by product that the inventor purchased that did not appear on the inventor's royalty statement, obvious omissions of a particular product the inventor knows is being sold, and the like.

Armed with that information, the inventor should then meet with the accounting firm. In addition to turning all of the above documents and information over to the firm, the inventor should also provide the accountants with a copy of the agreement governing the payment of royalties. The accountants will need to refer to that agreement in the course of the royalty audit.

10.3 CONDUCTING THE ROYALTY AUDIT

Armed with information provided by the inventor, the accountants will contact the toy company and set up an appointment to conduct the audit. Most toy companies have had audits conducted before and, as such, consider the matter little more than a business inconvenience.

After setting up the appointment, the accountant will send the company a list of the items that he will want to review in the course of the audit. This will include the accounting, sales and manufacturing records of the company relative to the product in question, as well as copies of the company's catalog and price lists for the relevant period. The accountant may also ask for production of all backup material used to prepare the inventor's royalty statement, as well as a list of all company locations including outlet and retail locations.

If the company has all of the requested material on hand at the time the accountant arrives to perform the audit, it should be a relatively easy procedure, frequently taking no more than a day or two. If not, the procedure may be arduous and the results may be inconclusive. The accountant should be able to make photocopies of the company's books and records as well as extract information. This will permit him to render a complete and meaningful report to the inventor, which can then be used in approaching the company if there is any evidence of under-reporting.

The obvious goal of any accountant in conducting a royalty audit is to compare the inventor's royalty statement against the actual sales records of the company to see whether the company accurately reported to the inventor. At the conclusion of the royalty audit, the accountant will render a formal report to the inventor, comparing the company's manufacturing and sales records against the inventor's royalty statements.

10.4 WHAT THE AUDIT MAY REVEAL

As noted above, most toy companies are honest. We live in the age of computers and most of the accounting and sales records of even the smallest companies are computerized. Royalty audits are common occurrences for the toy companies, both from the inventor side as well as from the character or sports licensing side (e.g., Disney, Major League Baseball, etc.). They are prepared for these audits, and frequently the audit numbers reconcile with what the company sold and what it reported.

There have, however, been instances where the numbers do

not reconcile and where it has been found that the company has under-reported sales to the inventor, thereby incurring a liability to the inventor for additional royalties. The reasons for this under-reporting vary. In virtually all instances, however, the company simply made an error.

According to Dan Jacobsen in an article that he had written on the subject for *The Licensing Journal*, (April 1987, at 10-11) the most common audit findings are:

> **Mathematical Errors.** Even in this age of computers, clerical and arithmetic errors do occur. Totals may be incorrectly carried over from one schedule to the next, and errors in simple arithmetic do occur.
>
> **Misclassifications.** Another common finding is the misclassification of an item. Was the sales invoice properly coded and posted as the sale of the licensed product? Was the sale misclassified as one bearing a lower royalty rate? Were expenses charged on the statements related to the license? Misclassification of items is commonly found by auditors.
>
> **Incorrect Royalty Base.** The license agreement typically establishes what is to be included in the royalty base and whether the royalty is to be based on list price or wholesale price. The auditor will determine whether the licensee has properly interpreted the contractual language and applied the correct royalty rate to the right base. Auditors frequently find instances where licensees have used a base for computing royalties which is different from the one permitted under the agreement.
>
> **Incorrect Rate.** Many agreements provide for changes in royalty rates at differing levels of sale and some provide for different rates in different territories. This is particularly true where there is a domestic royalty rate and an F.O.B. royalty rate. Many errors are found attributable to the use of the wrong royalty rate.
>
> **Sublicensing.** Does the license agreement permit sublicensing? Are the royalties to be reported based on the sublicensees' sales or on the amounts remitted by the sublicensee to the licensee?

Unaccounted for Production. Some of the most important records from the auditor's viewpoint are the production records and those records that reflect the licensee's purchases and inventory. The auditor will want to know the number of units that were available for sale to determine whether they have been sold or are in inventory. The failure of these records to reconcile may be the basis for a claim.

Affiliated Companies. Are sales to affiliates and related parties made at arms length prices? Often, a claim may arise for sales made to a related company at a special price resulting in an underpayment of royalties to the inventor.

Non-Contractual Deductions. The auditor will verify that deductions made by the licensee are provided for in the license agreement. Licensees will occasionally take deductions that are not permitted under the agreement.

Returns and Reserves. The auditor will verify that only actual returns have been deducted on the royalty statement. Occasionally, a licensee will set up a reserve for returns when only actual returns are permitted under the agreement.

Termination Period. If the term of the agreement has expired, has the licensee stopped manufacturing licensed products as required by the agreement? Has the licensee sold the licensed goods beyond the sell-off period? Have the unsold licensed goods been destroyed as required under the agreement?

At *The Licensing Journal*'s 1995 toy development seminars, Peggy Moizel, of the accounting firm of Deloitte & Touche, identified the following elements as the most misunderstood accounting practices leading to accounting irregularities:

1. Free Goods. No royalties are due on free sales, e.g., buy one, get one free, as most licensees consider them as discounts. This is quite commonly done by a licensee. The agreement should address the question of free goods and, if at all possible, provide for a maximum allowable percentage for free goods, e.g., 10%.

2. Close-outs or Discontinued Merchandise. Normally

no royalty is paid on close-outs or discontinued merchandise since the licensee makes no profit. The agreement should, however, clearly provide what constitutes a close-out, e.g., where the goods are sold at 50% or greater discounts.

3. Surplus Sales or Overstock Items. Overstock items are not discounted, per se, but in many instances they are offered at deep discounts to permit the toy company to reduce inventory. One problem that might develop is a situation where the goods that were dumped into the marketplace compete with full priced goods. Again, this is a question that should be addressed in the agreement.

4. Samples. The question of what constitutes a sample and how samples will be treated should be addressed in the agreement. Quantities must be reasonable and the circumstances defined. Limitations should be imposed to avoid any possible misunderstanding.

10.5 WHETHER OR NOT TO AUDIT

The mechanics for a royalty audit now being known, the inventor must make the difficult decision of whether to send in his accountants to conduct the audit. Two thoughts cross the inventor's mind: (1) will the company be offended? and (2) does it make business sense to have an audit conducted?

The inventor should quickly discount the first question. The Walt Disney Company retains teams of auditing personnel who regularly conduct these royalty audits throughout the world. Virtually every major character licensor regularly investigates its licensees. Why should the inventor be any different?

By and large, the toy companies will not blink when they receive the inventor's request to have a royalty audit conducted. While they may deem such an audit to be a business inconvenience, they recognize that audits have become an accepted business practice. For many licensors, these royalty audits are regularly conducted not out of a belief that their licensees are dishonest, but rather, simply to insure that their licensees have accurately reported royalty income.

Accordingly, the inventor should not concern himself as to whether such a request will negatively impact his relationship with the company. It should not. On the chance, however, that such a request might offend a particular company, the inventor should ask himself, why has the request met with objection (are they really hiding something) and does he really want to be doing business with that company in the future?

The second consideration is a much more relevant factor. Royalty audits are expensive. The cost of a single audit can easily run into the five figures although there are ways to reduce the cost, i.e., join in with a group of other inventors for a common audit or retain a contingent fee auditor.

Nevertheless, the inventor runs the risk of incurring substantial expenses with merely the hope of eventually recovering some uncertain amount of unpaid royalties. While the license agreement may provide for reimbursement of costs by the company if the audit reveals an underpayment that is greater than a certain amount, the inventor is betting that the audit will uncover such an underpayment.

The inventor should consider having a royalty audit conducted in three circumstances: (1) where he has evidence or a strong belief that the toy company is underreporting on sales of the licensed products; (2) where the earned royalties for the product in question are sufficiently high to justify the cost of such an audit; or (3) where the cost of conducting the audit is sufficiently low so as to justify the audit as a regular business practice.

10.6 TAX PLANNING

We will not even attempt to try to offer any tax advice or strategies to the toy inventor. In the vast majority of situations, the amount of time and money spent on developing tax shelters for licensed toy products is not justified. In any event, however, we would strongly counsel the toy inventor to consult with a qualified tax professional (either a tax attorney or accountant) who might be in a position to offer advice regarding tax minimization. The toy inventor should be aware that some licensors utilize an entity called an investment holding company to reduce state tax liability. Investment holding companies were historically used to hold stocks and bonds. In recent years, however, property rights owners have used them to hold intellectual property rights, i.e., patents, trademarks, copyrights.

Briefly stated, the parent company moves the property rights into a subsidiary company located in a state which does not have a state tax for income derived from licensing of that property right. The subsidiary would then pay a royalty to the parent corporation for use of the property. Delaware companies are very favorable for managing intangible assets, since there is no state tax liability in Delaware from the income derived from the utilization of such assets.

The trick in structuring a Delaware investment holding company is to make sure that all assets are retained in Delaware and the holding company is not doing business in another state where there is a state tax liability. Inventors should structure the Delaware company such that it is not doing business in another state. Practically, that means that the company must have a physical presence in Delaware, e.g., an office, employees, etc., and the Delaware company must be independent of the parent company relative to actual operations.

Investment holding companies are one of a number of different types of tax structures that the highly successful toy and game inventor may consider. Counsel should be sought from competent tax counsel prior to the adoption of any such mechanism.

Chapter Eleven:

INFRINGERS, COUNTERFEITERS, ME-TOO'S AND OTHER ANNOYANCES

Your product has now been introduced at Toy Fair to rave reviews. You've been contacted by CBS Evening News, and their anchor team wants to do a feature story on you and your new toy. The producer of NBC's Today Show has been calling daily to arrange for an interview with you at your home. You're anxiously waiting to actually see your "baby" on the shelves of the local toy store.

Then, disaster seemingly strikes. The marketing vice-president of the toy company that has introduced your product calls and tells you that XYZ Company out of the Far East has begun shipping a product into the major toy stores in this country which looks strikingly similar to your product. They want to know what you intend to do.

The inventor in this scenario has just experienced the final measure of success in this business. There is an old expression that imitation is the sincerest form of flattery. The new expression is that there are three sure things in life: death, taxes and that a successful product will be knocked off. Every successful toy product will be knocked off.

In years past, flights to the Far East were filled with people carrying in their briefcases photographs and drawings of the new toy products introduced at Toy Fair for the purpose of having the factories begin to work on competitive products. The advent of the fax machine has now reduced the cost and hastened the process. It is not uncommon for competing products to actually reach the United States market faster than the authentic ones introduced at Toy Fair. The inventor should not be discouraged, however. Most toy companies readily expect that their products will be imitated and are prepared to react aggressively against infringers. Often it is simply a question of degree.

11.1 WHO IS RESPONSIBLE FOR INFRINGERS?

The question of who (i.e., the inventor or the toy company) has the responsibility for pursuing infringers should be clearly spelled out by the license agreement. In many instances, the inventor will have the first right to pursue infringers. Normally, this is a discretionary right rather than a mandatory obligation. Typically, the inventor is given a limited period of time (e.g., 30 days) in which to commence an action against an infringement. In the event that the inventor does not bring such an action in that period, the toy company is typically given the right to bring such an action.

Most inventors will not want to get themselves involved in commencing and prosecuting infringement actions. Prosecuting an action for infringement may easily run into the hundreds of thousands of dollars in legal fees, with no guarantee of a recovery at the end of the day (at least a recovery that can financially justify the litigation). The primary consideration in deciding whether intellectual property litigation is worthwhile is whether it will be possible to quickly enjoin further sales of the infringing products. The prospect of a money recovery is a secondary factor.

Most agreements provide that the parties will cooperate with each other in connection with any legal action. Typically, the costs for such an action are borne by the party bringing the lawsuit. That party may also be responsible for paying any expenses incurred by the other party relative to such action.

A question to consider is what happens if there is a recovery from the infringer? Who will keep the money? In most situations, the party bringing the action will have the right to deduct "off the top" all costs incurred in bringing the action from any monies recovered. If anything is left over, the parties may agree to equitably divide the remainder. Some agreements provide for a 50/50 sharing of the net proceeds, while other agreements are less favorable to the non-participating party. Whatever the arrangement, it should be memorialized in the basic license agreement between the toy company and inventor to avoid any misunderstandings.

A typical provision concerning infringements in an inventor agreement is as follows:

(a) LICENSOR shall have the right, in its sole discretion, to prosecute lawsuits against third parties for infringement of LICENSOR's rights in the Property. If LICENSOR does not institute such an infringement suit within sixty (60) days after LICENSEE's written request that it do so, LICENSEE may institute and prosecute such suit.

(b) Any lawsuit shall be prosecuted solely at the expense of the party bringing suit and all sums recovered shall be divided equally between LICENSOR and LICENSEE after deduction of all reasonable expenses and attorneys' fees.

(c) The parties agree to fully cooperate with the other party in the prosecution of any such suit. The party bringing suit shall reimburse the other party for the expenses incurred as a result of such cooperation.

11.2 ACTIONS AGAINST INFRINGERS

The ability of the inventor and/or the toy company to stop imitators of their brand new product will depend, in large measure, on the steps the inventor and the company took relative to protecting the initial new product idea under the intellectual property laws. Further, it may depend upon the speed at which such protection was obtained, because frequently such protection has not been formally granted or issued as of the date of the initial product introduction. For example, prosecuting a patent application with the U.S. Patent & Trademark Office may take more than two years from the date of filing of the application. Assuming that intellectual property protection has been obtained for the underlying new product idea, the ability of the inventor and/or the company increases dramatically.

When considering bringing suit against an infringer, the first issue to be considered is whether the imitating product is close enough to the original to infringe the intellectual property rights. The standards for infringement are relatively simple. In order for a product to infringe another's patent, the patent must have issued and still be in force and one or more claims of the patent must "read on" the allegedly infringing product. That means that each and every element contained in one or more of the claims must be met by an exact (or potentially equivalent) element in the infringing product. It is not enough that merely some of the elements are met. They all must be met.

In order to establish a case for trademark infringement, the name or mark used by the alleged infringer must be "confusingly similar" to the owner's name or mark. Different courts have different standards for what constitutes confusing similarity, but the two most notable elements are the closeness of the marks themselves and of the goods or services on which they are used. Thus, the mark G.J. JOE for action figures would be confusingly similar to G.I. JOE® for action figures.

Where the mark used by the alleged infringer is identical to the owner's registered trademark and the goods are the same as covered by the owner's registration, the infringement rises to the level of "counterfeiting," which carries with it severe civil and even criminal penalties.

The standard for determining whether there is a case for copyright infringement is whether actual copying of the copyrighted work has occurred and whether the resulting copy is "substantially similar" to the original. Since it may be difficult to establish actual copying, the courts will typically assume that a copyrighted work is copied where the alleged infringer had access to the copyrighted work, and the two items in question are substantially similar.

Actions may be brought against infringers in both state and federal courts, depending upon the type of intellectual property sought to be enforced and the location of the parties. In addition, actions may be brought before the International Trade Commission to enjoin the importation of infringing products at the U.S. borders. The advantages of an ITC proceeding is the speed of action as well as the ability to enforce a judgment against a product rather than against an entity.

One effective tool used by inventors and companies alike is to register their intellectual property rights with the United States Customs Service which will impound products at the U.S. borders that infringe upon these registered rights. This is a particularly effective tool in the toy industry, where a substantial portion of the infringing products come from outside the United States.

Unfortunately, new products that are not protected under the intellectual property laws may have to withstand the competition that will certainly take place in the market from "copy cats." Without a patent, copyright or trademark covering the new product, it will be difficult to have any court or body enjoin sales of similar (or even identical) products on theories of trade dress infringement, palming off, passing off and the like (although if the financial implications are significant enough, any or all of these theories can be relied on as the basis for legal action).

11.3 THIRD PARTY CLAIMS OF INFRINGEMENT

There is a corollary to that refrain about the sure things in life. There is a fourth certainty: every successful product will draw out at least four entities that claim an ownership interest in it. Toy companies regularly receive cease and desist letters from individuals around the country and world claiming that the company's new product infringes upon a right that they believe they have.

In the vast majority of cases, these claims prove meritless and are withdrawn. Others, while also meritless, unfortunately become the subject of vexatious litigation, which is able to go forward because of our legal system's contingent fee arrangement and unscrupulous lawyers. A few, however, are legitimate and must be dealt with.

The manner in which the toy company receiving such a claim responds, however, depends in large measure on the agreement that they have with the inventor. In an earlier chapter, the question of inventor indemnification was explained. This is the real world application of that theoretical issue.

Most toy companies will seek some indemnification from the inventor relative to these third party claims. The extent and applicability of these indemnities, however, will depend upon the company and the circumstances. Some of these indemnifications are broader than others. It should be noted that few toy companies will seek to turn over the defense of such actions to the inventor. Instead, they prefer to control the litigation using counsel of their own choice, but look to the inventor for a financial contribution, if not payment of the entire cost of the defense.

An inventor should be prepared to represent and warrant that he has no actual knowledge of any third party rights that would be infringed by his new product idea. Similarly, the inventor should be prepared to indemnify the company in event that an infringement action is brought against the company based on third party rights known to the inventor. In such situation, however, the inventor should be able to cap or otherwise limit his indemnity obligation to the total amount of monies received by the inventor for the product in question. In other words, the inventor should be prepared to return to the company any monies that he received should it turn out that the product infringed such third party rights of which he was aware.

Some toy companies want more, however. They want inventors to totally indemnify them against all claims for infringement, regardless of whether the inventor knew of the rights or not. These companies might even insist upon the right to stop paying royalties to the inventor after receiving notice of such a claim. The company would thereupon begin paying future royalties into an escrow account where the monies are retained during the pendency of the claim. If it turns out that the claim was valid or should the company elect to settle the claim for whatever reason, they could use the monies in the escrow account to fund the judgment or settlement and thereafter cease paying any more royalties to the inventor.

Where the claim was meritless, however, some of these companies seek to use the monies in the escrow account to pay their legal fees and, should anything be left over, remit the balance to the inventor. Future royalties would, of course, continue.

To protect himself from this unenviable position, the inventor should carefully review and negotiate the indemnification provisions of his agreement to determine the extent of his potential liability to the company in the event of an infringement action.

Chapter Twelve:

CAPITALIZING ON YOUR SUCCESS

Once you have succeeded in actually licensing that first new product idea to a toy company, a whole new world is open. This is particularly true if that new product idea is a blockbuster hit.

Your telephone calls that heretofore were never returned by the gatekeepers at the major toy companies are now returned immediately. In fact, you may even begin receiving calls from those same toy company executives who only two years ago were not able to spare ten minutes of their time. They may even be asking you for your ideas on a certain new concept or line that the company is considering.

You find that your dinners during Toy Fair are no longer alone at Nedicks but, instead, you are a guest of the company's president at the Four Seasons. You are now on a first name basis, not only with the chairman of the board, but also with his (or her) significant other.

Television and radio talk show hosts and newspaper reporters find that you make great copy for their annual Toy Fair article as well as for feature articles on achieving the Great American Dream. You will also start receiving calls, letters and even product idea submissions from other toy inventors hoping to learn something from you or asking you to represent their product ideas.

Success breeds success. This old adage means more in the toy industry than in most other industries, since success is a fleeting thing, and a company that is on top one year can be on the bottom the next.

The successful toy inventor will find that a good track record means almost as much as a great product idea. A company is more likely to take a risk with an inventor who has an impressive array of toy products on the market than with one who has yet to place a new product idea. Companies will take more time with the experienced toy inventor than with the first timer. Heaven help the gatekeeper who management finds out failed to promptly return the call of someone who brought in $20,000,000 in sales to his last licensee. Success breeds success.

12.1 DRAWING FROM YOUR EXPERIENCE

The one thing that the successful toy inventor acquires on the path to success is an understanding of the process and a list of contacts who know him (or have heard of him). These contacts are not just names in the back of a book. Instead, they are individuals who will take the inventor's calls and respond to his requests for an opportunity to make a presentation. They are people who will make the time to review a new product submission and will think twice before simply saying "No" to the submission, fearing that it might turn into the next blockbuster hit (because the last one did).

As anyone in the toy industry will attest, the creativity to conceive and develop the next blockbuster hit is important, but it is only half the battle. There are hundreds (maybe even thousands) of potential blockbuster ideas that continue to sit on basement shelves gathering dust. They continue to sit on these shelves because their inventors lack a basic understanding of the toy industry and how new toy products are licensed. That is the very reason why most toy agents or brokers demand, and get, 50% of the royalty income from ideas they place. They view the task of actually selling a new product idea into the industry as representing at least half the job of new toy product development.

These agents are correct. The unsold blockbuster hit that does nothing more than gather dust is of no value to the inventor. It may be a brilliant idea and have all the market potential in the world. Unfortunately, however, it is not worth anything unless and until a toy company produces and sells the product.

12.2 CAPITALIZING ON YOUR CONTACTS

As a direct result of the success of your first product, you are now in the enviable position of being able to capitalize on your success. You now understand the way the game is played (no pun intended) and you know the players. Most importantly, the players know you. Your goal should be to parlay that success into the next one, and the one after that. In short, your initial success should be the basis of building a career in the business.

You might find yourself in the unique position of never having to work again — your initial product idea might have been that successful. That's rare and happens only once in a generation. If it does, learn to play golf, tell others to read this guide and go sail off into the sunset, because you've earned it.

Such success stories, however, are few and far between. Even for the handful of inventors who find themselves in the position of never having to work again, few actually give up the invention game. For the really successful ones, invention is in their blood. That may be the very reason for their initial success. Their very makeup drives them to continue to work to duplicate that first megahit. It is their genius.

For the vast majority, however, success is not lifetime security. Instead, it represents a great return on their initial investment, the pride and satisfaction of seeing their product on the shelves of Toys 'R' Us and the beginning of a new and satisfying career. Memories of past rejections and frustrations fade with the cashing of each royalty check.

For some inventors, the next idea is easier and better than the first. Without question, the job of selling it is much easier. This time, the companies take them seriously.

For these inventors, the first success represents the beginning of a toy development business. As the business grows, the inventor might even consider taking in a junior designer (or two) to develop the ideas that he has conceived. Cash flow from the initial toy product idea helps fund the development efforts for future product ideas.

The invention business is a numbers game and the use of additional contract designers permits the successful inventor to be able to create and present more ideas. More importantly, it permits the inventor to be able to buy the services of others in complimentary areas, e.g., electronics, etc. This can result in the creation of truly unique and different toys.

Successful inventors might even bring in a business manager (or, Heaven forbid, a lawyer) to allow them to devote their time to creative endeavors and not worry about the day-to-day pressures of the business.

No matter what direction the business may take, however, there is one constant. Because of the success of the initial product idea, the inventor will be able to at least have future new product ideas seen and considered by decision makers at the toy companies. That is an invaluable asset and one that should not be taken lightly. In a business where fifty percent of the game is attributable to marketing, the ability to get in the door of most major toy companies is a major asset.

This is not meant to imply that all inventors who achieve such initial success are able to duplicate that success. There are, in fact, many inventors who find that duplicating their first success is not as easy as they had originally thought it would be.

The reasons for subsequent failures are many. Many inventors of highly successful initial products have high expectations and simply cannot meet these expectations. They think that every new product must be licensed to a major toy company and sell at least a million pieces a year. In fact, few achieve those lofty heights. Other inventors find themselves complacent and cannot seem to get their creative juices flowing. For still others, their initial invention was a fluke. They may not have really been creative but came upon what turned out to be a great idea.

For whatever the reason, however, these successful first-time inventors find that they have no future in the business from the creative side. These individuals, however, should not discount the valuable asset they have — the ability to be heard. Successful inventors are regularly inundated with requests from other inventors and would-be inventors asking them to represent their new product ideas. Many invention development firms have been built on the inventions created by others. After all, the typical agent commission is up to fifty percent, and the successful inventor already has the contacts with the companies.

For those individuals, their ticket to future success may well be as toy agents or brokers. These inventors may decide to develop a cadre of internal and external designers and inventors to create new product ideas, using their contacts with the toy companies to get those ideas seen and considered.

12.3 IT'S A WONDERFUL LIFE

Think back to high school when you asked yourself what you would like to do for the rest of your life. You thought of your father's job and said to yourself, "There's no way I'm going to do that. It's boring. He hates it." You heard the stories of how he truly hated his boss, and you saw what the long commute to the job was doing to his temperament.

You vowed to yourself then that when you grew up, you would do something that you really enjoyed. Something that was fun, something that gave you satisfaction. You would be your own boss, make your own hours and work close to home. On top of all that, you would make a lot of money.

Congratulations, Mr. or Ms. Toy Inventor. You've accomplished your goal. The toy invention business is truly a wonderful life.

Appendices

APPENDIX 1
TMA STATISTICS 1995-1996*

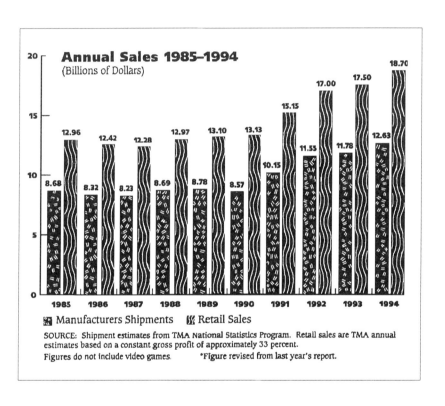

Annual Sales 1985–1994
(Billions of Dollars)

🖼 Manufacturers Shipments   🎰 Retail Sales

SOURCE: Shipment estimates from TMA National Statistics Program. Retail sales are TMA annual estimates based on a constant gross profit of approximately 33 percent.
Figures do not include video games.   *Figure revised from last year's report.

* All Statistics gathered by NPD; Statistics compiled by TMA
and originally published in the *1995-1996 Toy Industry Fact Book*

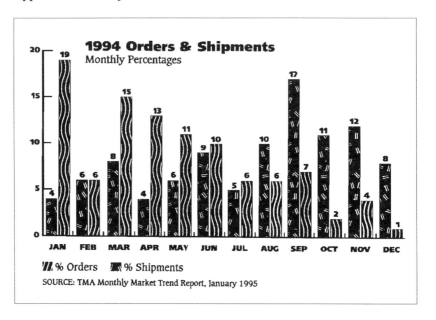

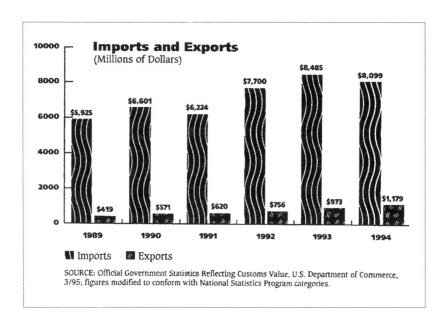

Estimated Manufacturers' Shipments By Product Category
Dollars (First Billing Value[1]) & Units 1994 vs. 1993
Volumes have been projected to reflect total industry levels (Estimated volumes in millions)

		DOLLARS			UNITS		
		1993	1994	% Change	1993	1994	% Change
I.	**Infant/Pre-School**	**$1,103**	**$1,157**	**4.9**	**163**	**167**	**2.5**
	Infant Toys	383	402		60	61	
	Pre-School Musical Toys	60	61		10	10	
	Pre-School Blocks/Accessories*	22	24		4	4	
	Pre-School Villages/Scenery Sets*	123	138		13	14	
	Pre-School Talking/Sound Toys	63	64		8	8	
	Pre-School Learning Toys*	55	50		8	7	
	Pre-School Tub Toys*	13	14		3	3	
	Pre-School Role Playing Toys*	143	148		20	20	
	Pre-School Push/Pull Toys	46	49		7	7	
	Pre-School Remaining*	195	207		30	33	
II.	**Dolls**	**$1,552**	**$1,668**	**7.5**	**208**	**215**	**3.4**
	Large Dolls	377	331		29	26	
	Large Doll Accessories	49	46		12	11	
	Fashion Dolls/Clothes/Accessories*	643	675		88	90	
	Mini Dolls	204	250		54	55	
	Mini Doll Accessories	29	90		3	9	
	Soft Dolls	37	31		6	6	
	Remaining Dolls/Accessories	115	115		9	9	
	Doll Houses/Furniture	98	130		7	9	
III.	**Plush**	**$ 870**	**$ 921**	**5.9**	**84**	**90**	**7.1**
	Musical/Electronic Plush/Accessories	125	120		8	8	
	Traditional Plush	727	782		73	79	
	Puppets	18	19		3	3	
IV.	**Male Action Toys**	**$ 709**	**$ 949**	**33.9**	**152**	**175**	**15.1**
	Action Figures	464	687		116	139	
	Action Figure Accessories	177	155		20	18	
	Male Role Playing	22	59		3	5	
	Mini Figures/Scene Sets	46	48		13	13	
V.	**Vehicles**	**$1,163**	**$1,274**	**9.5**	**227**	**244**	**7.5**
	Radio Controlled Vehicles*	242	285		11	12	
	Remote Controlled Vehicles***	37	34		5	4	
	Battery Operated Vehicles*	36	43		5	6	
	Other Powered Vehicles	20	24		6	7	
	Trains–Powered	22	20		2	2	
	Aircraft/Boats–Powered	23	24		4	4	
	Mini Vehicles*	237	282		135	147	
	Non-Powered Cars	40	46		8	9	
	Non-Powered Aircraft/Boats	30	34		9	10	
	Non-Powered Trucks	180	177		19	19	
	Vehicle Accessories	71	88		9	10	
	Electric Battery Car Sets/Accessories	47	42		2	2	
	Electric Train Sets/Accessories**	178	175		12	12	
VI.	**Ride-Ons**	**$ 655**	**$ 722**	**10.2**	**33**	**37**	**12.1**
	Metal Tricycles	22	22		1	1	
	Plastic Tricycles*	30	35		2	2	
	Other Pedal Ride-Ons*	30	35		1	1	
	Non-Pedal Ride-Ons	75	79		3	3	
	Stationary/Rocking/Spring Horses	13	14		1	1	
	Riding Sports**	305	331		23	26	
	All Other Riding Vehicles	180	206		2	3	

Notes
Number of companies responding = 73
Figures include imports
All sales are on a GROSS basis
Data are compiled through a process which includes a polling of major U.S. toy and game manufacturers, and a comparison of trends with the
U.S. Toy Market Index (TMI) and Toy Retail Sales Tracking Service (TRSTS)

	DOLLARS			UNITS		
	1993	1994	% Change	1993	1994	% Change
VII. Games/Puzzles	**$1,095**	**$1,179**	**7.7**	**204**	**206**	**1.0**
Card Games	60	66		16	17	
Dice Games	17	17		5	5	
Word Games	29	30		4	4	
Puzzle Games	17	18		4	5	
Standard Games	37	35		10	9	
Travel Games	38	35		8	8	
Children's Board Games	97	94		13	13	
Pre-School Games	45	40		8	7	
Family Board Games*	85	87		8	8	
Adult Board Games	113	90		9	7	
Children's Action Games	147	182		21	27	
Family Action Games	30	26		2	2	
Strategy Games	63	65		7	7	
Electronic Handheld/Tabletop Games**	195	280		13	22	
Cardboard Puzzles*	103	94		70	58	
Wood/Plastic/Other Puzzles	19	20		6	7	
VIII. Activity Toys	**$1,691**	**$1,829**		**534**	**552**	**3.4**
Building Sets	325	366		37	41	
Scientific Toys**	53	55		7	7	
Fashion Accessories*	105	108		32	30	
Powered Appliances	14	21		1	1	
Non-Powered Appliances	95	98		4	5	
All Other Household/Food Toys	73	75		17	19	
Educational Toys**	22	23		5	5	
Reusable Compounds	83	86		27	28	
Mechanical Design*	120	120		15	15	
Traditional Kits/Supplies	150	196		49	58	
Crayons/Markers/Chalk Etc.	245	255		181	182	
Crayons/Markers/Chalk Sets & Supplies	95	108		33	35	
Paint Sets/Supplies**	143	143		83	83	
Model Kits/Accessories*	115	123		25	26	
All Other Activity Toys**	53	52		18	17	
IX. All Other Toys	**$2,946**	**$2,939**	**-0.2**	**973**	**945**	**2.9**
Water/Pool/Sand Toys***	282	296		64	67	
Audio/Visual Toys	163	186		19	24	
Children's Furniture*	105	102		10	10	
Electronic Learning Aids Hardware*	175	225		6	7	
Electronic Learning Aids Software	15	15		2	2	
Sports Activities	414	408		71	70	
Musical Instruments	27	35		2	2	
Pre-School Playground Equipment	120	127		2	3	
Guns/Weapons & Accessories***	220	187		58	48	
Swingsets/Gym Sets & Accessories**	80	89		2	3	
Trading Cards & Accessories**	1,060	954		612	561	
Miscellaneous Toys***	285	315		125	148	
Total Toy Industry	**11,784**	**12,638**	**7.2**	**2,578**	**2,631**	**2.1**
Video Games	**$3,828**	**$3,755**	**-1.9**	**99**	**97**	**2.0**
TV Video Hardware	1,077	948		11	9	
TV Video Software	1,718	1,804		48	49	
TV Video Accessories*	266	280		13	13	
Portable Video Hardware	343	290		5	4	
Portable Video Software	341	358		16	16	
Portable Video Accessories	83	75		6	6	
Total Industry with Video Games	**$15,612**	**$16,393**	**5.0**	**2,677**	**2,728**	**1.9**

*1993 Figures Revised   **Limited Sample   ***Both 1993 Figures Revised and Limited Sample
+First Billing Value: first price paid for an item in the U.S.

Data compiled by The NPD Group in conjunction with Toy Manufacturers of America

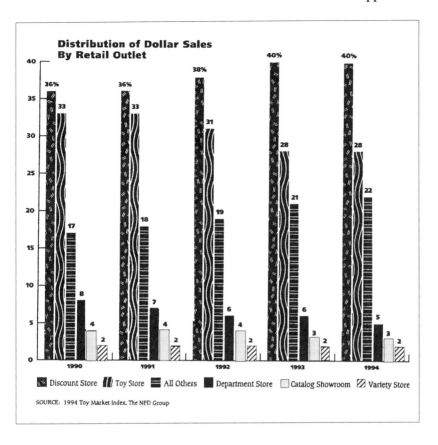

SOURCE: 1994 Toy Market Index, The NPD Group

Top Toy Retailers Estimated Dollar Share of U.S. Toy Industry

Rank	Retailer	Type	1994 ($) SHARE(%)	1993 ($) SHARE(%)	# of STORES
1	TOYS 'R' US	Toy	20.7	20.2	618
2	WAL–MART	Discount	13.6	12.7	2119
3	KMART	Discount	7.1	7.3	2240
4	TARGET	Discount	5.7	5.3	628
5	KAY BEE/TOY WORKS	Toy	4.7	4.5	1050
6	JC PENNEY	Department	1.9	2.0	1232
7	SERVICE MERCHANDISE	Cat. Showroom	1.8	1.6	410
8	SEARS	Department	1.4	1.6	798
9	HILLS	Department	1.3	1.0	156
10	CALDOR	Discount	1.1	1.2	161

SOURCE: 1994 Toy Market Index, The NPD Group

APPENDIX 2
LIST OF RESOURCES FOR THE TOY INVENTOR

1. Associations

Game Manufacturers Association, 803 Fourth Avenue, Grinnel, IA 50112 (515) 236-5027.

Licensed Industry Merchandisers Association ("LIMA"), Ste. 6210, 350 Fifth Avenue, New York, NY 10118-0110 (212) 244-1944.

Toy Manufacturers of America, Ste. 740, 200 Fifth Avenue, New York, NY 10010 (212) 675-1141.

2. Books

BEST OF THE LICENSING JOURNAL — THE TOY INDUSTRY, Kent Communications, Ltd., Stamford, CT (1994).

Levy & Weingartner, FROM WORKSHOP TO TOY STORE, Fireside, Simon & Schuster, New York, NY (1992).

Peek, Steve, THE GAME INVENTOR'S HANDBOOK, Betterway Books, Cincinnati, OH (1993).

Revoyr, Jack, A PRIMER ON LICENSING, Second Edition, Kent Communications, Ltd., Stamford, CT (1995).

Revoyr & Harrison, LICENSEE SURVIVAL GUIDE, Kent Communications, Ltd., Stamford, CT (1995).

Stern, Sydney Ladensohn and Schoenhaus, Ted, TOYLAND, THE HIGH-STAKES GAME OF THE TOY INDUSTRY, Contemporary Books, Inc., Chicago, IL (1990).

Toy Manufacturers of America, TOY INVENTOR/DESIGNER GUIDE, Toy Manufacturers of America, New York, NY (1994).

3. Periodicals

Gift & Decorative Accessories, Geyser-McAllister Publications, Inc., 51 Madison Avenue, New York, NY 10010-1675 (212) 689-4411.

The Licensing Journal, Kent Communications, Ltd., P.O. Box 1169, Stamford, CT 06904-1169 (203) 358-0848.

Licensing Letter, EPM Communications, Inc., 488 East 18th Street, Brooklyn, NY 11226 (718) 469-9330.

Licensing Trends, Geyser-McAllister Publications, Inc., 51 Madison Avenue, New York, NY 10010-1675 (212) 689-4411.

Playthings, Geyser-McAllister Publications, Inc., 51 Madison Avenue, New York, NY 10010-1675 (212) 689-4411.

Toy Book/Licensing Book, Adventure Publishing, 264 W. 40th Street, New York, NY 10018 (212) 575-4510.

4. Articles

Beller, Miles, "Jim Becker & Andy Mayer; Aw Guys, Quit Playing Around," *Los Angeles Magazine,* V. 31:18. Jan. 1986.

Brown, Caryne, "Making Money Making Toys: How Black Inventors Are Bringing Innovative Ideas to the Toy Market," *Black Enterprise,* V. 24:68. Nov. 1993.

Cho, Erin, "Lincoln Logs: Toying with the Frontier Myth," *History Today,* V. 43:31. April 1993.
Darrow, Barbara, "The Exciting, but Serious, *World of Toy Design,*" Design News, V. 42:56. Dec. 1, 1986.

Gardner, Dana, "DFM Adds Sparkle to Toy Line," *Design News,* V47:62. July 8, 1991.

Gardner, Dana, "The Walking Piano," *Design News*, V44:60. December 19, 1988.

Pereira, Joseph, "The Toy Industry, Too, is Merging Like Crazy to Win Selling Power," *Wall Street Journal*, V. CCXXIV, No. 84:1 Oct. 28, 1994.

5. Major Trade Shows

American International Toy Fair, February, New York, NY. c/o Toy Manufacturers of America, 200 Fifth Avenue, New York, NY 10010 (212) 675-1141.

British Toy and Hobby Fair, January, London, England.

Canadian Toy and Decoration Fair, January, Toronto, Canada.

Dallas Toy Shows, Spring and Fall, c/o Dallas Market Center, 2100 Stemmons Freeway, Dallas, TX 74207 (800) 521-0977.

GENCON, August, Lake Geneva, WI.

Harrogate International Toy Fair, January, North Yorkshire, England.

Hong Kong Toy & Games Fair, January, Hong Kong.

International Toy Fair, January, Paris, France.

Licensing Expo, LIMA, June, New York City.

Milan Toy Fair, January, Milan, Italy.

Nuremberg Toy Fair, February, Nuremberg, Germany.

Pacific Northwest Toy Association Show, Spring, Seattle, WA c/o PNTA, 2601 Elliot Avenue, Ste. 5105, Seattle, WA 98121 (206) 441-1881.

Western States Toy & Hobby Show, Spring, Pomona, CA c/o WTHRA, 11100 Valley Blvd., Ste. 340-20, El Monte, CA 91731 (818) 442-1635.

6. Courses in Toy Design

Fashion Institute of Technology, Toy Design Department, 227 West 27th Street, Room B231, New York, New York 10001 (212) 760-7133.

APPENDIX 3
COPYRIGHT APPLICATION FORM (FORM VA)

FORM VA

UNITED STATES COPYRIGHT OFFICE

REGISTRATION NUMBER

VA ⌒501 963
VA   ⊢ VAU

EFFECTIVE DATE OF REGISTRATION

MAY 1 1 1992
Month   Day   Year

DO NOT WRITE ABOVE THIS LINE. IF YOU NEED MORE SPACE, USE A SEPARATE CONTINUATION SHEET.

1

TITLE OF THIS WORK ▼

FISHER-PRICE SLEEPYTIME PUFFALUMP

NATURE OF THIS WORK ▼ See instructions

SOFT SCULPTED TOY

PREVIOUS OR ALTERNATIVE TITLES ▼

SLEEPYTIME PUFFALUMP

PUBLICATION AS A CONTRIBUTION If this work was published as a contribution to a periodical, serial, or collection, give information about the collective work in which the contribution appeared.   Title of Collective Work ▼

If published in a periodical or serial give: Volume ▼   Number ▼   Issue Date ▼   On Pages ▼

2 a

NAME OF AUTHOR ▼

FISHER-PRICE, INC.

DATES OF BIRTH AND DEATH
Year Born ▼ Year Died ▼

Was this contribution to the work a "work made for hire"?

XX Yes
☐ No

AUTHOR'S NATIONALITY OR DOMICILE
Name of Country

OR { Citizen of ▶_____USA_____
Domiciled in▶_____USA_____

WAS THIS AUTHOR'S CONTRIBUTION TO THE WORK

Anonymous?   ☐ Yes XX No
Pseudonymous?   ☐ Yes XX No

If the answer to either of these questions is "Yes," see detailed instructions.

NOTE

NATURE OF AUTHORSHIP   Check appropriate box(es).   See instructions

XX 3-Dimensional sculpture   ☐ Map   ☐ Technical drawing
☐ 2-Dimensional artwork   ☐ Photograph   ☐ Text
☐ Reproduction of work of art   ☐ Jewelry design   ☐ Architectural work
☐ Design on sheetlike material

NAME OF AUTHOR ▼

DATES OF BIRTH AND DEATH
Year Born ▼ Year Died ▼

Was this contribution to the work a "work made for hire"?

☐ Yes
☐ No

AUTHOR'S NATIONALITY OR DOMICILE
Name of Country

OR { Citizen of ▶_____
Domiciled in▶_____

WAS THIS AUTHOR'S CONTRIBUTION TO THE WORK

Anonymous?   ☐ Yes ☐ No
Pseudonymous?   ☐ Yes ☐ No

If the answer to either of these questions is "Yes," see detailed instructions.

NATURE OF AUTHORSHIP   Check appropriate box(es).   See instructions

☐ 3-Dimensional sculpture   ☐ Map   ☐ Technical drawing
☐ 2-Dimensional artwork   ☐ Photograph   ☐ Text
☐ Reproduction of work of art   ☐ Jewelry design   ☐ Architectural work
☐ Design on sheetlike material

3 a

YEAR IN WHICH CREATION OF THIS WORK WAS COMPLETED   This information must be given   Year in all cases.

1991

b DATE AND NATION OF FIRST PUBLICATION OF THIS PARTICULAR WORK   Complete this information ONLY if this work has been published.

Month ▶ 9   Day ▶ 9   Year ▶ 1991

USA   ◀ Nation

4

COPYRIGHT CLAIMANT(S) Name and address must be given even if the claimant is the same as the author given in space 2. ▼

FISHER-PRICE, INC.
636 GIRARD AVENUE
EAST AURORA, NEW YORK 14052

TRANSFER If the claimant(s) named here in space 4 are different from the author(s) named in space 2, give a brief statement of how the claimant(s) obtained ownership of the copyright. ▼

See instructions before completing this space.

APPLICATION RECEIVED
MAY 11 1992
ONE DEPOSIT RECEIVED
MAY 11 1992
TWO DEPOSITS RECEIVED

REMITTANCE NUMBER AND DATE

DO NOT WRITE HERE
OFFICE USE ONLY

MORE ON BACK ▶   · Complete all applicable spaces (numbers 5-9) on the reverse side of this page.
· See detailed instructions.   · Sign the form at line 8.

DO NOT WRITE HERE

Page 1 of __2__ pages

VA 501 963

EXAMINED BY
CHECKED BY

☐ CORRESPONDENCE
Yes

FORM VA

FOR
COPYRIGH
OFFICE
USE
ONLY

DO NOT WRITE ABOVE THIS LINE. IF YOU NEED MORE SPACE, USE A SEPARATE CONTINUATION SHEET.

PREVIOUS REGISTRATION Has registration for this work, or for an earlier version of this work, already been made in the Copyright Office?
☐ Yes XXNo If your answer is "Yes," why is another registration being sought? (Check appropriate box) ▼
a. ☐ This is the first published edition of a work previously registered in unpublished form.
b. ☐ This is the first application submitted by this author as copyright claimant.
c. ☐ This is a changed version of the work, as shown by space 6 on this application.
If your answer is "Yes," give: Previous Registration Number ▼   Year of Registration ▼

5

DERIVATIVE WORK OR COMPILATION Complete both space 6a & 6b for a derivative work; complete only 6b for a compilation.
a. Preexisting Material Identify any preexisting work or works that this work is based on or incorporates. ▼

6

See instruction
before complet
this space.

b. Material Added to This Work Give a brief, general statement of the material that has been added to this work and in which copyright is claimed. ▼

DEPOSIT ACCOUNT If the registration fee is to be charged to a Deposit Account established in the Copyright Office, give name and number of Account.
Name ▼   Account Number ▼

FISHER-PRICE LEGAL SERVICES   DA065137

7

CORRESPONDENCE Give name and address to which correspondence about this application should be sent.   Name/Address/Apt/City/State/Zip ▼
TONI GREEN / LEGAL SERVICES
FISHER-PRICE RESEARCH & DEVELOPMENT
636 GIRARD AVENUE
EAST AURORA, NEW YORK 14052
Area Code & Telephone Number▶   (716) 687-3872

Be sure to
give your
daytime pho
number

CERTIFICATION* I, the undersigned, hereby certify that I am the
Check only one ▼
☐ author
☐ other copyright claimant
☐ owner of exclusive right(s)
XX authorized agent of _____ FISHER-PRICE, INC. _____
Name of author or other copyright claimant, or owner of exclusive right(s) ▲

8

of the work identified in this application and that the statements made
by me in this application are correct to the best of my knowledge.

Typed or printed name and date ▼ If this application gives a date of publication in space 3, do not sign and submit it before that date.
TONI GREEN   date▶   5/8/92

Handwritten signature (X) ▼
Toni Green

**MAIL
CERTIFI-
CATE TO**

Name ▼
FISHER-PRICE, INC. / ATTN: TONI GREEN

Certificate
will be
mailed in
window
envelope

Number/Street/Apartment Number ▼
636 GIRARD AVENUE

City/State/ZIP ▼
EAST AURORA, NEW YORK 14052

• Complete all necessary spaces
• Sign your application in space 8

1. Application form
2. Nonrefundable $20 filing fee
   in check or money order
   payable to Register of Copyrights
3. Deposit material

Register of Copyrights
Library of Congress
Washington, D.C. 20559

9

*17 U.S.C. § 506(e): Any person who knowingly makes a false representation of a material fact in the application for copyright registration provided for by section 409, or in any written statement filed in connec

153

APPENDIX 4
SAMPLE PATENT FOR AN ACTION TOY

US005250002A

United States Patent [19]

Kinberg

[11] Patent Number: 5,250,002

[45] Date of Patent: Oct. 5, 1993

[54] INFLATABLE PLAY GYM

[76] Inventor: Benjamin Kinberg, 425 Riverside Dr., Apt. 5A, New York, N.Y. 10025

[21] Appl. No.: 726,345

[22] Filed: Jul. 5, 1991

[51] Int. Cl.⁵ A63H 33/00
[52] U.S. Cl. 446/220; 446/227
[58] Field of Search 446/227, 220, 236, 419,
446/265, 221, 222, 223, 224, 225, 226;
248/163.1, 163.2

[56] References Cited

U.S. PATENT DOCUMENTS

1,318,024	10/1919	Sundell	446/227
2,927,383	3/1960	Longino	446/221 X
3,008,265	11/1961	Converse	446/265 X
3,559,332	2/1971	Stephens	446/226
4,232,477	11/1980	Lin	446/220 X
4,391,064	7/1983	Lakin et al.	446/227
5,076,520	12/1991	Bro	446/227 X
5,088,952	2/1992	Goldblatt	446/220

FOREIGN PATENT DOCUMENTS

149296	7/1985	European Pat. Off.	446/227
1250880	12/1960	France	446/220

Primary Examiner—Mickey Yu
Attorney, Agent, or Firm—Grimes & Battersby

[57] ABSTRACT

An infant's inflatable play gym for use either as a crib toy or floor toy which includes a pair of opposed upright end supports for rotatably supporting therebetween an inflatable chamber. Within the inflatable chamber are a plurality of loosely disposed amusing playthings which are free to tumble within the inflatable chamber as the chamber is rotated. To impart a tumbling motion to the playthings within the inflatable chamber are a plurality of transversely extending vanes which are radially and circumferentially spaced therein. The chamber is also provided with a valve through which air may be pumped to inflate or to exhaust to deflate the chamber.

12 Claims, 3 Drawing Sheets

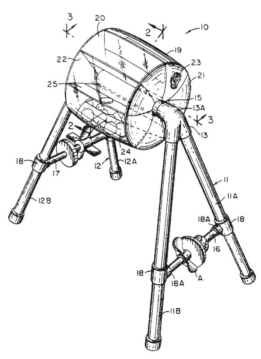

U.S. Patent   Oct. 5, 1993   Sheet 1 of 3   5,250,002

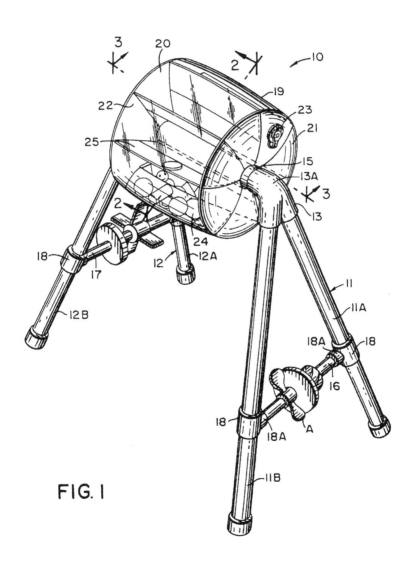

FIG. I

FIG. 2

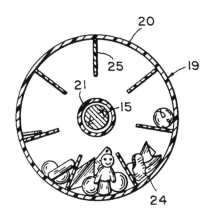

FIG. 3

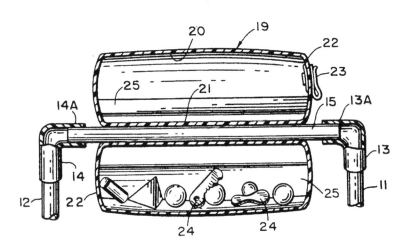

FIG. 4

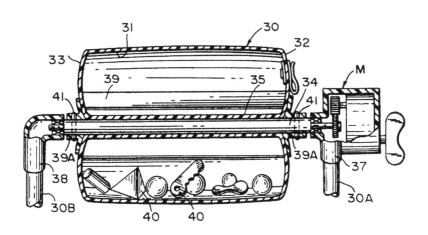

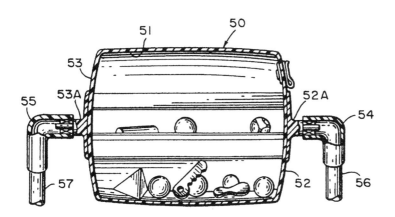

FIG. 5

5,250,002

1

INFLATABLE PLAY GYM

This invention is related to a child's play gym and more specifically to an infant's play gym which can be readily used as a crib attraction or a floor attraction for infants of three months to one year or more.

DESCRIPTION OF THE PRIOR ART

Heretofore, children's play gyms are well known. Generally, such play gyms comprise full scale swing sets formed by a pair of end supports for supporting therebetween a cross bar from which one or more swing sets are supported and on which children of various ages can play. Toy swing sets or play gyms are also known. One such small child's toy play gym comprises a pair of opposed end supports having connected therebetween a cross bar. Various amusing play things in the form of loops, dolls and other amusing toy items are dependently suspended from the cross bar with which a small child can amuse itself. Such toy gym sets were usually made of rigid plastic tubing or the like. These known toy play gyms provided limited amusement to a child and not particularly of interest to an infant who is too young to crawl or walk.

OBJECTS OF THE PRESENT INVENTION

An object of this invention is to provide an infant's toy gym set which can be utilized either as a crib toy or floor toy that is particularly amusing to an infant.

Another object is to provide an infant's toy gym set which is relatively simple in construction, inexpensive to fabricate and which is positive in operation.

Another object is to provide an infant's toy gym set having an action feature which is pleasing and amusing to an infant.

Another object is to provide an infant's toy gym set having an inflatable chamber formed as an integral part thereof which can be readily inflated and deflated, which when inflated, enhances the play value of the toy gym set and when deflated provides ease of shipment and/or storage when not in use.

SUMMARY OF THE INVENTION

The foregoing objects are attained by an infant's toy gym set which comprises a pair of opposed upright end supports for supporting therebetween an inflatable chamber which is rotatably mounted between the end supports. The chamber is provided with a suitable valve for inflating and deflating the chamber. Disposed within the chamber are a plurality of various playthings that are free to tumble within the chamber when the chamber is rotated. To enhance the tumbling effect of the playthings within the chamber, there is provided a plurality of transversely extending vanes circumferentially spaced within the chamber. In one form of the invention, the chamber is formed integral to a cross bar which is rotatably supported between the end supports. In another form of the invention, the chamber is formed with a center sleeve through which the cross bar extends. In another embodiment, the inflatable chamber is provided with opposed side trunnions which are rotatably supported to the end supports. Each of the end supports includes a pair of leg members which are secured at their upper ends by a V fitting having a lateral offset socket for supporting the chamber.

2

BRIEF DESCRIPTION OF THE DRAWINGS

A feature of the invention resides in providing a toy play gym with an inflatable chamber rotatably supported between the end supports and having disposed therein a plurality of playthings which are free to tumble therein and which are rendered appealing to infants.

Another feature resides in the provision of a plurality of vanes circumferentially spaced within the inflatable chamber to enhance the tumbling effect of the playthings disposed therein.

Other features and advantages will become more readily apparent when considered in view of the drawings and specifications in which:

FIG. 1 is a perspective view of an infant's play gym set embodying the invention.

FIG. 2 is a sectional view taken along line 2—2 on FIG. 1.

FIG. 3 is a sectional view taken along line 3—3 on FIG. 1.

FIG. 4 is an elevational view of a modified form of the invention having parts shown in section.

FIG. 5 is a perspective view of another modified form of the invention.

DETAIL DESCRIPTION OF THE PREFERRED EMBODIMENTS

Referring to the drawings and in particular to FIGS. 1 to 3, there is illustrated an infant's toy gym set embodying the present invention. Infant, as used herein, is defined as a child ranging between three months to one year of age. As shown, the toy gym set 10 of FIG. 1 comprises a pair of opposed upright supports 11 and 12. Each upright support 11 and 12 includes a pair of leg members 11A, 11B and 12A, 12B which are arranged to converge toward the upper ends thereof. The upper ends of the respective leg members 11A, 11B and 12A, 12B are connected by a fitting 13 and 14 respectively. As seen, the fittings 13 and 14 comprise a generally V-shape fitting having a pair of sockets for slid ably receiving the upper ends of the corresponding leg members. The arrangement is such that the leg members are frictionally received within the corresponding sockets of the respective fitting. Each fitting 13 and 14 is also provided with a laterally off-set socket 13A and 14A respectively which provides the end support for a cross bar 15; which is preferably round in cross-section. To stabilize the end supports 11 and 12, a tie bar 16 and 17 is interconnected between the respective pair of leg members 11A, 11B and 12A, 12B. This is readily attained by a T-shape fitting 18 which is slipped onto the respective legs whereby the cross arm of the fitting 18 slides onto the respective leg whereby the cross arm of the fitting 18 slides onto the respective leg with the tie bar fitted between the opposed stem 18A portion of the T fitting 18. Rotatably and slidably mounted on the respective tie bars 16 and 17 are a plurality of beads, propellers and other amusing articles A which can be readily manipulated by an infant or its parents for imparting additional play value or activity to the toy 10.

In accordance with this invention, an inflatable means or chamber 19 is rotatably mounted on the cross bar 15. In the illustrated form of the invention, the inflatable chamber 19 is defined by a cylindrical outer shell 20 formed of a suitable plastic material. Disposed axially of the shell 20 is a center sleeve 21 for receiving the cross bar 15 about which the chamber 19 is free to rotate. Opposed end walls 22, 22 are secured between the outer

5,250,002

3

shell 20 and sleeve 21 to define an air tight chamber 19. A suitable valve 23 is provided to allow for inflating and/or deflating the chamber 19.

Disposed within the chamber 19 and free to tumble therein as the chamber 19 is rotated are a plurality of individual playthings or beads. It will be understood that the playthings 24 may simulate any figure or shape that may appeal to an infant. To facilitate the tumbling of the playthings within the chamber when rotated, the chamber is provided with a plurality of circumferen- 10 tially spaced internal vanes 25 which are radially disposed therein. Thus, it will be apparent that as the chamber is rotated about the cross bar 15, the internal vanes will cause the playthings to be caught thereby and released when the vanes reach the zenith of its 15 rotation. The rotating chamber thus presents an amusing and appealing attraction to an infant as the playthings 24 disposed therein rise and fall upon the continued rotation of the chamber. The tumbling of the playthings within the chamber also produces a random 20 sound which also supplements the visual appeal. If desired, the outer shell may be suitably decorated in colors which may also impart thereto a kaleidoscope effect.

Within the construction described, it will be apparent that the toy gym set 10 may be mounted above a crib 25 and utilized as a crib toy or it can stand on a floor and be utilized as a floor toy. In either event, the infant lying below the inflatable chamber can be readily amused by the action, sound and sight of the rotating chamber and the tumbling playthings disposed therein. 30

FIG. 4 illustrates a modified form of the invention. In this form of the invention, the end supports 30A, 30B are constructed as hereinbefore described. In this form of the invention, the inflatable chamber 30 comprises an outer shell 31 which is cylindrical in shape and sealed at 35 the ends by end walls 32 and 33. As shown in FIG. 4, the cross bar 34 is projected through the sleeve 35 extending between side walls 32, 33 and sealed thereat to define an annular chamber 31, which is supported on the cross bar 35. The cross bar in turn is rotatably jour- 40 nalled in the support fittings 37 and 38. As hereinbefore described, the inflatable chamber includes the internal vanes 39 and internally disposed playthings 40. In this form of the invention, rotation of the inflatable chamber 30 is effected by rotation of the cross bar 35 to which 45 the inflatable chamber is fixed, e.g. pins 41 extending to mounting sleeves 39A connected to the end walls 32, 33 of the inflatable chamber. If desired, a motor means M may be connected in driving relationship to the cross bar 35 as shown to effect rotation of the chamber 30 50 connected to the cross bar 35. In the illustration embodiment, the motor M comprises a spring wound motor which is suitably geared to one end of the cross bar as shown to effect rotation thereof. A small electrical motor may be substituted in lieu thereof. In all other 55 respects, the embodiment of FIG. 4 is similar to that of FIGS. 1 to 3.

FIG. 5 illustrates a further embodiment of the invention. This form of the invention differs from that hereinbefore described in that the inflatable chamber 50 com- 60 prises an outer shell 51 which is sealed by end walls 52 and 53. Connected to the respective end walls 52 and 53 is an outwardly projecting trunnion or axle 52A, 53A respectively. The outer ends of the trunnions 52A, 53A are rotatably supported in the end fittings 54, 55 respec- 65 tively of the end supports 56, 57. In all other respects, the toy gym set is similar to that hereinbefore described with respect to FIG. 1

4

While the embodiments herein described are constructed so as to permit the inflatable chambers 19 and 50 to be manually rotated, it will be understood that if desired, the inflatable chamber could be motorized by a small mechanical or electrical motor as shown in FIG. 4, which can be suitably geared to effect rotation of the chamber when the motor is activated. Also, it will be understood that a music box can be suitably associated with the rotating chamber which is actuated when the chamber is rotated.

Although the preferred embodiment has been illustrated and described, it will be obvious to those skilled in the art that various modifications may be made without departing from the spirit and scope of this invention.

What is claimed is:

1. An inflatable play gym comprising:
   a pair of spaced apart end supports;
   a cross bar interconnected between said pair of end supports;
   an inflatable chamber connected to said cross bar and rotatable therewith between said pair of end supports, said inflatable chamber having a plurality of circumstantially spaced vanes disposed therein; and
   at least one plaything disposed within said inflatable chamber, said at least one plaything being loosely retained within said inflatable chamber, whereby said at least one plaything is freely movable within said inflatable chamber and is adapted to be captured and released by said plurality of vanes as said inflatable chamber is rotated between said pair of end supports.

2. An inflatable play gym as defined in claim 1, wherein said at least one plaything includes a plurality of playthings.

3. An inflatable play gym as defined in claim 1, wherein said vanes extend transversely of said inflatable chamber.

4. An inflatable play gym as defined in claim 1, further comprising valve means that provides an inlet and an outlet for inflating and deflating said inflatable chamber.

5. An inflatable play gym as defined in claim 1, wherein said inflatable chamber comprises a cylindrical outer shell and opposed end walls, said outer shell being connected to and between said opposed end walls.

6. An inflatable play gym comprising:
   a pair of spaced apart end supports;
   a cross bar interconnected between said pair of end supports, said cross bar being mounted on said pair of end supports;
   an inflatable chamber connected to said cross bar in sealing relationship therewith, whereby said inflatable chamber is free to rotate therewith, said inflatable chamber having a plurality of circumstantially spaced vanes disposed therein; and
   at least one plaything disposed within said inflatable chamber, said at least one plaything being free to tumble within said inflatable chamber and be captured and released by said plurality of vanes during rotation of said inflatable chamber.

7. An inflatable play gym comprising:
   a pair of spaced apart upright end supports each having an upper end,
   a cross bar interconnected between the upper ends of said pair of upright end supports;
   an inflatable means rotatably journalled about said cross bar; and

5,250,002

5

at least one plaything disposed within said inflatable means whereby said plaything is free to tumble within said inflatable means as said inflatable means rotates about said cross bar.

8. An inflatable play gym as defined in claim 7, wherein said inflatable means comprises an air tight chamber, said air tight chamber including:

an outer cylindrical shell;

a center sleeve having a diameter slightly greater than the diameter of said cross bar;

a pair of annular end walls interconnected to said outer shell and said center sleeve;

said cross bar extending transversely through said center sleeve; and

valve means for inflating and deflating said air tight chamber.

9. An inflatable play gym as defined in claim 8, further comprising a plurality of circumferentially spaced vanes extending transversely between said pair of annular end walls for randomly tumbling said at least one plaything within said chamber as said chamber is rotated relative to said cross bar.

10. An inflatable play gym as defined in claim 7, wherein said pair of upright end supports each includes a pair of upwardly extending leg members, said leg members converging toward one another at the upper ends thereof, a connector for receiving and securing the upper ends of said leg members together, said connector

6

including an angularly disposed socket for receiving and supporting an end portion of said cross bar to said pair of upright end supports, and a tie rod interconnected between said leg member intermediate the ends thereof, and a rotatably journalled plaything mounted on said tie rod.

11. An inflatable infant play gym comprising:

a pair of spaced apart end supports;

a cross bar interconnected between said pair of end supports;

an inflatable means having a center sleeve through which said cross bar extends and about which said inflatable means is adapted to rotate, said inflatable means including a cylindrical outer shell having a pair of opposed ends;

an end wall connected to each opposed end of said cylindrical shell;

at least one plaything loosely disposed within said cylindrical shell; and

a plurality of vanes disposed within said cylindrical shell to impart a tumbling effect to said plaything disposed within said cylindrical shell during rotation of said cylindrical shell.

12. An inflatable play gym as defined in claim 6, wherein said at least one plaything includes a plurality of playthings.

* * * * *

160

APPENDIX 5
SAMPLE PATENT FOR A BOARD GAME

US005120065A

United States Patent [19]

Driscoll et al.

[11] Patent Number: **5,120,065**

[45] Date of Patent: **Jun. 9, 1992**

[54] ELECTRONIC TALKING BOARD GAME

[75] Inventors: **Robert W. Driscoll**, Northampton; **Daniel J. Marceau**, Springfield, both of Mass.

[73] Assignee: **Hasbro, Incorporated**, Pawtucket, R.I.

[21] Appl. No.: **653,068**

[22] Filed: **Feb. 8, 1991**

[51] Int. Cl.⁵ A63F 3/00; G09B 7/04

[52] U.S. Cl. 273/237; 273/243; 434/169

[58] Field of Search 273/237, 243; 434/169, 434/201

[56] **References Cited**

U.S. PATENT DOCUMENTS

4,505,682 3/1985 Thompson 434/335

4,958,837 9/1990 Russell 273/237

FOREIGN PATENT DOCUMENTS

WO90/00429 1/1990 PCT Int'l Appl. 273/237

OTHER PUBLICATIONS

Popular Electronics "Computers: Monopoly Program" p. 44, May 1981.

Primary Examiner—Benjamin Layno
Attorney, Agent, or Firm—Donald Brown

[57] **ABSTRACT**

A talking board game having a board and an electronic computer system providing speech information to the players, and cards which can be read by the electronic computer system.

12 Claims, 5 Drawing Sheets

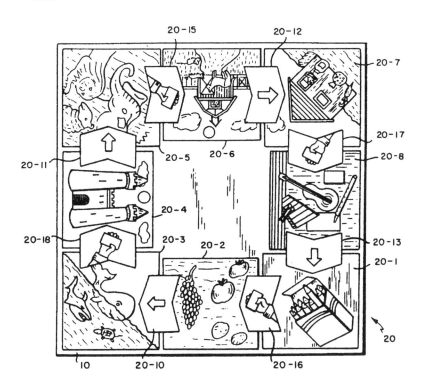

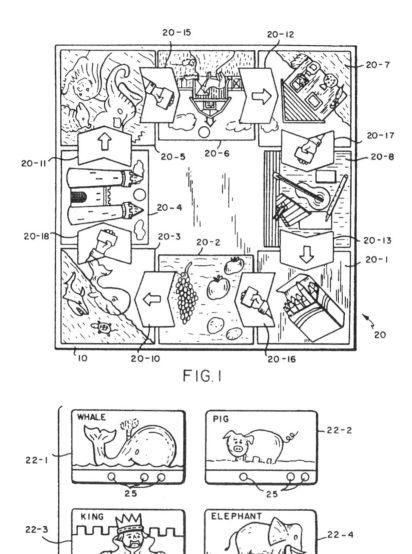

FIG. 1

FIG. 2

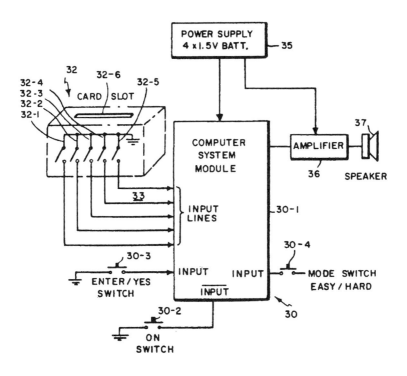

FIG. 3

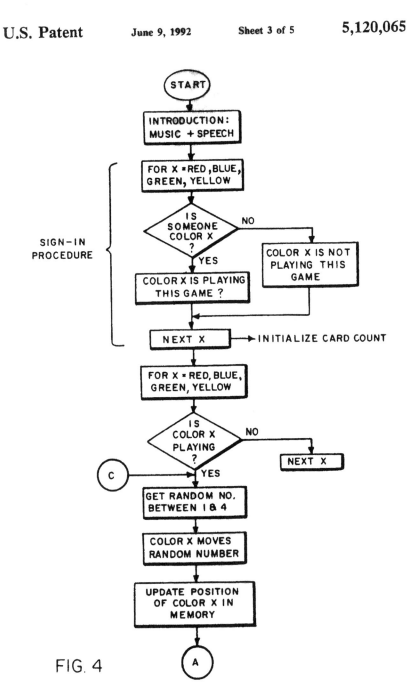

FIG. 4

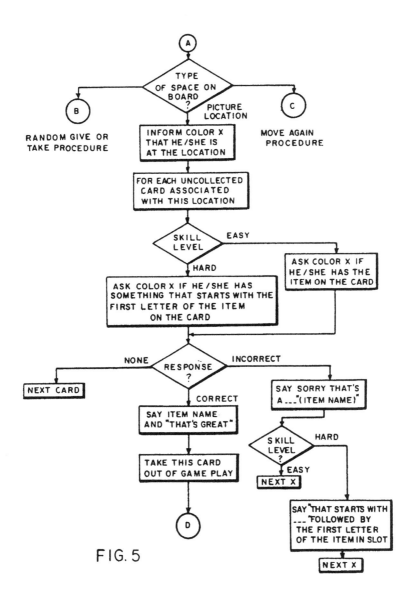

FIG. 5

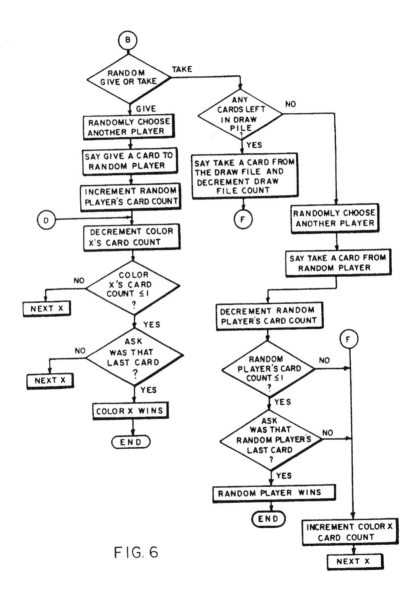

FIG. 6

5,120,065

1

ELECTRONIC TALKING BOARD GAME

BACKGROUND OF THE INVENTION

This invention relates to electronic learning aids, teaching machines and electronic games. More particularly, this invention relates to electronic learning aids in the form of a game and using synthesized sounds, a game board and cards to teach the user information, such as letters in the alphabet.

Many games, toys and etc., have been produced over the years for teaching children to learn their letters, numbers, arithmetic and spell correctly, and/or learn other information. Examples of such systems are to be found in U.S. Pat. Nos. 3,584,398 and 4,516,260. Systems such as U.S. Pat. No. 4,516,260, have included voice synthesizers.

The present invention provides another way of particularly teaching children information such as letters, words, etc., in a way which combines learning with playing a competitive board game with their peers or even parents.

The preferred embodiment of the game as shown herein, combines sound for instructional purposes and pictorial cards as learning aids together with a game board. The preferred embodiment permits two to four children to play the game while learning information, such as the alphabet.

It is therefore an object of this invention to provide a new learning device, which combines teaching with a competitive board game.

It is a further object of this invention to provide a learning experience, which can be enjoyed while reinforcing learning of such information as the alphabet, words and etc.

It is yet another object of this invention to provide a board game which not only will provide voice directions and questions to the user, but will by use of a game board get the user involved in a learning situation in which each correct answer results in a reward and which ultimately will result in the user providing correct answers having the best chance of winning the game.

The foregoing objects are achieved as will be described in the brief description of the invention and as described in the description of the preferred embodiment of the invention.

BRIEF DESCRIPTION OF THE DRAWINGS

FIG. 1, represents a game board of the talking board game;

FIG. 2, is a diagram illustrating some of the cards of the talking board game;

FIG. 3 is a schematic view of the computer system hardware of the talking board game to be used in conjunction with the game board and cards of FIGS. 1 and 2;

and

FIGS. 4 to 6, represent a flow chart representing the steps carried out by the computer system hardware of FIG. 3 and which may be implemented by a computer program stored in the computer system hardware, corresponding to the steps in the flow chart.

BRIEF DESCRIPTION OF THE INVENTION

The invention comprises a playing (game) board and a computer system controlled by software as will be

2

described with reference to the flow chart shown in the drawings

The playing board in its preferred form, comprises 16 spaces: 8 location spaces, 4 move again spaces and 4 give / take a card spaces. There are 26 cards, 1 for each letter of the alphabet Each card has a picture of an item related to one of the 8 location spaces (e.g., 3 or 4 cards for each location). Each card preferably includes the name of the item. Preferably each card will carry a picture, e.g., "turtle", associated with each location. There are four playing pieces, e.g., pawns in the shape of coins, etc., (e.g., red, blue, green and yellow), one for each player. The players throughout the game will be instructed by referring to the color pawn they selected.

The computer system determines who is playing through a sign-in procedure. The computer system knows where each player is starting. The board and/or voice instructions indicates to each player where to initially place their colored pawns. The software initializes card counts for each player based on the number of players starting the game. The computer system therefore knows how many cards will be in a draw pile at the start of a game. The computer system will not know which cards each of the players have.

The computer system keeps track of the location of each player through the game play software. The computer system insures that each player stays in agreement with the software, as far as location is concerned, through the use of speech. For example, the player using a red pawn is 3 spaces away from the jungle space when the computer says "red move 3", after pausing for enough time to let the player move. the computer system through speech, asks the player if the player has landed on a space, which has items (pictorially represented on the cards, e.g., apples) associated with that location, which also had apples shown thereon. If the player has moved to the wrong space, he/she can now correct the mistake. The computer also keeps track of the card count, i.e., the number of cards in the players possession for each player (identified by color). If a player puts the correct card in the card reader slot of the computer system, then the computer system will respond with an affirmative answer and the player for each card. The software then decrements that players' card count and takes that card out of the game. If a player lands on a give/take card space then the computer system tells that player which other player to give a card to, or take a card from or to take a card from the draw pile (if there are cards remaining in the draw pile). The computer software then updates the card count for each player involved in the transaction.

When a player is at a location space, the computer system does not ask for cards which are no longer in play and asks if the player has any of the remaining cards associated with that location. If any player has provided one of his/her last two cards to another player, or inserted the card in the card slot of the computer system, then the computer system will ask that player if that was their last card. If the response is "yes", then the game is over and the player with no cards left is a winner of the game.

In order to help in understanding the game the following information is provided relating to the game, including the verbal information provided to the player.

I. PARTS

4 pawns (red, blue, green and yellow)
26 cards (1 for each letter in the alphabet)

5,120,065

3

1 board with electronics module (114 words)

The game parts include a game board and 4 pawns (e.g., red, blue, green and yellow), one for each player and the player is identified during the game as red, blue, green or yellow, 26 cards (1 for each letter in the alphabet), which have means thereon for permitting the cards to be identified by the game board computer system, e.g., holes to be identified (electronics module) and a computer system having a card reader, processor, memory, power supply, voice synthesizer, amplifier and a speaker.

II. SET-UP

Shuffle cards and deal out 24 cards to all players. (12 (2 players), 8 (3 players), or 6 (4 players)). Put the 2 left-over cards in the draw pile.

Turn the power on to start the game and players then sign-in.

To begin the game, the players each select a colored pawn. The cards are shuffled and 24 cards in all are dealt out to all players (12, 8 or 6), depending if there are respectively 2, 3 or 4 players. The two cards left over, are placed in the draw pile. The computer system is then turned on, the players sign in and the play proceeds according to the instructions and information provided to each player according to that shown in the flow chart of the drawings.

III. POWER-ON

3.1. Select Skill Level:

When you depress the "ON" switch the computer will read the ENTER switch. If the enter switch is also depressed then the game will be played at the higher (hard) skill level.

3.1.1. In normal (easy) skill level mode, the computer system asks each player if he/she has a certain object.

3.1.2. In higher (hard) skill level mode, the computer system asks each player if he/she has an object that starts with a certain letter.

3.2. After the power is turned on, the following introduction occurs:

3.2.1. The computer system plays a musical tune.

3.2.2. And then greets the players by saying "Hi, I'm Bird. Let's Play".

4. Sign-In Procedure:

This game is for 1 to 4 players (red, blue, green and yellow).

4.1. The following then occurs by the computer system asking the following questions and/or making the following statements:

FIRST CHANCE:

"Is someone red?" (blue, green or yellow).

4.1.1. Enter switch hit:

Beep!"0.K., you're red". (this color is playing).

4.2.2 Enter switch NOT hit (not closed): Go to 4.2.

4.2. SECOND CHANCE:

"No one is red?" (blue, green or yellow).

4.2.1. Enter switch hit (switch temporarily closed):

Beep! "0.K., you're red". (now he/she is playing)

4.2.2. Enter switch NOT hit:

Go on to next color (this color is not playing)

5. Starting a Turn:

The computer system randomly chooses 1 to 4 or chooses a move event. Turns do not have to be balanced for each player, because there is no advantage in big numbers.

5.1. The computer system announces move as follows:

4

5.1.1. Normal move:

"Red, go one". (two, three or four)

"Move ahead" can randomly replace "GO" for variety.

5.1.2. The computer system describes the move event as follows:

"Red, go to the garden".

"Red, go to the jungle".

"Red, go to the farm".

"Red, go to the ocean".

"Red, go to the castle".

"Red, go to the music store".

"Red, go to the art store".

"Red, go to the house".

6. Move Verification:

VERY IMPORTANT NOTE:

The computer will keep track where each player ends his/her turn, so it will announce the results, which will confirm the player's move.

6.1. The player is supposed to landed on one of the eight locations:

6.1.1. The computer system announces the location as follows:

"You're in the garden". (Apple, Grapes, Oranges)

"You're in the jungle". (Elephant, Lion, Mouse, Zebra)

"You're in the farm". (Horse, Nest, Pig)

"You're in the ocean". (Shark, Turtle, Whale)

"You're in the castle". (Dragon, King, Queen)

"You're in the music store". (Flute, Violin, Xylophone)

"You're in the art store". (Blue, Red, Yellow Crayons)

"You're in the house". (Cat, Ice, Jar, Umbrella)

6.1.2. If all the items from this area have been turned in, then the computer system says the following: "Gosh, I already have everything from there".

6.1.3. If not, the computer system asks for a card: Only ask for cards which have not been turned in yet.

6.1.3.1. Normal Skill Level:

The computer system randomly chooses an item from the location.

"Do you have an Apple?"

6.1.3.1.1 Correct Answer (detected by insertion a card in the card reader:

Beep! "An Apple, you're smart!"

("Super" or "Very Good" are also interchangeably used, instead of "Smart").

6.1.3.1.2. Incorrect Answer (the computer system states the following:

Beep! "Sorry, that is a cat".

6.1.3.1.3. No Answer: (either time for action runs out, or enter switch hit)

Repeat question with new item.

6.1.3.2. Higher Skill Level:

The computer system randomly chooses a letter that starts with one of the items from the garden, e.g., apple.

"Do you have something that starts with "A"?

6.1.3.2.1. Same as 6.1.3.1.1.

6.1.3.2.2. Same as 6.1.3.1.2., plus following (the computer system says):

"That starts with "C".

6.1.3.2.3. Same as 6.1.3.1.3.

6.2. Landed on a GIVE/TAKE card box:

Randomly choose between give or take. The computer keeps track of how many cards each player has.

5

6.2.1. Give Card (the computer system says):
"Oh boy! Give a card to red". (blue, green, yellow).
6.2.2. Take Card (the computer system says):
"Uh oh! Take a card from the pile". (1st two times)
OR
"Uh oh! Take a card from red". (blue, green, yellow)
6.3. Landed on move box (the computer system says):
"Oh Boy! Move ahead one". (two, three or four)
The computer will then determine where the player
should end up and continue his/her turn at 6.1.
7. End of Game:
Whenever a player has answered correctly, the computer will respond with:
"Can I have it please?"
This lets the child (player) know that he/she
should turn the card into the already used card
stack. If the computer determines that the player
who turned the card in might be out of cards, it will
ask:
"Was that you last card?"
If the enter button is not depressed, then the game
will continue. If the enter button is hit (closed),
then the computer will announce:
"That's great? YOU WIN?"
And the game is over.

DETAILED DESCRIPTION OF THE
INVENTION

Reference should now be had to FIG. 1, which shows
the game board 20 for this invention The game board
has sixteen spaces, eight "location spaces" shown at
20-1, 20-2, 20-3, 20-4, 20-5, 20-6, 20-7 and 20-8, four
"move again" spaces shown at 20-10, 20-11, 20-12 and
20-13. and four "give/take a card" spaces shown at
20-15 to 20-16.
FIG. 2 shows four of the cards 22-1, 22-2, 22-3 and
22-4 of the twenty-six cards used in the game. Each of
the cards have holes 25 representing a unique code, so
that the card reader 32 may identify which card is inserted in the card reader of the computer system.
Reference should now be had to FIG. 3, which shows
the computer system hardware 30 according to this
invention. The computer system hardware comprises at
30-1 a processor, memory and a voice synthesizer, and
the normal controls. A conventional Texas Instrument
synthesizer module No. 50C11 chip may be used to
provide the processor, memory, voice synthesizer and
control functions. The computer system is controlled by
a computer program, written in accordance with the
flow chart functions as set forth in FIGS. 4 through 6.
Providing information to the processor is input
switches, namely switch 30-2, which turns on the computer hardware, switch 30-3, which acts as the ENTER/yes switch, and an optional mode switch 30-4,
which determines if the questions asked to the game
players will be easy or hard. The switch 30-4 may normally be closed for the easy mode and be opened to
instruct the module 30-1 to ask more difficult questions
to the game players.
A conventional card reader 32 is provided for detecting which of the twenty-six cards 22-1, etc., are inserted
into a slot 32-6, so that the presence or absence of holes
25 in the card 22-1, etc., may be sensed by the five
switches 32-1 to 32-5. The switches close if the respective switch contact makes contact to the underlying
switch stationary portion as is conventional. Clearly
cards could be sensed using magnetic card readers as
used with credit cards, optical readers and many others

6

which are conventional in the art. The module 30-1 and
a power amplifier 36 are powered by a battery unit 35.
The amplifier 36 acts to amplify the electrical signal
output from the voice synthesizer of the module 30-1
and a conventional speaker 37 is used to generate the
audible instructions and questions posed to the players.
At this time, reference should now be had to FIGS. 4,
5 and 6, which depict a flow chart representing the play
of the game.
The flow chart is implemented by a computer program, which is then stored (loaded) in the memory of
the module 30-1 and in which the program is then implemented by the processor of the module. The program may be easily written by any person skilled in the
art, as will be apparent by reviewing the flow chart.
As shown in the flow chart (FIG. 4), after the "on"
switch 30-2 is turned on, the program provides introductory audible music and speech instructions directing
the players in the procedures of the game (e.g., how
many cards to choose, based on the number of players),
how to sign on to the computer, how to select pieces
and where each colored piece should initially be placed
on the board locations.
Other instructions, e.g., how may cards to deal out,
when to put a card in the card reader slot are also provided in written form to the players. However, when
more cost effective speech hardware is available, all
instructions relating to play of the game may be provided by the computer system in speech form.
The players are then asked to sign on and the sign on
procedure is implemented, so the computer system will
know who is playing. For example, if only two players
are playing the game, the players will enter "yes" using
the ENTER/yes switch 30-3 when the color they each
selected has been mentioned. If no player has selected
green, then switch 30-3 will remain open to indicate to
the computer that no one is using green. Alternatively,
a separate "NO" switch can be used to indicate that the
green colored pawn is not being used. This procedure
also lets the processor and memory determine the number of cards 22-1, etc., each player is supposed to have
(but not the specific cards each player has) and the
location on the game board where each player is to
initially place the colored pawn selected.
After all the players sign "on" the computer, the play
begins. The computer system 30-1 now generates a
random instruction and tells the player, e.g., red to
move forward or backwards 1 to 4 spaces in accordance
with a random generated number. The computer then
updates the position of the color "X" (e.g., red) pawn in
memory. Only players who have signed "on" will be
asked to move.
Turning now to FIG. 5 (A to A), the computer determines the type of space (location) on which the players,
pawn should be positioned and tells the player which
space the pawn should be on and allows time for the
player to go to the correct position.
The computer system then determines which cards
remain and which cards are associated (e.g., by picture
with the particular location) and asks the player (assuming the mode switch is in the hard question mode) if
he/she has a card that starts with the first letter of the
item on the card (e.g., "W" in whale). Based on written
game instructions (or oral instructions by Mom or Dad),
the player (child) (X =color) will insert the card with
the "W" into the slot of the card reader 32 (i.e., if he/-
she has the card asked for or thinks he/she has the card
asked for).

7

5,120,065

8

If the card inserted is correct, then the flow chart path (D to D) is followed (see FIG. 6), and then the card is removed from the game. The players' card count is decremented and then the player is asked if that was his/her last card. If this player has no cards left, the player is a winner and the game ends. If there are cards left in the players hand, the next player takes a turn.

Now, if the situation occurs and there is no response to the question, "IF HE/SHE has something that starts with the first letter of the item of the card?" (e.g., in 5 seconds), the computer asks about another card (NONE PATHWAY). However, if the player inserts the wrong card (INCORRECT PATHWAY) in the card reader, the player is told that his/her answer is incorrect and the player (the computer does not ask for the card) retains the card. The person's turn is over and the next player is told to move.

Going back to FIG. 5, there are shown B and C pathways, which are followed if a player lands on a give and/or take spaces 20–15 to 20–18. In the pathway (B to B, see FIG. 6), the memory for the computer is decremented and/or added to reflect, which of the players (e.g., X = red pawn) gave a card and which player (X = green pawn) received a card. If a player is told to take a card (see. FIG. 6), the path shown is taken and the questions shown in the flow chart (FIG. 6) are asked depending on the "yes" or "no" answer given.

If a player pawn lands on a move again space 20-10 to 20-13, pathway C is followed (see FIGS. 4 and 5) and the player is instructed to continue to play and receives another turn.

If the easy skill level option is included in the game and used, the respective pathway shown in the flow chart (FIGS. 4 through 6) is followed. In the easy mode, the player could be asked if he/she has a specific card with, e.g., a cat on it. Now instead of having to search for a word that starts with a certain letter, the player only has to look for the item on the card.

Although the invention has been described with reference to a specific embodiment, this description is not meant to be construed in a limiting sense. Various modifications of the disclosed embodiment as well as alternative embodiments of the invention will become apparent to persons skilled in the art upon reference to the description of the invention. It is therefore contemplated that the appended claims will cover any such modifications or embodiments that fall within the true scope of the invention.

We claim:

1. A game comprising a game board having a plurality of defined locations, a plurality of pawns for moving on the game board one pawn for each of the game players, a plurality of cards having machine readable information thereon, said cards also containing machine readable identification information, first machine means for asking questions of the game players and directing the players to move the pawns on the game board, the second machine means for identifying the game cards by reading the machine readable information and deter-

mining if the player has selected the card having information responsive to game questions.

2. The game according to claim 1, in which said first machine means provides said instructions and questions as voice signals.

3. The game according to claim 1, in which said first machine means includes third means for keeping track of the position of each player's pawn on the game board.

4. The game according to claim 3, said first machine means including fourth machine means for producing audible reinforcing information to the players' so that they can correct their position on the board if their pawn has been moved by the player to the wrong location.

5. The game according to claim 1, in which the written information on each of the cards starts with a different letter of the English alphabet.

6. The game according to claim 1, in which said second machine means instructs the player who selected a correct card to discard the correct card.

7. The game according to claim 1, in which said second machine also keeps track of the number of cards held by each player.

8. The game according to claim 1, in which said second machine information comprises one or more holes in said cards and in which said second means includes hole detecting means for reading said holes.

9. A method of teaching information to players of a game having pawns, one for each player, a game board having a plurality of locations and a plurality of cards for each player, and machine means for directing the play of the game, said cards having machine readable information and information to assist the player in learning, said method comprising said machine means instructing the player to move a pawn along a game board, said machine means then audibly asking questions of said player relating to cards in the possession of said player and the determining by reading said machine means readable information if said player has a card responsive to the question asked.

10. The method according to claim 9, in which said machine means instructs said player to select a card from a pile of said cards or to take a card or give a card to another player.

11. The method according to claim 9, in which said method includes said machine means indicating to said player whether or not the player has picked a card responsive to the question asked.

12. A talking board game comprising a playing board having eight "place" locations, four "take or give a card locations" and four "play again" locations, pawns for each player to be used on the game board, a plurality of cards having machine readable information for identifying the card, a card reader and first machine means for directing the play of the game, said first means comprising second machine means for providing instructions to each player for moving a pawn on the game board, and third machine means for asking the player if the player has a card with the information thereon responsive to the question asked.

* * * * *

65

170

APPENDIX 6
TRADEMARK APPLICATION (USE BASED)

IN THE UNITED STATES PATENT AND
TRADEMARK OFFICE

Applicant: CHILDREN'S TOY COMPANY,
                                    a New York Corporation
Applicant's Address: 200 Fifth Avenue,
                                    New York, NY 00000
Mark: FLAPPERS
Class: 28
Attorney Docket No.:   TOY002UST

Hon. Assistant Commissioner of Patents
 and Trademarks
2900 Crystal Drive
Arlington, VA 22202-3513

The above-identified applicant requests that the mark shown in the accompanying drawing be registered in the United States Patent and Trademark Office on the Principal Register established by the Trademark Act of July 5, 1946 for the following goods:

CLASS 28 - BOARD GAMES, JIGSAW PUZZLES AND EDU-CATIONAL TOYS

Applicant is using the mark in interstate commerce on or in connection with the above-identified goods. Applicant first used the mark on or in association with the goods at least as early as JULY 1, 1993, and first used the mark in interstate commerce on or in association with the goods at least as early as JULY 1, 1993, and the mark is still in use in such commerce.

The mark is used by applying it to the goods, applying it to packaging for the goods and in advertisements for the goods.

Three specimens for each class covered by the application evidencing the use of the mark accompany the application.

DECLARATION AND POWER OF ATTORNEY

The undersigned, JOSEPH YARBROUGH, declares that: he is the Vice President of applicant and is authorized to execute this declaration on behalf of applicant; that applicant believes itself to be owner of the mark sought to be registered or, if the application is being filed under 15 U.S.C. 1051 (b) believes it is entitled to use such mark in commerce; to the best of his knowledge and belief no other person, firm, corporation or association has the right to use said mark in commerce, either in the identical form or in such near resemblance thereto as to be likely, when applied to the goods/services of such other person, firm, corporation or association, to cause confusion or to cause mistake or to deceive; that all statements made herein of his own knowledge are true and that all statements made on information and belief are believed to be true; and further, that these statements were made with the knowledge that willful false statements and the like so made are punishable by fine or imprisonment or both, under Section 1001 of Title 18 of the United States Code and that such willful false statements may jeopardize the validity of the application or document or any registration resulting therefrom.

Applicant hereby appoints Charles W. Grimes, Gregory J. Battersby, George W. Cooper, Leora Herrmann and James G. Coplit, of the law firm of Grimes & Battersby with offices at 3 Landmark Square, Suite 405, Stamford, Connecticut 06901, as its attorneys with full power of substitution, association and revocation to prosecute this application, to transact all business in the United States Patent and Trademark Office in connection therewith and to receive the Certificate of Registration. Address all correspondence to:

Grimes & Battersby
P.O. Box 1311
Stamford, CT 06904-1311

_____   _____
(sign full name)   (insert date of signing)

DRAWING

Applicant:	CHILDREN'S TOY COMPANY, a New York Corp.
Applicant's Address:	200 Fifth Avenue, New York, NY 00000
For:	Board Games, Jigsaw puzzles and educational toys (class 28)
Basis for Registration:	15 U.S.C. 1051(a)
First Use:	At least as early as July 1, 1993
Use in Commerce:	At least as early as July 1, 1993

FLAPPERS

SPECIMENS

Applicant: CHILDREN'S TOY COMPANY

Applicant's Address: 00 Fifth Avenue,
                              New York, NY 00000

Mark: FLAPPERS

For: Board Games, Jigsaw puzzles and
                              educational toys (class 28)

Basis for Registration: 15 U.S.C. 1051(a)

(Attach Specimens Here)

APPENDIX 7
TRADEMARK APPLICATION FORM (INTENT TO USE)

IN THE UNITED STATES PATENT AND
TRADEMARK OFFICE

Applicant: CHILDREN'S TOY COMPANY,
                                  a New York Corporation
Applicant's Address: 200 Fifth Avenue,
                                  New York, NY 00000
Mark: ZAPPERS
Class: 28
Attorney Docket No.: TOY001UST

Hon. Assistant Commissioner of Patents
and Trademarks
2900 Crystal Drive
Arlington, VA 22202-3513

The above-identified applicant requests that the mark shown in the accompanying drawing be registered in the United States Patent and Trademark Office on the Principal Register established by the Trademark Act of July 5, 1946 for the following goods:

CLASS 28 - BOARD GAMES, JIGSAW PUZZLES AND EDUCATIONAL TOYS

Applicant has a bona fide intention to use the mark in commerce on or in connection with the above-identified goods.

The mark will be used by applying it to the goods, on packaging for the goods and on labels attached to the goods.

DECLARATION AND POWER OF ATTORNEY

The undersigned, JOSEPH YARBROUGH, declares that: he is the Vice President of applicant and is authorized to execute this declaration on behalf of applicant; that applicant believes itself to be owner of the mark sought to be registered or, if the application is being filed under 15 U.S.C. 1051 (b) believes it is entitled to use such mark in commerce; to the best of his knowledge and belief no other person, firm, corporation or association has the right to use said mark in commerce, either in the identical form or in such near resemblance thereto as to be likely, when applied to the goods/services of such other person, firm, corporation or association, to cause confusion or to cause mistake or to deceive; that all statements made herein of his own knowledge are true and that all statements made on information and belief are believed to be true; and further, that these statements were made with the knowledge that willful false statements and the like so made are punishable by fine or imprisonment or both, under Section 1001 of Title 18 of the United States Code and that such willful false statements may jeopardize the validity of the application or document or any registration resulting therefrom.

Applicant hereby appoints Charles W. Grimes, Gregory J. Battersby, George W. Cooper, Leora Herrmann and James G. Coplit, of the law firm of Grimes & Battersby with offices at 3 Landmark Square, Suite 405, Stamford, Connecticut 06901, as its attorneys with full power of substitution, association and revocation to prosecute this application, to transact all business in the United States Patent and Trademark Office in connection therewith and to receive the Certificate of Registration. Address all correspondence to:

Grimes & Battersby
P.O. Box 1311
Stamford, CT 06904-1311

_____   _____
(sign full name)   (insert date of signing)

DRAWING

Applicant:	CHILDREN'S TOY COMPANY, a New York Corporation
Applicant's Address:	200 Fifth Avenue, New York, NY 00000
For:	Board Games, Jigsaw puzzles and educational toys (class 28)
Basis for Registration:	15 U.S.C. 1051(b)

ZAPPERS

APPENDIX 8
SAMPLE CONFIDENTIAL DISCLOSURE AGREEMENT

CONFIDENTIAL DISCLOSURE AGREEMENT

This Agreement is made as of the 1st day of January, 1995 between CHILDREN'S TOY COMPANY, a New York Corporation with offices at 555 Fifth Avenue, New York, NY 10011 (the "Corporation") and XYZ PROPERTIES, INC., with offices at 111 Madison Avenue, New York, NY 10022 ("XYZ").

WHEREAS, Corporation and XYZ mutually desire to engage in discussions which may lead to a business relationship; and

WHEREAS, the parties in the course of their dealings may furnish to each other "Confidential Information" as defined in paragraph 1 and do not wish to convey any interest or right therein to the other or make such Confidential Information public or common knowledge;

NOW, THEREFORE, in consideration of the joint nature of the disclosure and the business relationship between the parties, it is hereby agreed as follows:

1. CONFIDENTIAL INFORMATION. For purposes of this agreement, the term "Confidential Information" shall mean the following:

(a) Any information, know-how, data, process, technique, design, drawing, program, formula or test data, work in process, engineering, manufacturing, marketing, financial, sales, supplier, customer, employee, investor or business information, whether in oral, written, graphic, or electronic form, or (b) any document, diagram, drawing, computer program or other communication which is either conspicuously marked "confidential," known or reasonably known by the other party to be confidential, or is of a proprietary nature and is learned or disclosed in the course of discussions, studies, or other work undertaken between the parties.

The above notwithstanding, "Confidential Information" shall not include Non-Protected Information as defined in paragraph 5.

2. JOINT UNDERTAKING. Both Corporation and XYZ and their respective employees and agents agree that during the period of their discussions and/or business relationship and for a period of five years after the later of the termination of such discussions or termination of such relationship, the recipient of Confidential Information will not at any time disclose to any person or use for its own benefit or the benefit of anyone, Confidential Information of the other party without the prior express written consent of said party.

3. CONSULTANTS. Prior to disclosure of any Confidential Information to consultants working for a party, the recipient will obtain from all such consultants a written agreement (1) to hold all Confidential Information in confidence and not to use such confidential information for any purpose except as it relates to discussions between the parties or any subsequent business relationship between the parties; (2) to return all Confidential Information received immediately after consultant has completed its work to the party from whom said confidential information was received.

4. RETURN OF CONFIDENTIAL INFORMATION. Upon termination of the discussions and/or business relationship between the parties, the recipient of Confidential Information shall promptly deliver to the other party any and all such Confidential Information in its possession or under its control, including, without limiting the foregoing, any and all copies thereof which the recipient may have made, may have access to, or may receive or possess during the period of its discussions and/or business relationship, except as the parties by prior express written permission or agreement have agreed to retain.

5. NON-PROTECTED INFORMATION. The parties agree that their mutual covenant not to disclose Confidential Information shall not apply to any information or data or other materials imparted to the extent that any of the following conditions exist or come into existence:

(a) Information, which at the time access is gained, is already in the recipient's possession or available to it or its employees from any other source having no obligation to the party which is the source of said information.

(b) Such information which is, or any time hereafter becomes, available to the public through acts not attributable to recipient.

(c) Such information which, after access is gained to the disclosure, is at any time obtained by the recipient from any other person, firm or company having no obligation to or relationship with the source of said information.

6. NO CONVEYANCE OR LICENSE. Nothing in this agreement shall be construed to convey to the recipient of Confidential Information any right, title or interest in any Confidential Information, or any license to use, sell, exploit, copy or further develop any such Confidential Information. This agreement does not in any way bind the parties to enter into a business relationship with the other of any type.

7. GOVERNING LAW. This agreement shall be construed for all purposes in accordance with the law of the state of New York.

8. SEVERABILITY. If any provision of this agreement is declared void or unenforceable, such provision shall be severed from this agreement which shall otherwise remain in full force and effect.

9. REMEDIES. The parties agree that if there is a breach of this agreement by either party, the other shall have remedy in law and/or equity including, but not limited to, appropriate injunctive relief of specific performance as may be granted to a court of competent jurisdiction.

10. ATTORNEY'S FEES. In the event any suit or other action is commenced to construe or enforce any provision of this agreement, the prevailing party, in addition to all other amounts such party shall be entitled to receive from the other party, shall be entitled to recover its reasonable attorney's fees and court costs.

11. ENTIRE AGREEMENT. This agreement constitutes the entire agreement between the parties with respect to the subject matter addressed herein. This agreement may not be amended or modified except by a writing signed by both parties.

12. COURT ORDERED DISCLOSURE. Neither Corporation nor XYZ shall be liable for disclosure of Confidential Information if made in response to a valid order of a court or authorized agency of government; provided that ten days notice must first be given to the other party so a protective order, if appropriate, may be sought by such party.

13. ASSIGNEES AND SUCCESSORS. This agreement shall be binding upon the parties hereto and their respective assigns and successors.

IN WITNESS WHEREOF, this agreement has been duly executed by the parties hereto as of the latest date set forth below.

CHILDREN'S TOY COMPANY   XYZ PROPERTIES, INC.

By: _____   By: _____

    Terry Adams   Jim Lookgood
Title: Vice-President   Title: Vice-President
Date: January ,___1995   Date: January,____1995

APPENDIX 9
SAMPLE CONFIDENTIALITY WAIVER AGREEMENT

CONFIDENTIALITY WAIVER AGREEMENT

THIS AGREEMENT, made as of December 1, 1995 by and between CHILDREN'S TOY COMPANY, a New York corporation with offices at 200 Fifth Avenue, New York, NY 00000 ("CTC"), and JOE JONES, whose address is 1 North Street, Anywhere, NY 10111 ("Submitter").

WHEREAS, Submitter has developed a product, concept, design or other artwork, of which the name, description and any pictures or illustrations pertaining to the product, design or artwork are attached hereto as Exhibit A (hereinafter known as "The Item"); and

WHEREAS, Submitter is willing to make a voluntary disclosure of the Item to CTC for the purpose of permitting CTC to evaluate said Item;

NOW, THEREFORE, in consideration of the mutual promises and covenants set forth below, it is hereby agreed as follows:

1. Submitter agrees to disclose the Item and all information pertaining to it to CTC for the purpose of enabling CTC to evaluate said Item. Submitter understands that for the purposes of its review, CTC may disclose the Item to its employees or other third parties if, in the sole opinion of CTC, such disclosures are necessary and required for the proper evaluation of the Item.

2. Submitter hereby agrees to outline all features of the Item which Submitter believes to be unique. Submitter further understands that CTC's review of the Item and/or offer to negotiate with Submitter is not an admission of novelty, priority or originality and does not prejudice CTC's rights to contest any existing or future patents or copyrights on the Item.

3. Submitter warrants and represents that:

(a) Submitter is the sole and exclusive originator and owner of the Item and that Submitter has the sole and exclusive rights to the Item;

(b) to the best of Submitter's knowledge and belief, the Item has not been in public use and is not in the public domain;

(c) Submitter has the full right to make the Item and to offer to license it to CTC;

(d) this agreement does not violate any other agreement which the Submitter has entered into concerning the Item; and

(e) Submitter has no knowledge or reason to believe that the Item infringes upon the proprietary rights of any other party.

Submitter understands that the acceptance of the Item by CTC for the purposes of review or for any other purpose is based upon the representations made herein.

4. In return for receiving, reviewing and evaluating the Item, Submitter agrees to release and indemnify CTC from any liability in connection with CTC's receipt, reviewing and evaluating of the Item or in connection with CTC's use or disclosure to others of any portion of the Item, except as to such liability that may accrue under any valid patents or copyrights that Submitter now or hereafter owns or controls.

5. Submitter understands and acknowledges that the submission of the Item to and the acceptance of the Item by CTC does not give rise to any type of agreement between the parties concerning the Item, except as specifically set forth herein. No obligation of any kind is assumed by CTC unless and until a formal written agreement has been entered into, and then the obligation shall be only such as is expressed in the formal written agreement executed by an officer of CTC. CTC alone shall determine whether compensation shall be paid to Submitter, and if paid, the amount of such compensation.

6. Submitter understands and acknowledges that no confidential relationship between Submitter and CTC is established or is to be implied by CTC's entering into this agreement and/or CTC's consideration of the Item, and the Item is not to be considered submitted "in confidence."

7. Upon the written request of Submitter, CTC shall deliver to Submitter the documents and material in its possession concerning the Item, including but not limited to, all documents and materials furnished to CTC by Submitter. Submitter understands and acknowledges that a copy of all said items will be retained by CTC for its records. Submitter further understands and acknowledges that CTC has no obligation to compensate Submitter for any damage to the Item which may occur in shipment.

8. Submitter understands and acknowledges that no employee or representative of CTC is authorized to solicit any disclosure or to do any act or make any representations from which any relationship may be implied other than that expressed in this document.

9. This Agreement constitutes the entire understanding of the parties and revokes and supersedes all prior agreements between the parties and is intended as a final expression of their Agreement. It shall not be modified or amended except in writing signed by both parties hereto and specifically referring to this Agreement. This Agreement shall take precedence over any other documents which may be in conflict with said Agreement and shall be governed by the laws of Illinois.

IN WITNESS WHEREOF, the parties hereto, intending to be legally bound hereby, have each caused to be affixed hereto its or his/her hand and seal the day indicated.

CHILDREN'S TOY COMPANY   SUBMITTER

_____   _____
         Name and Date   Name and Date

EXHIBIT A

(Attach description of the Item)

APPENDIX 10
SAMPLE PRODUCT DISCLOSURE FORM

PRODUCT DISCLOSURE FORM

		PAGE
		OF
SUBMITTOR NAME		DATE

I AM INTERESTED IN PRESENTING FOR YOUR CONSIDERATION MY PROPOSAL FOR NEW PRODUCT. THIS PRODUCT IS DESCRIBED AS FOLLOWS: (IDENTIFY EACH PRODUCT BY NAME)

P.D.F. NO.	PRODUCT NAME	HOLD	P.D.F. NO.	PRODUCT NAME	HOLD

DESCRIPTION (USE FOR FIRST PRODUCT NAME ONLY, OTHER PRODUCT NAMES TO BE DESCRIBED ON CONTINUATION SHEET)

THE FOLLOWING PROTECTIVE STEPS HAVE BEEN TAKEN

☐ WITNESSED BY OTHER PERSONS   ☐ PATENT APPLIED FOR   ☐ COPYRIGHTED

☐ PHOTOGRAPHED, DATED, AND WITNESSED   ☐ PATENTED   ☐ OTHER

ITEMIZE THE FOLLOWING

NUMBER OF DRAWINGS	NUMBER OF PHOTOGRAPHS	NUMBER OF VIDEOTAPES

(DO NOT SEND MODELS UNLESS REQUESTED)

NUMBER OF MODELS

I understand your caution in permitting me to disclose to you my ideas, suggestions, inventions, designs, sketches, models, of other materials including any additional or supplemental disclosures (all hereinafter referred to as "ideas") because your company has developed or had suggested to you many ideas for future products and there is the possibility that some of such ideas are similar to those which I might disclose to you. I understand that this submission to you is not made in confidence and that no obligation is assumed by _____ unless and until a formal written contract is agreed to and entered into, and then the obligation shall be only that which is expressed in the formal, written contract. I understand that _____ willingness to review these ideas is not admission by _____ of novelty, priority, or originality and does not impair _____ right to contest existing or future patents claiming the ideas. I hereby represent that I have the right to disclose these ideas and to make the present agreement. It is also understood by me that you cannot and will not be bound in any manner by ideas of a general nature which are not in such form when disclosed that they can be protected under the Patent and Copyright Statutes of the United States of America. I therefore agree that you assume no liability in reviewing these ideas and agree to rely solely upon such protection for these ideas as may be afforded under the Patent and Copyright Statutes of the United States of America. The foregoing terms and conditions shall apply to any further information of the idea that I elect to submit.

PLEASE PRINT

NAME

COMPANY

ADDRESS (STREET, CITY, STATE AND ZIP CODE)

TELEPHONE NUMBER (AREA CODE)

( )

SIGNATURE	DATE

INTERVIEWER'S COMMENTS

INTERVIEWED BY

☐ ACCEPTED (INITIALS)	☐ REJECTED (INITIALS)	☐ MODEL REQUESTED (INITIALS)	☐ ADD. WORK SUBMITTOR (INITIALS)	☐ REVIEW TAPE/RESPON (INITIALS)

DISTRIBUTION: WHITE-File; CANARY-Submittor

185

APPENDIX 11
SAMPLE OPTION AGREEMENT

OPTION AGREEMENT

Date: January 1, 1995

For the below stated, non-refundable, option payment and subject to the following terms, XYZ Properties, Inc. ("XYZ") hereby grants Children's Toy Company ("Toy Company") an option to further evaluate the following product concepts:

Product Concept Name	Option Payment
BIG AL DOLL	$1,500
TOMMY JR. DOLL	$1,500
DANNY BOY DOLL	$1,500
TOTAL OPTION PAYMENT	$4,500

1. The option will expire sixty (60) days from the above date.

2. During the option period, XYZ will not show the noted product concepts to any other party.

3. The Toy company may exercise its option by:

a. notifying XYZ in writing of such intention prior to expiration of the option period; and

b. simultaneously paying XYZ a non-refundable fee in the amount of ONE THOUSAND DOLLARS ($1,000.00) per product concept.

4. Thereupon, XYZ and the Toy Company shall enter into a formal license agreement within 30 days. The advance on royalties in the license agreement shall be TWO HUNDRED PERCENT (200%) of the option payment and the royalty rate shall be FIVE PERCENT (5%). All monies paid by the Toy Company in connection with the option shall be credited, on a concept by concept basis, against such advances and such advances shall be credited, on a concept-by-concept basis, against royalties.

5. In the event that the Toy Company does not exercise its option or enter into a license agreement with XYZ for a product concept, all rights in that product concept shall revert to XYZ who shall be free to commercialize the product concept. Further, in such event, the Toy Company shall:

a. turn over to XYZ all materials relating to the product concept including materials generated by the Toy Company; and

b. not use or disclose to any third party information relating to the product concept.

XYZ PROPERTIES, INC. CHILDREN'S TOY COMPANY

By: _____ By: _____
  Jim Lookgood   Terry Adams
  Title: Vice-President   Title: Vice-President
  Date: January ___, 1995 Date: January ___,1995

APPENDIX 12
SAMPLE TOY AGENT AGREEMENT

AGENT AGREEMENT

This agreement is made this 1st day of January 1996 by and between JOHN JONES, an individual who resides at 74 Meadowlands Drive, East Rutherford, NH 11111 (the "Owner") and LICENSING COMPANY, LTD., a New York corporation with offices at 200 Fifth Avenue, New York, New York 10010 (the "Agent").

WITNESSETH:

WHEREAS, it is understood and agreed that the Owner is the sole and exclusive owner of all rights in and to the properties described and/or illustrated in Schedule A attached to this Agreement ("the Properties") including, but not limited to, the Trademark(s) listed in Schedule B attached hereto ("the Trademarks"); and

WHEREAS, the Owner has no binding contractual obligation with any other agent or person having the duty or authority to negotiate on behalf of the Owner for the license of the Properties and/or the Trademarks; and

WHEREAS, the Agent is willing to develop a public relations, advertising, and marketing program relative to said Properties and/or said Trademarks and to commercialize said Properties and/or Trademarks through third party licensees who will use the Properties and/or Trademarks on or in association with various and sundry products.

THEREFORE, in consideration of the promises and agreements set forth herein, the parties, each intending to be legally bound hereby, do promise and agree as follows:

1. Agent Grant

(a) For the Term of this Agreement and during any extensions or renewals thereof, the Owner hereby grants to the Agent the exclusive right to represent the Owner in the United States and Canada (the "Territory") in the implementation of a plan using third party licensees (the "Licensees") to commercialize, license and/or sell various products in the Territory which bear or otherwise incorporate the Properties and/or the Trademarks (the "Licensed Products").

(b) During the Term of this Agreement and during any extensions or renewals thereof, the Owner agrees not to retain the services of any other person, persons or firm to represent it in the Territory in the implementation of such a plan to commercialize, license and/or sell Licensed Products through third party Licensees. It is understood and agreed, however, that the Owner may retain the services of other firms to represent it in the implementation of such a plan in countries outside the Territory.

2. Term

(a) This Agreement shall commence upon its execution by both parties and shall extend for an initial "Term" of eighteen (18) months, unless terminated sooner pursuant to one or more provisions of this Agreement.

(b) If the Agent fully performs according to all terms and conditions hereof during the initial Term and, during that initial Term, produces gross compensation for the Owner (after deduction of the Agent's fees and expenses) of at least Two Million United States Dollars ($2,000,000), the Term of this Agreement shall automatically be extended by a term of two (2) years commencing immediately upon expiration of the preceding Term. The Agreement may, thereafter, be extended by further terms of two (2) years, provided that the Agent continues to fully perform in accordance with all terms and conditions of this Agreement and further, produces gross compensation for the owner (after deduction of the Agent's fees and expenses) during the preceding Term of at least Three Million United States Dollars ($3,000,000). In the event that the Agent does not fully perform in accordance with all terms and conditions of this Agreement and/or does not achieve the enumerated minimum gross compensation, this Agreement shall terminate on the normal termination date.

(c) In the event of termination of this Agreement by the Owner, the Owner's obligations to the Agent relative to agreements with Licensees negotiated and/or concluded by Agent during the Term(s) of this Agreement shall survive termination of this Agreement subject to the following provisions:

(1) Upon termination of the Agreement with the Agent, the Agent shall promptly turn over to the Owner all books and records relative to each Licensee and shall immediately close out all accounts Agent had opened on behalf of the Owner;

(2) All future royalty payments made by Licensees shall be made directly to the Owner or to its duly appointed representative; and

(3) The Agent's commission for agreements entered into during the Term of this Agreement shall be proportionally reduced after termination in accordance with Paragraph 4, infra.

3. Agent's Duties and Obligations

(a) Subject to the conditions herein specified, the Agent shall use its best efforts during the Term of this Agreement to find and conclude business arrangements with Licensees which are advantageous to the Owner. With respect to any such business arrangements, it is understood and agreed that the Owner shall have the right of final refusal as to the particular Licensee and/ or the terms and conditions of the arrangement negotiated by the Agent.

(b) It is understood and agreed that the owner has properties and trademarks other than the Properties and/or the Trademarks which form part of this Agreement and such properties and/or trademarks do not form any part of this Agreement.

(c) It is understood and agreed that the Agent may render other similar services on behalf of other clients and nothing contained in this Agreement shall preclude the Agent from rendering such services.

(d) In furtherance of the Agent's duties as herein specified, the Agent agrees to and will:

(1) Seek out the best potential Licensees for the Properties and/or the Trademarks in terms of financing, manufacturing, and marketing a quality item in the product areas for which a license will be granted to them. This includes an in-depth review of each Licensee's position in the industry involved and a personal inspection of each Licensee's factory and showroom.

(2) Negotiate on behalf of the Owner the business terms and conditions of a license agreement which is supplied by the Owner.

(3) Monitor and oversee the licensing program with the third party Licensees to insure that the Licensee's royalties, minimums, and sales reports are promptly submitted.

(4) At least twice per year review each of the Licensee's Licensed Products and complete sets of their promotional, advertising and packaging material relative to the Licensed Products to insure that the quality control provisions of the license agreements with the Licensees are being complied with and to insure that the Licensee's promotional, advertising and sales programs are being carried out.

(5) If necessary and with the express written authorization of the Owner, conduct a personal visit to the Licensee's manufacturing facilities to insure that the quality control provisions of the license agreements with the Licensee are being complied with.

(6) Submit to the Owner a written report after each of said reviews and visits.

(7) Conduct a comprehensive review of the product categories and markets to determine the appropriate mix of Licensed Products and a targeted approach for market entry.

(8) Plan and execute a complete advertising and promotional support program including public relations, media creative development, and special merchandising opportunities.

(9) Collect all minimums and royalties due under the agreements negotiated with third party Licensees between the Owner and the Licensees during the Term of this agreement or its renewals. All payments from third party Licensees are to be transmitted to the Agent by check, money order or transfer payable to the Owner and are to be deposited by the Agent in a separate account in the name of the Owner to which the Agent, during the Term of this Agreement, shall have access. Within thirty (30) days after receipt of any payment under any license agreement

with a third party Licensee, the Agent shall deduct its percentage compensation and remit the balance of the payment to the Owner.

(10) The Agent shall not use in any manner, directly or indirectly, or in whole or in part, the Properties and/or the Trademarks, except in the manner and to the extent consistent and necessary to complete the goals of this Agreement. For other uses, Agent shall obtain the Owner's specific consent in writing. Upon termination of this Agreement, Agent shall discontinue all use of the Properties and/or the Trademarks and shall return to the Owner all facsimiles of any products manufactured or distributed under such Properties and/or Trademarks.

(11) The Agent, within thirty days after execution of this Agreement, shall submit to the Owner a written budget covering all of the above duties for Owner's approval. All budgeted and approved expenses, including out-of-pocket expenses incurred by the Agent with the Owner's prior express written authorization, shall be reimbursed to the Agent by the Owner as expended. In the event that within thirty (30) days after submission of such proposed budget, an agreement cannot be reached as to the amount of the budget, the Owner shall have the right to terminate this Agreement upon thirty (30) days' written notice to the Agent.

4. Agent's Compensation

(a) In consideration for the services rendered by the Agent, the Owner, during the Term of this Agreement, agrees to and shall pay the Agent a commission based on a percentage of gross revenues received by the Owner from all Licensees in the Territory, whether generated as a result of the efforts of the Agent or otherwise, in accordance with the following schedule:

Percentage	Gross Revenues
40%	0-$2,000,000
35%	> $2,000,000

(b) "Gross Revenues" shall include all income received by the Owner (prior to deduction of the Agent's commission) from all Licensees within the Territory, pursuant to any contract or agreement for the sale, lease, license or other disposition of the

Properties and/or the Trademarks, regardless of whether such Licensees were obtained by the Agent, the Owner or a third party.

(c) After termination of this Agreement, the Agent shall be entitled to an ongoing commission based on contracts or agreements with Licensees in the Territory which were entered into during the Term of this Agreement for which the Agent would have received a commission had the Agreement not been terminated. In such event, however, the Agent's commission relative to such Licensees shall be proportionally reduced after termination in accordance with the following post-termination schedule:

Calendar Year Following Termination	Percentage of Gross Compensation
1	40%
2	25%
3	10%
4	0

5. Warranties and Indemnifications

(a) The Owner warrants and represents that it is the owner of all rights in and to the Properties and/or the Trademarks and that it has the right and power to license and/or sell such Properties and/or Trademarks and it further represents that it has not granted anyone else the right or authority to act for it during the Term hereof in the capacity in which it has employed the Agent.

(b) The Owner hereby agrees to defend, indemnify and hold the Agent, its shareholders, directors, officers, employees, agents, parent companies, subsidiaries, and affiliates, harmless from and against any and all claims, liabilities, judgments, costs and expenses (including, without limitation, reasonable attorneys' fees) incurred in connection therewith, which any of them may incur or to which any of them may be subjected, arising out of or relating to the Owner's warranty.

(c) The Agent hereby agrees to defend, indemnify and hold

the Owner, its shareholders, directors, officers, employees, agents, parent companies, subsidiaries and affiliates and any of its related entities harmless from and against any and all claims, liabilities, judgments, costs and expenses (including without limitation, reasonable attorneys' fees) incurred in connection therewith, which any of them may incur or to which any of them may be subjected, arising out of any breach of this Agreement by Agent, or any action or omission by the Agent other than as it may relate to the Owner's warranty stated above.

6. Statements and Payments

(a) The Agent shall provide the Owner with monthly statements of the Owner's account, including any expenses incurred in the promotion and development of the Properties and/or the Trademarks, and shall notify the Owner promptly and specifically relative to any pending negotiations.

(b) The Agent agrees to keep accurate books of account and records at its principal place of business covering all transactions relating to the licenses being granted herein. The Owner and its duly authorized representatives shall have the right, at all reasonable hours of the day, to examine the Agent's books of account and records and all other documents and material in the possession or under the control of the Agent with respect to the subject matter and the terms of this Agreement and to make copies and extracts thereof.

(c) The receipt or acceptance by the Owner of any of the statements furnished or payments made hereunder to the Owner (or the cashing of any royalty checks paid hereunder) shall not preclude the Owner from questioning the correctness thereof at any time, and, in the event that any inconsistencies or mistakes are discovered in such statements or payments, they shall immediately be rectified and the appropriate payment shall be made by the Agent.

(d) Upon demand by the Owner, but not more than once each year, the Agent, shall at its own expense, furnish the Owner with a detailed statement by an independent certified public accountant of the Agent's choice and acceptable to the Owner showing the pricing information of all Licensed Products including the number and description of the Licensed products distributed and/or sold by the Agent up to the date of the statement.

(e) All books of account and records of the Agent relating to this Agreement or any third party Licensees shall be retained for inspection by the Owner for at least three (3) years after the expiration or termination of this Agreement.

7. Assignment

(a) Nothing contained in this Agreement shall be construed as an assignment or grant to the Agent of any right, title or interest in and to the Properties and/or the Trademarks, it being understood that all rights relating thereto are expressly reserved by the Owner except for the rights being licensed hereunder.

(b) This Agreement is personal to the Agent and its rights and/or obligations hereunder shall not be assigned by any act of the Agent or by operation of law. The Agent shall have no right to grant any licenses or sublicenses without the Owner's prior express written approval. Any attempt on the part of Agent to license or assign to third parties its rights or obligations under this Agreement shall constitute a material breach of this Agreement.

(c) The Owner shall have the right to assign its rights and obligations under this Agreement without the prior approval of the Agent.

8. Default

If the Agent shall violate any of its obligations under this Agreement including its payment obligations, the Owner shall have the right to terminate this Agreement by giving written notice of termination to the Agent and termination shall be effective thirty (30) days after notice is mailed to the Agent unless the Agent, in the interim, shall remedy the violation and reasonably satisfy the Owner that such violation has been remedied. Delinquent payment two or more times in a year shall be cause for termination without a cure period.

9. Insolvency

If the Agent files a petition in bankruptcy or is adjudicated a bankrupt or insolvent, or makes an assignment for the benefit of creditors, or an arrangement pursuant to any bankruptcy law, or if the Agent discontinues its business or if a receiver is appointed for the Agent or the Agent's business, who is not discharged within thirty (30) days, the License granted hereunder shall automatically be terminated forthwith without any notice whatsoever being necessary.

10. Effect of Termination

(a) After the expiration or termination of this Agreement, all rights granted to the Agent shall forthwith revert to the Owner who shall be free to contract with others to commercialize the Properties and/or Trademarks. The Agent shall refrain from further efforts to commercialize the Properties and/or the Trademarks or any further reference to them, direct or indirect.

(b) The Agent acknowledges that its failure to perform under the terms of this Agreement will result in immediate and irreparable damage to the Owner. The Agent acknowledges and admits that there is no adequate remedy at law for Agent's failure to perform and the Agent agrees that in the event of such failure, the Owner shall be entitled to equitable relief by way of injunctive relief and such other relief as any court with jurisdiction may deem just and proper.

11. Final Statement Upon Termination or Expiration

Within thirty (30) days after termination or expiration of this Agreement, the Agent shall deliver to the Owner a statement indicating the number and description of all license agreements with Licensees which it has entered into on behalf of the Owner and a copy of each and every such license agreement.

12. Notices

All notices or other communications required or desired to be sent to either party shall be in writing and sent by Registered or Certified Mail, postage prepaid, return receipt requested, or by telefax, telex or telegram, charges prepaid to the addresses indicated above. Either party may change such address by notice in writing to the other party.

13. Relationship of the Parties

This Agreement does not create a partnership or joint venture between the parties and the Agent shall have no power or obligation to bind the Owner in any manner whatsoever.

14. Applicable Law

This Agreement shall be governed by the law of the State of New York and any claims arising hereunder shall, at the Owner's election, be prosecuted in the appropriate state court of the State of New York or in the U. S. District Court having jurisdiction for causes of action arising in the District in which the Owner is located.

15. Captions

The captions used in connection with the paragraphs and subparagraphs of this Agreement are inserted only for purpose of reference. Such captions shall not be deemed to govern, limit, modify or in any other manner affect the scope, meaning or intent of the provisions of this Agreement or any part thereof nor shall such captions otherwise be given any legal effect.

16. Waiver

No waiver by either party of a breach or a default hereunder shall be deemed to be a waiver by such party of a subsequent breach or default of a like or similar nature.

17. Survival of Rights

Notwithstanding anything to the contrary contained herein, such obligations which remain executory after expiration of the Term of this Agreement shall remain in full force and effect until discharged by performance and such rights as pertain thereto shall remain in force until their expiration.

18. Integration

This Agreement represents the entire understanding between the parties hereto with respect to the subject matter hereof and this Agreement supersedes all previous representations, understandings or agreements, oral or written, between the parties with respect to the subject matter hereof and cannot be modified except by a written instrument signed by the parties hereto.

By their execution below, the parties hereto have agreed to all of the terms and conditions of this Agreement.

LICENSING COMPANY, LTD.

_____ By:_____
      John Jones   Simon Workhard

                                  Title: President
      Date: Date:

Schedule A

Description of the Property

Corporate Trademarks of PROPERTY OWNER, INC. as identified in Schedule B.

Schedule B

TRADEMARKS	U.S. TRADEMARK REG. No.
Property	444,444
Property and Design	555,555
Worker & Design	666,666

APPENDIX 13
SAMPLE LETTER OF INTENT

December 1, 1995

Mike Marshall
Dodgertown Novelties, Inc.
1 Baseball Blvd.
Los Angeles, California 99999

Dear Mike:

Re: Letter of Intent

In accordance with our discussion, XYZ Properties, Inc. ("Licensor") would be willing to grant Dodgertown Novelties, Inc. ("Licensee") an exclusive license to use the proprietary property of XYZ Properties, Inc. described and/or illustrated in the attached Schedule A (the "Property") and the trademark(s) listed in the attached Schedule B (the "Trademarks") for the products listed in the attached Schedule C (the "Licensed Products") subject to the following terms and conditions:

1. The license will extend for an initial "First Term" of eighteen (18) months from the date of execution by both parties of the license and will include "Options" for two one-year "Extended Terms" provided that the Licensee's sales during the existing period will have resulted in "Actual Royalties" of at least One Million United States Dollars ($1,000,000).

2. The license will cover the countries listed in the attached Schedule D (the "Licensed Territory").

3. In exchange for such license, the Licensee will pay Licensor an Actual Royalty of Seven Percent (7%) based on Net Sales of Licensed Products. The Licensee will pay Licensor a Guaranteed Minimum Royalty per Term of Fifty Thousand United States Dollars ($50,000) in the event Actual Royalties for any Term are below such amount. A portion of the Guaranteed Minimum Royalty for the First Term in the amount of Ten Thousand United States Dollars ($10,000) will be paid upon execution of the Agree-

ment as an Advance against the Actual or Guaranteed Minimum Royalties.

4. If the Licensee requires artwork to be prepared by the Licensor, an Artwork Fee will be charged by the Licensor.

5. Licensee agrees to maintain product liability and advertising insurance in the amount of Two Million Dollars ($2,000,000) with no deductible naming Licensor as an additional insured.

6. The Property and the Trademarks are owned by and shall remain the exclusive property of the Licensor.

7. The parties agree to enter into a definitive license agreement within thirty (30) days after execution of this letter of intent by both parties. In the event that such a definitive license agreement is not entered into by such date, the terms recited in this letter of intent will automatically expire.

If the above terms and conditions are acceptable to you, kindly indicate your approval thereof at the appropriate place below and we will promptly transmit to you a formal license agreement.

We look forward to a long and mutually profitable relationship between our companies.

Very truly yours

XYZ Properties, Inc.
By: _____
Jim Lookgood
Vice-President

Approved:
Dodgertown Novelties, Inc.
By: _____
Mike Marshall
Title: President
Date: December 1995

Schedule A

Property:

The name and character representations of the Diamond Kids as illustrated below.

Schedule B

Trademarks:

DIAMOND KIDS
SWIFTY
PINE-TAR
HARD HAT
BULLPEN

Schedule C

Licensed Products:

Children's T-shirts to size 20
Children's sweat shirts to size 20
Cloth baseball caps
Poplin jackets

Schedule D

Licensed Territory:

United States
Canada
Mexico
Puerto Rico
Japan

APPENDIX 14:
SAMPLE TOY LICENSE AGREEMENT

TOY LICENSE AGREEMENT

THIS AGREEMENT is entered into this 1st day of December, 1995 by and between TOY INVENTION ENTERPRISES, a New York corporation with offices at 10 East Tenth Street, New York, NY 00000 ("LICENSOR") and CHILDREN'S TOY COMPANY, a New York corporation with offices at 200 Fifth Avenue, New York, NY 00000 ("LICENSEE").

WITNESSETH:

WHEREAS, LICENSOR is the sole and exclusive owner of the Property or Properties identified more fully in Schedule A attached hereto (the "Property"); and

WHEREAS, LICENSOR has the power and authority to grant to LICENSEE the right, privilege and license to use, manufacture and sell those types of licensed products which incorporate or are otherwise based on the Property as identified in Schedule A attached hereto (the "Licensed Products"); and

WHEREAS, LICENSEE has represented that it has the ability to manufacture, market and distribute the Licensed Products in the countries identified in Schedule A attached hereto (the "Licensed Territory");

WHEREAS, LICENSEE desires to obtain from LICENSOR an exclusive license to use, manufacture, have manufactured and sell Licensed Products in the Licensed Territory; and

WHEREAS, both LICENSEE and LICENSOR have agreed to the terms and conditions upon which LICENSEE shall use, manufacture, have manufactured and sell Licensed Products.

NOW, THEREFORE, in consideration of the promises and agreements set forth herein, the parties, each intending to be legally bound hereby, do promise and agree as follows:

1. LICENSE

(a) LICENSOR hereby grants to LICENSEE for the Term of this Agreement the exclusive right and license to use, manufacture, have manufactured and sell the Licensed Products in the Licensed Territory. The license includes a license under all patents and copyrights and any applications therefore with respect to the Property. It is understood, however, that this license grant and LICENSEE's obligation to pay royalties hereunder are not predicated or conditioned on LICENSOR seeking, obtaining or maintaining any patent or copyright protection for the Property. LICENSOR hereby retains all merchandising or ancillary product licensing rights.

(b) LICENSEE shall also have the right to grant sublicenses to third parties to manufacture or sell the Licensed Products in countries in the Licensed Territory other than the United States subject to LICENSOR's prior express written approval of each such sublicense.

(c) LICENSEE shall not make, use or sell the Licensed Products or any products which are confusingly or substantially similar thereto in any country outside the Licensed Territory and will not knowingly sell the Licensed Products to persons who intend to or are likely to resell them in a country outside the Licensed Territory.

2. TERM

This Agreement shall be effective as of the date of execution by both parties and shall extend for so long as LICENSEE or its sublicensees or distributors continue to manufacture or sell the Licensed Products (the "Term").

3. COMPENSATION

(a) In consideration for the license granted hereunder, LICENSEE agrees to pay to LICENSOR the royalty recited in Schedule A (the "Royalty") based on LICENSEE's Net Sales of Licensed Products.

(b) Should LICENSEE grant any approved sublicenses in countries outside the United States, LICENSEE shall pay LICENSOR Fifty Percent (50%) of the gross income received by LICENSEE from such sublicensees.

(c) The Royalty owed LICENSOR shall be calculated on a quarterly calendar basis (the "Royalty Period") and shall be payable no later than thirty (30) days after the end of the preceding calendar quarter, except that the first and last calendar quarters may be "short" depending on the effective date of this Agreement.

(d) For each Royalty Period, LICENSEE shall provide LICENSOR with a written royalty statement in a form acceptable to LICENSOR. Such royalty statement shall be certified as accurate by a duly authorized officer of LICENSEE reciting, on a country by country basis, the stock number, item, units sold, description, quantity shipped, gross invoice, amount billed customers less discounts, allowances, returns and reportable sales for each Licensed Product. Such statements shall be furnished to LICENSOR regardless of whether any Licensed Products were sold during the Royalty Period or whether any actual Royalty was owed.

(e) LICENSEE agrees to pay to LICENSOR an Advance against Royalties in the amount recited in Schedule A which may be credited against LICENSEE's actual royalty obligation to LICENSOR.

(f) During each calendar year of the Term of this Agreement, LICENSEE agrees to pay LICENSOR a Guaranteed Minimum Royalty as recited in Schedule A, which may be credited against LICENSEE's actual royalty obligation to LICENSOR. The Guaranteed Minimum Royalty shall be calculated at the end of each calendar year. In the event that LICENSEE's actual Royalties paid LICENSOR for any calendar year are less than the Guaranteed Minimum Royalty for such year, LICENSEE shall, in addition to paying LICENSOR its actual earned Royalty for such Royalty Period, pay LICENSOR the difference between the total earned Royalty for the year and the Guaranteed Minimum Royalty for such year.

(g) "Net Sales" shall mean LICENSEE's gross sales (the gross invoice amount billed customers) of Licensed Products, less discounts and allowances actually shown on the invoice (except cash discounts which are not deductible in the calculation of Royalty) and, further, less any bona fide returns (net of all returns actually made or allowed as supported by credit memoranda actually issued to the customers) up to the amount of the actual sales of the Licensed Products during the Royalty Period. No other costs incurred in the manufacturing, selling, advertising, and distribution of the Licensed Products shall be deducted nor shall any deduction be allowed for any uncollectible accounts or allowances.

(h) A Royalty obligation shall accrue upon the sale of the Licensed Products regardless of the time of collection by LICENSEE. A Licensed Product shall be considered "sold" when such Licensed Product is billed, invoiced, shipped, or paid for, whichever occurs first.

(i) If LICENSEE sells any Licensed Products to any affiliated or related party at a price less than the regular price charged to other parties, the Royalty shall be computed at the regular price.

(j) The receipt or acceptance by LICENSOR of any royalty statement or payment shall not prevent LICENSOR from subsequently challenging the validity or accuracy of such statement or payment.

(k) Upon expiration or termination of this Agreement, all Royalty obligations, including the Guaranteed Minimum Royalty, shall be accelerated and shall immediately become due and payable.

(l) LICENSEE's obligations for the payment of Royalties shall survive expiration or termination of this Agreement.

(m) All payments due LICENSOR shall be made in United States currency by check drawn on a United States bank, unless otherwise specified by LICENSOR.

(n) Late payments shall incur interest at the rate of ONE PERCENT (1%) per month from the date such payments were originally due.

4. RECORD INSPECTION AND AUDIT

(a) LICENSOR shall have the right, upon reasonable notice, to inspect LICENSEE's books and records and all other documents and material in LICENSEE's possession or control with respect to the subject matter of this Agreement. LICENSOR shall have free and full access thereto for such purposes and may make copies thereof.

(b) In the event that such inspection reveals an underpayment by LICENSEE of the actual Royalty owed LICENSOR, LICENSEE shall pay the difference, plus interest calculated at the rate of ONE PERCENT (1%) per month. If such underpayment is in excess of ONE THOUSAND UNITED STATES DOLLARS ($1,000.00) for any Royalty Period, LICENSEE shall also reimburse LICENSOR for the cost of such inspection.

(c) All books and records relative to LICENSEE's obligations hereunder shall be maintained and made accessible to LICENSOR for inspection at a location in the United States for at least two (2) years after termination of this Agreement.

5. WARRANTIES & OBLIGATIONS

(a) LICENSOR represents and warrants that it has the right and power to grant the license granted herein and that there are no other agreements with any other party in conflict with such grant.

(b) LICENSOR further represents and warrants that it has no actual knowledge that the Property as submitted to LICENSEE infringes any valid rights of any third party.

(c) LICENSEE represents and warrants that it will use its best efforts to promote, market, advertise, sell and distribute the Licensed Products in the Licensed Territory and agrees to the Advertising Commitment recited in Schedule A.

(d) LICENSEE shall be solely responsible for the manufacture, production, sale and distribution of the Licensed Products and will bear all costs associated therewith.

(e) LICENSEE shall introduce the Licensed Products in all countries in the Licensed Territory before the Product Introduction Date recited in Schedule A and commence shipment of Licensed Products in all countries in the Licensed Territory before the Initial Shipment Date recited therein. This is a material provision of this Agreement.

(f) LICENSEE shall not be entitled to materially modify or change the Property without the prior written consent of LICENSOR, which consent shall not be unreasonably withheld. If such modification or change is later incorporated in an improved or modified product by LICENSEE, such improved product shall be subject to the payment of a Royalty in accordance with the terms hereof. Further, if LICENSEE incorporates any dominant feature of the Property in other products, such other products shall be subject to the payment of a Royalty in accordance with the terms hereof.

6. NOTICES & SAMPLES

(a) LICENSEE shall fully comply with the marking provisions of the intellectual property laws of the applicable countries in the Licensed Territory.

(b) The Licensed Products and all promotional, packaging and advertising material shall include all appropriate legal notices as required by LICENSOR.

(c) The Licensed Products shall be of a high quality which are at least equal to comparable products manufactured and marketed by LICENSEE and in conformity with a standard sample approved by LICENSOR.

(d) If the quality of a class of the Licensed Products falls below the quality previously approved by LICENSOR, LICENSEE shall use its best efforts to restore such quality. In the event that LICENSEE has not taken reasonable steps to restore such quality within thirty (30) days after notification by LICEN-SOR, LICENSOR shall have the right to terminate this Agreement.

(e) At least once during each calendar year, LICENSEE shall submit to LICENSOR three (3) samples of the Licensed Products for review.

7. NOTICES

Any notice required to be given pursuant to this Agreement shall be in writing and mailed by certified or registered mail, return receipt requested or delivered by a national overnight express service.

8. PATENTS, TRADEMARKS AND COPYRIGHTS

(a) LICENSOR may, but is not obligated to seek, in its own name and at its own expense, appropriate patent, trademark or copyright protection for the Property. LICENSOR makes no representation or warranty with respect to the validity of any patent, trademark or copyright which may be granted with respect to the Property.

(b) In the event that LICENSOR has not sought patent protection for a particular feature of the Property or in a particular country, LICENSEE may request that LICENSOR apply for such protection and LICENSOR shall take reasonable steps to obtain such protection. In such event, LICENSEE shall advance LICENSOR the costs of obtaining and maintaining such protection.

(c) It is understood and agreed that LICENSOR shall retain all right, title and interest in the original Property and to any modifications or improvements made to the Property by LICENSEE.

(d) The parties agree to execute any documents reasonably requested by the other party to effect any of the above provisions.

(e) LICENSEE acknowledges LICENSOR's exclusive rights

in the Property and that the Property is unique and original to LICENSOR and that LICENSOR is the owner thereof. Unless otherwise permitted by law, LICENSEE shall not, at any time during or after the effective Term of the Agreement, dispute or contest, directly or indirectly, LICENSOR's exclusive right and title to the Property or the validity thereof.

9. TERMINATION

The following termination rights are in addition to the termination rights which may be provided elsewhere in the Agreement:

(a) Immediate Right of Termination. LICENSOR shall have the right to immediately terminate this Agreement by giving written notice to LICENSEE in the event that LICENSEE does any of the following:

(1) fails to obtain or maintain product liability insurance in the amount and of the type provided for herein; or

(2) files a petition in bankruptcy or is adjudicated a bankrupt or insolvent, or makes an assignment for the benefit of creditors, or an arrangement pursuant to any bankruptcy law, or if the LICENSEE discontinues or dissolves its business or if a receiver is appointed for the LICENSEE or for the LICENSEE'S business and such receiver is not discharged within thirty (30) days.

(b) Immediate Right to Terminate a Portion. LICENSOR shall have the immediate right to terminate the portion of this Agreement relating to any Licensed Product and/or country in the Licensed Territory if LICENSEE, for any reason, fails to meet the Product Introduction Date or the Initial Shipment Date specified in Schedule A with respect to such Licensed Product or country or if, after the commencement of manufacture and sale of a particular Licensed Product in a particular country, LICENSEE ceases to sell commercial quantities of such Licensed Product in such country for three (3) consecutive Royalty Periods. In such event, that Licensed Product or country shall be deemed severed from the Agreement and revert to LICENSOR with no restrictions.

(c) Right to Terminate on Notice. Either party may terminate this Agreement on thirty (30) days' written notice to the other party in the event of a breach of any provision of this Agreement by the other party, provided that, during the thirty (30) days period, the breaching party fails to cure such breach.

(d) LICENSEE Right to Terminate. LICENSEE shall have the right to terminate this Agreement at any time on sixty (60) days' written notice to LICENSOR, such termination to become effective at the conclusion of such sixty (60) day period.

10. POST TERMINATION RIGHTS

(a) Not less than thirty (30) days prior to the expiration of this Agreement or immediately upon termination thereof, LICENSEE shall provide LICENSOR with a complete schedule of all inventory of Licensed Products then on-hand or in the process of manufacture (the "Inventory");

(b) Upon expiration or termination of this Agreement, except for reason of a breach of LICENSEE's duty to comply with the quality control or legal notice marking requirements, LICENSEE shall be entitled, for three (3) months (the "Sell-Off Period") and on a non-exclusive basis, to continue to sell such Inventory. Such sales shall be made subject to all the provisions of this Agreement including the payment of a Royalty which shall be due within thirty (30) days after the close of the Sell-Off period. At the conclusion of the Sell-Off Period, LICENSOR may require that the LICENSEE either destroy any product still on hand or, alternatively, LICENSOR may purchase it from LICENSEE at a price equal to 50% of LICENSEE's Net Selling Price.

(c) Upon the expiration or termination of this Agreement, all rights granted to LICENSEE under this Agreement shall forthwith terminate and immediately revert to LICENSOR and LICENSEE shall discontinue all use of the Property and the like.

(d) Upon expiration or termination of this Agreement, LICENSOR may require that the LICENSEE transmit to LICENSOR, at no cost, all material relating to the Property including all artwork, color separations, prototypes and the like, and any market studies or other tests conducted by LICENSEE with respect to the Property.

(e) In the event of termination of this Agreement, all monies paid to LICENSOR shall be deemed non-refundable and LICENSEE's obligation to pay the Guaranteed Minimum Royalty for the year in which such termination becomes effective as well as for the year thereafter shall be accelerated and shall immediately become due and payable.

11. INFRINGEMENTS

(a) LICENSOR shall have the right, in its sole discretion, to prosecute lawsuits against third persons for infringement of LICENSOR's rights in the Property. If LICENSOR does not institute an infringement suit within thirty (30) days after LICENSEE's written request that it do so, LICENSEE may institute and prosecute such lawsuit.

(b) Any lawsuit shall be prosecuted solely at the expense of the party bringing suit and all sums recovered shall be divided equally between LICENSOR and LICENSEE after deduction of all reasonable expenses and attorney's fees.

(c) The parties agree to fully cooperate with the other party in the prosecution of any such suit. The party bringing suit shall reimburse the other party for the expenses incurred as a result of such cooperation but such monies shall be recoverable before any award is split.

12. INDEMNITY

(a) LICENSEE agrees to defend, indemnify and hold LICENSOR, its officers, directors, agents and employees, harmless against all costs, expenses and losses (including reasonable attorneys' fees) incurred through claims of third parties against LICENSOR based on the manufacture or sale of the Licensed Products including, but not limited to, actions founded on product liability.

(b) LICENSOR agrees to defend, indemnify and hold LIC-ENSEE, its officers, directors, agents and employees, harmless against all costs, expenses and losses (including reasonable attorneys' fees) incurred through claims of third parties against LICENSEE based on a breach by LICENSOR of any representation and warranty made in this Agreement, provided, however, that such indemnity shall only be applicable in the event of a final decision by a court of competent jurisdiction from which no appeal of right exists and, further, shall be limited to the lower of the amount of the actual monies received by LICENSOR for the Property in question under this Agreement or FIFTY PER-CENT (50%) of LICENSEE's costs, expenses and losses (including reasonable attorneys' fees).

13. INSURANCE

LICENSEE shall, throughout the Term of the Agreement, obtain and maintain at its own cost and expense from a qualified insurance company licensed to do business in New York, standard Product Liability Insurance naming LICENSOR as an additional insured. Such policy shall provide protection against all claims, demands and causes of action arising out of any defects or failure to perform, alleged or otherwise, of the Licensed Products or any material used in connection therewith or any use thereof. The amount of coverage shall be as specified in Schedule A attached hereto. The policy shall provide for ten (10) days' notice to LICENSOR from the insurer by Registered or Certified Mail, return receipt requested, in the event of any modification, cancellation or termination thereof. LICENSEE agrees to furnish LICENSOR a certificate of insurance evidencing same within thirty (30) days after execution of this Agreement and, in no event, shall LICENSEE manufacture, distribute or sell the Licensed Products prior to receipt by LICENSOR of such evidence of insurance.

14. JURISDICTION & DISPUTES

This Agreement shall be governed by the laws of New York and all disputes hereunder shall be resolved in the applicable state or federal courts of New York. The parties consent to the jurisdiction of such courts, agree to accept service of process by mail, and waive any jurisdictional or venue defenses otherwise available.

15. AGREEMENT BINDING ON SUCCESSORS

This Agreement shall be binding upon and shall inure to the benefit of the parties hereto, their heirs, administrators, successors and assigns.

16. ASSIGNABILITY

The license granted hereunder is personal to LICENSEE and may not be assigned by any act of LICENSEE or by operation of law unless in connection with a transfer of substantially all the assets of LICENSEE or with the consent of LICENSOR.

17. WAIVER

No waiver by either party of any default shall be deemed as a waiver of any prior or subsequent default of the same or other provisions of this Agreement.

18. SEVERABILITY

If any provision hereof is held invalid or unenforceable by a court of competent jurisdiction, such invalidity shall not affect the validity or operation of any other provision and such invalid provision shall be deemed to be severed from the Agreement.

19. INTEGRATION

This Agreement constitutes the entire understanding of the parties, and revokes and supersedes all prior agreements between the parties and is intended as a final expression of their Agreement. It shall not be modified or amended except in writing signed by the parties hereto and specifically referring to this Agreement. This Agreement shall take precedence over any other documents which may be in conflict herewith.

IN WITNESS WHEREOF, the parties hereto, intending to be legally bound hereby, have each caused to be affixed hereto its or his/her hand and seal the day indicated.

TOY INVENTION   CHILDREN'S TOY
ENTERPRISES   COMPANY

By: _____   By: _____
Joseph Yarbrough   Dick Smith
Title: President   Title: Vice President
Date: Date:

SCHEDULE A

1. Property

The Property is defined as follows:

The toy concept developed under the working title FLAP-PERS, as more fully described in the material attached hereto as Exhibit A.

2. Licensed Products

The Licensed Products are as follows:

Board games, jigsaw puzzles and children's educational toys.

3. Licensed Territory

The following countries shall constitute the Licensed Territory:

Worldwide

4. Royalty Rate

The Royalty Rate is as follows: FIVE PERCENT (5%).
The Royalty Rate for F.O.B. sales (including F.O.B. sales from Licensee's foreign affiliates to unaffiliated entities) is as follows: EIGHT PERCENT (8%).

5. Advance

The following Advance shall be paid upon execution of this Agreement: Ten Thousand Dollars ($10,000.00).

6. Guaranteed Minimum Royalty

During each year of the Term of this Agreement, LICENSEE hereby guarantees that LICENSOR shall receive a minimum royalty of: Fifteen Thousand Dollars ($15,000.00)

7. Product Liability Insurance

Five Million Dollars ($5,000,000) combined single limit, with a deductible amount not to exceed Twenty Five Thousand Dollars ($25,000), for each single occurrence for bodily injury and/or for property damage.

8. Product Introduction/Initial Shipment

The Product Introduction Date for all Licensed Products in the United States shall be New York City Toy Fair, 1996.

The Initial Shipment Date for all Licensed Products in the United States shall be June, 1996.

The Product Introduction Date and Initial Shipment Date for all other countries shall be one year after the applicable date in the United States.

9. Advertising Commitment

LICENSEE shall spend at least Twenty-five Thousand Dollars ($25,000.00) on media purchases to advertise the Licensed Products during each year of this Agreement.

EXHIBIT A

(Attach description/drawings of the toy property.)

APPENDIX 15:
LIST OF TOY AGENTS/BROKERS

Robert Anderson
Cactus Marketing Services
1553 South Military Highway
Chesapeake, VA 23230
(804)366-9907

Jim Becker
Anjar, Inc.
200 Fifth Avenue, Suite 1305
New York, NY 10010
(212)255-4720

Andrew Berton
Excel Development Group, Inc.
1721 Mount Curve Avenue
Minneapolis, MN 55403-1017
(612)374-3233

Tom Braunlich
Technical Game Services
239 Wood Avenue
Bainbridge, WA 98110
(206)842-5104

George Chanos
Game Makers
12950-101 Carmel Creek Road
San Diego, CA 92130
(619)481-8697

George Delaney
Delaney Product Development
6956 Hawthorne Lane
Hanover Park, IL 60103
(708)289-1583

Walter Dobosz
Fun 'N Games
340 Collingwood Avenue
Fairfield, CT 06430
(203)576-0794

Jerry Houle, III
Bliss House
11 Hampton Street
Springfield, MA 01103
(413)737-0757

Benjamin Kinberg
Benj. Kinberg & Associates
200 Fifth Avenue
New York, NY 10010
(212)989-1610

Daniel Lauer
Lauer Enterprises, Inc.
8008 Carondelet Ave,
Suite 101
Clayton, MO 63105
(314)727-8697

Paul Lapidus
The Together Group
9882 Cow Creek Drive
Palo Cedro, CA 96073
(800)846-0701

Richard Moore
Peachtree Products, Inc.
210 Rolling Ridge Court
Roswell, GA 30075
(404)998-0806

Barry Piehls
Robert McDarren
Link Group
341 West Lane
Ridgefield, CT 06877
(203)438-9807

Carol Rehtmeyer
Rehtmeyer Design
26 West 144 Durfee Road
Wheaton, IL 60187
(708)668-1406

Mel Taft
Mel Taft Associates
10 Crane Avenue
East Longmeadow, MA 01028
(413)525-4405

Arthur Venditti
Invention Incubator Network
29 Cummings Park, Suite 422
Woburn, MA 01801
(617)933-8824

APPENDIX 16
DIRECTORY LISTING OF TOY COMPANIES

ABALONE GAMES CORPORATION
128 Columbus Street
Grand Haven, MI 49417
Telephone: 616-846-0200   Telefax: 616-846-9828
Matt Mariani, Marketing Manager
    Games, Board & Card

ACE NOVELTY CO., INC.
13434 N.E. 16th Street
Bellevue, WA 98005
Telephone: 206-644-1820   Telefax: 206-641-5035
Kati White, Licensing Manager
    Action Figures & Accessories   Character Products
    Construction Toys & Sets   Furniture, Juvenile
    Inflatable Toys   Magic Sets
    Novelties   Premiums & Promotional Items
    Pre-School Toys & Playsets   Stuffed Toys

ACTIVITIES UNLIMITED
510 Metairie Road
Metairie, LA 70005
Telephone: 504-837-5615   Telefax: 504-837-5658
Fred H. Shear, President
    Construction Toys & Sets   Educational Toys & Games
    Infant Toys   Pre-School Toys & Playsets
    Wooden Toys

AIR POGO BY HYPERGEE, INC.
909 Adeline Street
Hattiesburg, MS 39401
Telephone: 601-545-7646   Telefax: 601-545-7646
Sarah Webb, President
    Athletic Products   Backyard Play Equipment

AJF TOYS INTERNATIONAL
610 Wall Street
Los Angeles, CA 90014
Telephone: 213-624-5062   Telefax: 213-624-0669
Kay Ta, Vice President

Action Figures & Accessories
Animals & Figures (Hard)
Cars & Trucks
Educational Toys & Games
Remote Control Toys
Trains

Airplanes & Accessories
Battery-Operated Toys
Construction Toys & Sets
Pre-School Toys & Playsets
Stuffed Toys

ALEX
25 Smith Street
Englewood, NJ
Telephone: 201-569-5757   Telefax: 201-569-7944
Richard Amdur, Owner

Books-Coloring
Costumes and Masks
Crayons and Markers
Model Kits
Play Cosmetics & Make-up
Science Kits
Stuffed Toys

Chalk & Chalkboards
Crafts, Kits and Supplies
Educational Toys and Games
Paint Sets
Rubber Stamps
Stickers

ALL STAR TOY COMPANY
P.O. Box 9348
Rancho Santa Fe, CA 92067
Telephone: 619-759-0405   Telefax: 619-759-0814
David M. Dahlberg, Research & Development

Action Figures & Accessories
Animal & Figures (Hard)
Backyard Play Equipment
Character Products
Construction Toys and Sets
Crafts, Kits & Supplies
Educational Toys & Games
Games, Adventure
Games, Trivia
Halloween Novelties
Infant Toys
Musical Toys & Instruments
Paint Sets
Pre-School Toys & Playsets
Stuffed Toys

Airplanes & Accessories
Athletic Products
Cars & Trucks
Christmas Products
Costumes & Masks
Dolls, Collector
Games, Action & Skill
Games, Board & Card
Guns
Housekeeping & Cooking Toys
Inflatable Toys
Novelties
Premiums & Promotional Items
Robots
Wooden Toys

ALPAK INDUSTRIES, INC.
222 Route 9W, Suite 1201
Haverstraw, NY 10927
Telephone: 914-457-3102   Telefax: 914-354-3188
Douglas Taub, President
   Corrugated Fiber-Board Products

AMERICAN TOY & FURNITURE CO., INC.
8950 Gloss Point Road
Skokie , IL 60077
Telephone: 708-966-5500   Telefax: 708-966-5610
Susan Zagorin, Director of Marketing/Product Development

Athletic Products	Backyard Play Equipment
Chalk & Chalkboards	Character Products
Construction Toys and Sets	Crafts, Kits and Supplies
Doll Accessories	Educational Toys & Games
Furniture, Juvenile	Games, Action & Skill
Games, Adventure	Horses, Hobby, Rocking etc.
Housekeeping & Cooking Toys	Musical Toys & Instruments
Pre-School Toys & Playsets	Science Kits
Wading Pools & Summer Toys	Wooden Toys

ANJAR CO.
200 Fifth Avenue
New York, NY 10010
Telephone: 212-255-4720 ext. 22 Telefax: 212-633-1183
Roger Becker, Partner

ARTS OF AVALON
P.O. Box 289
Santa Cruz, CA 95061-0289
Telephone: 408-459-9499
Kristin Putney or Zoe Morelli, Owners
   Costumes and Masks

AVALON HILL GAME CO., THE
4517 Harford Road
Baltimore, MD 21214
Telephone: 410-254-9200
Phyllis Opolko

Computer Software	Games, Action & Skill
Games, Adventure	Games, Board & Card
Games, Trivia	

BADGER BASKET COMPANY
111 Lions Drive, Suite 220
Barrington, IL 60010
Telephone: 708-381-6200   Telefax: 708-381-6218
Jon Rasmussen, President
    Doll Accessories (Doll Furniture)   Furniture, Juvenile
    Infant Toys   Wooden Toys

BEPUZZLED
22 East Newberry Road
Bloomfield, CT 06002
Telephone: 203-769-5700   Telefax: 203-769-5799
Sue Braun, Creative Assistant
    Books & Cassettes   Books—Word/Picture
    Educational Games   Games, Action & Skill
    Games, Adventure   Games, Board & Card
    Games, Electronic & Video   Premiums & Promotional Items
    Puzzles   Crosswords & Word Puzzles

BERK CORP.
2500 Crow Foot Lane
Diamond Bar, CA 91765
Telephone: 909-613-0036   Telefax: 909-613-0227
Jackson Lai, President
    Educational Toys & Games   Pre-Schools & Playsets
    Puzzles

BETA TOYS, INC.
2850A E. Cedar Street
Ontario, CA 91761
Telephone: 909-923-6988
Telefax: 909-923-2688
John Stamford, Director, Sales & Marketing
    Stuffed Toys

BINARY ARTS
5601 Vine Street
Alexandria, VA 22310
Telephone: 703-971-3401   Telefax: 703-971-3403
Bill Ritchie, President
    Puzzles

BINNEY & SMITH
1100 Church Lane
Easton, PA 18044-0431
Telephone: 215-253-6271   Telefax: 215-250-5862
Ellyn Scott, Manager, Consumer Communications
    Chalk & Chalkboards   Crafts, Kits and Supplies
    Crayons and Markers

BLAZE INTERNATIONAL PRODUCTIONS, INC.
245 Fifth Avenue, Suite 1704
New York, NY 10016
Telephone: 212-213-0050   Telefax: 212-213-0055
Steven Bloom, Director
    Books and Cassettes   Books-Coloring
    Books-Word/Picture   Crafts, Kits & Supplies
    Educational Toys & Games   Halloween Novelties
    Novelties   Premiums & Promotional Items
    Pre-School Toys & Playsets

BLUE BOX TOYS, INC.
200 Fifth Avenue, Suite 838
New York, NY 10010
Telephone: 212-255-8388   Telefax: 212-255-8520
Rick McNeely, Executive Vice President
    Action Figures & Accessories   Airplanes & Accessories
    Animals & Figures (Hard)   Backyard Play Equipment
    Battery Operated Toys   Bubbles & Sets
    Cars & Trucks   Chalk & Chalkboards
    Character Products   Construction Toys & Sets
    Crafts, Kits & Supplies   Dolls, Fashion
    Doll Accessories   Educational Toys & Games
    Electronic Toys   Games, Action & Skill
    Games, Adventure   Games, Electronic & Video
    Housekeeping & Cooking Toys   Infant Toys
    Mechanical Toys   Musical Toys & Instruments
    Play Cosmetics & Make-up   Premiums & Promotional Items
    Pre-School Toys & Playsets   Roller Skates & Blades
    Wading Pool & Summer Toys

BRADLEY IMPORT CO.
1400 N. Spring Street
Los Angeles, CA 90012
Telephone: 213-221-4162   Telefax: 213-221-8272
Benson Goldenberg, General Manager
    Dolls, Collector   Dolls, Fashion
    Doll Accessories

BRAVO INTERNATIONAL CORPORATION
1421 Kirkwall
Court   Inverness, IL 60010
Telephone: 708-304-1620   Telefax: 708-304-0232
Manager New Products & Ventures

Airplanes & Accessories	Beach Toys
Educational Toys and Games	Games, Action & Skill
Premiums & Promotional Items	Flying Toys

BRIK TOY COMPANY
2630 Fountain View #218
Houston, TX 77053
Telephone: 713-780-2745   Telefax: 713-780-4826
Barry Stiles, Vice President, Operations

Action Figures & Accessories	Backyard Play Equipment
Beach Toys	Character Products
Construction Toys & Sets	Educational Toys & Games
Furniture, Juvenile	

C WORKS
P.O. Box 53742
San Jose, CA 95153
Telephone: 408-226-2981   Telefax: 408-972-2096
Charles Rath, Owner

Crafts, Kits & Supplies	Educational Toys & Games
Novelties	Premiums & Promotional Items
Puppets	Wooden Toys

CAP TOYS
26201 Richmond Road
Bedford Heights, OH 44146
Telephone: 216-292-6363   Telefax: 216-292-4815
Jill Tapper, Director of Marketing

Action Figures & Accessories	Battery Operated Toys
Beach Toys	Bubbles & Sets
Cars & Trucks	Character Products
Dolls, Fashion	Novelties
Pre-School Toys & Playsets	Remote Control Toys
Stuffed Toys	

CAPTIVATION CORPORATION
7894 S. Locust Ct.
Englewood, CO 80112
Telephone: 303-220-9372   Telefax: 303-20-9373
Bruce Miller, President

Games, Board & Card	Games, Trivia

CARLISLE CO.
P.O. Box 21029
Carson City, NV 89721
Telephone: 702-246-7822   Telefax: 702-246-7826
Alan Carlisle, President
  Animals & Figures (Hard)   Books, Coloring
  Educational Toys & Games   Inflatable Toys
  Premiums & Promotional Items   Puzzles
  Rubber Stamps   Science Kits
  Stickers

CAVANAGH GROUP INTERNATIONAL
1000 Holcomb Woods Pkwy. 440B
Roswell, GA 30076
Telephone: 770-643-1175   Telefax: 770-643-1172
John F. Cavanagh, President
  Action Figures & Accessories   Animals & Figures (Hard)
  Athletic Products   Character Products
  Christmas Products   Halloween Novelties
  Premiums & Promotional Items   Stuffed Toys

CEACO, INC.
124 Watertown Street
Watertown, MA 02172
Telephone: 617-926-8080   Telefax: 617-924-7554
Lisa Casella, Art Director
  Puzzles

CHIMERIC INC.
4301 F. Amherst Ave., Ste. 308
Denver, CO 80222
Telephone: 303-756-5696   Telefax: 303-756-5574
Chip Brunk, President
  Crafts, Kits & Supplies   Educational Toys & Games

CLOVER TOYS, INC.
16261 Phoebe Avenue
La Mirada, CA 90638
Telephone: 714-994-1372   Telefax: 714-994-0523
Roger Richards, Vice President
  Backyard Play Equipment   Bicycles
  Bubbles & Sets   Cars & Trucks
  Construction Toys & Sets   Electronic Toys
  Furniture Juvenile   Pre-School Toys & Playsets
  Remote Control Toys   Riding Vehicles

COBURN CORPORATION
1650 Corporate Road West
Lakewood, NJ 08701
Telephone: 908-367-3511   Telefax: 908-367-2908
John White, Vice President, Marketing
    Character Products   Crafts, Kits & Supplies
    Stickers

COLLEGEVILLE/IMAGINEERING L.P.
P.O. Box 808
Collegeville, PA 19426
Telephone: 610-489-0100   Telefax: 610-489-2190
Lawrence J. Liff, Vice President, R&D
    Halloween Novelties

COLORFORMS
133 Williams Drive
Ramsey, NJ 07446
Telephone: 201-327-2600   Telefax: 201-327-2506
Jeri Weiss, Account Executive

COME ALIVE PUBLICATIONS
53 Hillcrest Road
Concord, MA 01742
Telephone: 508-369-0680   Telefax: 508-369-7291
Carol Bowen; Ilona Stashko, Partner; President
    Books & Cassettes   Books, Word/Picture
    Costumes & Masks   Educational Toys & Games

COMMONWEALTH TOY & NOVELTY CO. INC.
45 West 25th Street
New York, NY
Telephone: 212-242-4070
Jeffrey A. Bialosky, Vice President, Marketing & Product Development
    Athletic Products   Battery Operated Toys
    Character Products   Christmas Products
    Costumes and Masks   Dolls, Collector
    Dolls, Fashion   Doll Accessories
    Infant Toys   Premiums & Promotional Items
    Puppets   Stuffed Toys

CONCEPT MARKETING
P.O. Box 1705
Santa Rosa, CA 95402
Telephone: 707-545-4171   Telefax: 707-575-3707
Ian T. Allison, President
    Halloween Novelties   Stickers

COX PRODUCTS, INC.
475 N. Sheridan Street
Corona, CA 91720
Telephone: 909-278-1282   Telefax: 909-278-2981
Mr. Larry Renger, Director of Engineering
    Airplanes & Accessories   Electronic Toys
    Mechanical Toys   Model Kits
    Remote Control Toys   Road Racing Sets

CREATIVE CONCEPTS UNLIMITED, INC.
985 Mancherter Place, Suite 100
Atlanta, GA 30378
Telephone: 404-252-4640   Telefax: 404-955-4059
George Anderson, President
    Books & Cassettes   Character Products
    Infant Toys   Puppets
    Stuffed Toys

CREATIVE GROUP, THE
400 Main Street, Suite 210
Stamford, CT 06901
Telephone: 203-359-3500   Telefax: 203-978-1919
Gary Ahlert, President

Action Figures & Accessories	Animals & Figures (hard)
Athletic Products	Backyard Play Equipment
Balloons	Balls
Battery-Operated Toys	Books & Cassettes
Books-Coloring	Books-Word/Picture
Bubbles & Sets	Cars & Trucks
Character Products	Computer Software
Construction Toys & Sets	Crafts, Kits & Supplies
Crayons & Markers	Dolls, Collector
Dolls, Fashion	Doll Accessories
Educational Toys & Games	Electronic Toys
Games, Action & Skill	Games, Adventure
Games, Board & Card	Games, Electronic & Video
Games, Trivia	Housekeeping & Cooking Toys
Infant Toys	Inflatable Toys
Magic Sets	Mechanical Toys
Model Kits	Musical Toys & Instruments
Novelties	Play Cosmetics & Make-up

Premiums & Promotional Items
Remote Control Toys
Robots
Stuffed Toys
Wooden Toys

Pre-School Toys & Playsets
Road Racing Sets
Roller Skates & Blades
Trains

CREATIVE TOYS PRODUCTS, INC.
P.O. Box 290120/2117 87th Trail N.
Minneapolis, MN 55429
Telephone: 612-495-4751
J. Anthony Burnett, President

Action Figures & Accessories
Animals & Figures
Bicycles
Books-Coloring
Bubbles & Sets
Character Products
Computer Software
Educational Toys & Games
Games, Adventure
Games, Electronic & Video
Horses, Hobby, Rocking
Musical Toys & Instruments
Premiums & Promotional Items
Puppets
Robots
Science Kits
Wooden Toys

Airplanes & Accessories
Balloons
Books & Cassettes
Books-Word/Picture
Cars & Trucks
Christmas Products
Construction Toys & Sets
Games, Action & Skill
Games, Board & Card
Games, Trivia
Mechanical Toys
Novelties
Pre-School Toys & Playsets
Puzzles
Rubber Stamps
Trains

D & K ENTERPRISES, INC.
3216 Commander Drive, Ste. 101
Carrollton, TX 75006
Telephone: 214-248-9100   Telefax: 214-248-9750
J. Pushaw /M. Rudiger, Director/President

Books & Cassettes
Books-Word/Picture
Clocks & Watches
Crafts, Kits & Supplies
Novelties
Stuffed Toys

Books-Coloring
Character Products
Computer Software
Educational Toys & Games
Premiums & Promotional Items

DAMERT COMPANY
2476 Verna Street
San Leandro, CA 94577
Telephone: 510-895-6500   Telefax: 510-895-5454
Fred DaMert, President/Creative Director

Bubbles & Sets	Chalk & Chalkboards
Computer Software	Construction Toys & Sets
Educational Toys & Games	Games, Action & Skill
Games, Adventure	Games, Board & Card
Games, Electronic & Video	Games, Trivia
Magic Sets	Mechanical Toys
Puzzles	Robots
Science Kits	

DAVIS LIQUID CRYSTALS
14722 Wicks Blvd.
San Leandro, CA 94577
Telephone: 510-351-2295   Telefax: 510-351-2328
Alan Friedman, Sales Manager
    Color Change Products

DEE'S DELIGHTS, INC.
3150 State Line Road
North Bend, OH 45052
Telephone: 513-353-3390   Telefax: 513-353-3933
Jerry Hacker, President
    Doll Houses

DELVAR INC.
2020 14th Street
Santa Monica, CA 90405
Telephone: 310-452-7098   Telefax: 310-450-8635
Spyros Dellaportas, C.E.O.

Educational Toys & Games	Games, Action & Skill
Games, Adventure	Games, Board & Card
Games, Trivia	Premiums & Promotional Items
Pre-School Toys & Playsets	Puzzles

DESIGN SCIENCE TOYS, LTD.
1362 Route 9
Tivoli, NY 12491
Telephone: 914-756-4221   Telefax: 914-756-4223
Patty Turner, New Product Coordinator

Construction Toys & Sets	Crafts, Kits & Supplies
Educational Toys & Games	Infant Toys
Kites and Windsocks	Model Kits
Musical Toys and Instruments	Premiums & Promotional Items
Pre-School Toys & Playsets	Puzzles
Science Kits	Wooden Toys

DISGUISE INC.
37-11 35th Avenue
Astoria, NY 11101
Telephone: 718-361-8601
Steven Cohen, Vice President
Halloween Novelties

DIVERSIFIED SPECIALISTS, INC.
1100 West Sam Houston Parkway
North   Houston, TX 77043
Telephone: 713-526-2888   Telefax: 713-526-5049
Rick McNeely, Executive Vice President

Action Figures & Accessories	Athletic Products
Backyard Play Equipment	Balls
Battery Operated Toys	Cars & Trucks
Clocks & Watches	Educational Toys & Games
Electronic Toys	Guns
Musical Toys & Instruments	Novelties
Pre-School Toys & Playsets	Road Racing Sets
Robots	Trains
Wading Pools & Summer Toys	

DOC'S HI TECH
4140 Garner Road
Riverside, CA 92501
Telephone: 909-784-2710   Telefax: 909-784-7709
Don Reisinger, President

Computer Software	Electronic Toys
Games, Electronic & Video	

DOODLETOP COMPANY
1807 Contra Costa Street
Sand City, CA 93955
Telephone: 408-393-9000   Telefax: 408-393-9013
Chris McKay, President

Action Figures & Accessories
Character Products
Crafts, Kits & Supplies
Educational Toys & Games
Novelties
Tops

Animals & Figures (Hard)
Construction Toys & Sets
Crayons & Markers
Games, Action & Skill
Premiums & Promotional Items

DRAGONS ARE TOO SELDOM INC.
1501 Pine Heights
Rapid City, SD 57701
Telephone: 605-343-8200   Telefax: 605-343-8226
Claire Scholz, President

Backyard Play Equipment
Bubbles & Sets
Educational Toys & Games
Infant Toys
Premiums & Promotional Items
Puppets
Wading Pools & Summer Toys

Beach Toys
Christmas Products
Furniture, Juvenile
Inflatable Toys
Pre-School Toys & Playsets
Science Kits
Wooden Toys

DUNCAN TOYS
15981 Valplast Road
Middlefield, OH 44062
Telephone: 216-632-1631   Telefax: 216-632-1581
Michael Caffrey, Marketing Manager

Balls
Skill Toys
Yo-yos

Construction Toys & Sets
Spin Tops

DYNASTY DOLLS/DIVISION OF CARDINAL INC.
400 Markley Street
Port Reading, NJ 07064-0099
Telephone: 908-636-6160   Telefax: 908-636-6215
Anne L. Dolan/Donna R. Rovner, Merchandise Manager/Associate
Merchandise Manager

Dolls, Collector
Doll Accessories

Dolls, Fashion

ECHELON KIDS INC.
P.O. Box 3071
Boulder, CO 80307
Telephone: 303-499-6444   Telefax: 303-499-0890
  Backyard Play Equipment   Cars & Trucks
  Construction Toys & Sets   Housekeeping & Cooking Toys
  Inflatable Toys   Pre-School Toys & Playsets

EDEN TOYS, INC.
812 Jersey Avenue
Jersey City, NJ 07310
Telephone: 201-656-3331   Telefax: 201-656-3070
Tracey Tsontakis, Vice President, Product Development
  Character Products   Dolls, Collector
  Dolls, Fashion   Doll Accessories
  Educational Toys & Games   Infant Toys
  Musical Toys & Instruments   Pre-School Toys & Playsets
  Puppets   Stuffed Toys
  Wooden Toys

EDUCATIONAL INSIGHTS, INC.
19560 S. Rancho Way
Dominguez Hills, CA 90220
Telephone: 310-884-1931
Livian Perez, Submissions Editor
  Computer Software   Crafts, Kits & Supplies
  Educational Toys & Games   Electronic Toys
  Games, Board & Card   Games, Trivia
  Magic Sets   Rubber Stamps
  Science Kits

EFFANBEE DOLL COMPANY
1026 W. Elizabeth Avenue
Linden, NJ 07036
Telephone: 908-474-8000   Telefax: 908-474-8001
Stanley Wahlberg, President
  Dolls, Collector   Dolls, Fashion
  Doll Accessories

EPI
250 Pequot Avenue
Southport, CT 06490
Telephone: 203-255-1112   Telefax: 203-255-3313
Merryl Lambert, Senior Vice President Marketing

Books, Wood/Picture	Educational Toys & Games
Environmental Toys	Premium & Promotional Items
Stuffed Toys	

ESTES
1295 H Street
Penrose, CO 81240
Telephone: 719-372-6565   Telefax: 719-372-3419
R&D Manager

Airplanes & Accessories	Model Kits
Rockets & Related Accessories	Science Kits

EUROPEAN TOY COLLECTION/CROCODILE CREEK
6643 Melton Road
Portage, IN 46368
Telephone: 219-763-3234   Telefax: 219-762-1740
Kristen Scott, New Product Coordinator

Books & Cassettes	Books, Coloring
Books, Word/Picture	Chalk & Chalkboards
Character Products	Costumes & Masks
Educational Toys & Games	Games, Board & Card
Infant Toys	Novelties
Pre-School Toys & Playsets	Puppets
Puzzles	Science Kits
Stuffed Toys	Wooden Toys

FABLE TOY INC.
1710 Flushing Avenue, #302
Ridgewood, NY 11385
Telephone: 718-456-8500   Telefax: 718-417-7166
Kenneth Guerin, Designer

Character Products	Christmas Products
Stuffed Toys	

FANTASY DOLL WORKS
2845 Lakeview Drive
Santa Cruz, CA 95062
Telephone: 408-475-3443
Dianne Carter, Partner

FISHER-PRICE, INC.
636 Girard Avenue
East Aurora, NY 14052
Telephone: 716-687-3000

Backyard Play Equipment
Cars & Trucks
Construction Toys & Sets
Dolls, Fashion
Educational Toys & Games
Furniture, Juvenile
Games, Board & Card
Infant Toys
Mechanical Toys
Pre-School Toys & Playsets
Remote Control Toys
Roller Skates & Blades
Wading Pools & Summer Toys

Bubbles & Sets
Chalk & Chalkboards
Crafts, Kits & Supplies
Doll Accessories
Electronic Toys
Games, Action & Skill
Housekeeping & Cooking Toys
Magic Sets
Musical Toys & Instruments
Puzzles
Riding Vehicles
Stuffed Toys

FLORIDA POOL PRODUCTS, INC.
14480 62nd Street North
Clearwater, FL 34620
Telephone: 800-937-5154   Telefax: 813-536-8066
Jim Eisch, President

Athletic Products
Balls
Educational Toys & Games
Infant Toys
Wading Pools & Summer Toys

Backyard Play Equipment
Battery-Operated Toys
Games, Action & Skill
Inflatable Toys

FORECEES
P.O. Box 153
Vicksburg, MI 49097
Telephone: 616-649-2900   Telefax: 616-649-2900
Cyndee Decker, General Manager

Construction Toys & Sets
Infant Toys

Educational Toys and Games

FORTE SPORTS, INC.
314 E. Main Street, Suite 1
Newark, DE 19711
Telephone: 302-731-0776   Telefax: 302-731-0298
Larry DiMaio, Creative Director

Action Figures & Accessories
Animals & Figures (Hard)
Balls
Novelties
Stuffed Toys

Airplanes & Accessories
Athletic Products
Games, Action & Skill
Premiums & Promotional Items

FRANK SCHAFFER PUBLICATIONS
23740 Heathorne Blvd.
Torrance, CA 90505
Telephone: 800-421-5533   Telefax: 310-375-5090
Bonnie Carter, National Sales Manager
    Educational Toys & Games

FUN & JAMES, INC.
P.O. Box 2511
Bartlesville, OK 74006
Telephone: 918-335-1001   Telefax: 918-335-2685
James Duval, Chairman
    Educational Toys & Games   Games, Action & Skill
    Games, Adventure   Games, Board & Card
    Games, Electronic & Video   Games, Trivia

FUN-TIME INTERNATIONAL INC.
1530 Locust Street, Ste. 15F
Philadelphia, PA 19102
Telephone: 215-546-2880   Telefax: 215-545-2858
Eric Lipson, President
    Animals & Figures (Hard)   Character Products
    Christmas Products   Halloween Novelties
    Novelties   Premiums & Promotional Items

FUNDEX GAMES
P.O. Box 22128, 3750 West 16th Street
Indianapolis, IN 46222
Telephone: 317-263-9869   Telefax: 317-263-0038
Pete Voigt, Vice President
    Crafts, Kits & Supplies   Games, Board & Card
    Puzzles

GALISON BOOKS/MUDPUPPY PRESS
36 West 44th Street
New York, NY 10010
Telephone: 212-354-8840   Telefax: 212-391-4037
Mary Goodwin, Editorial Director
    Books and Cassettes   Books-Coloring
    Books-Word/Picture   Christmas Products

GAMES & GADGETS ENTERPRISES INC.
3873 Airport Way, Unit 338
Bellingham, WA 98226
Telephone: 604-241-4583   Telefax: 604-241-7578
D. Michael Briard, President
   Animals & Figures (Hard)   Construction Toys & Sets
   Educational Toys & Games   Games, Board & Card
   Games, Trivia   Inflatable Toys
   Wading Pools & Summer Toys

GAMESOURCE LTD.
4308 Hockaday
Dallas, TX 75229
Telephone: 214-358-1633   Telefax: 214-351-0220
H. Hudson Dobson
   Educational Games   Games, Action & Skill
   Games, Adventure   Games, Board & Card
   Games, Trivia

GARY PRODUCTS GROUP
624 North 8th Street, Suite 102
Manitowoc, WI 54220
Telephone: 414-683-9990   Telefax: 414-683-9999
Jerry Waak, Vice-President Sales/Marketing
   Backyard Play Equipment   Christmas Products
   Furniture, Juvenile

GBD GAME CONCEPTS, INC.
1335 Dublin Road, Suite 200-A
Columbus, OH 43215-1000
Telephone: 614-481-3512   Telefax: 614-481-3501
Gary Bogan, President/CEO
   Doll Accessories   Games, Board & Card

GEMMY INDUSTRIES
1780 Hurd Drive
Irving, TX 75038
Telephone: 214-550-7979   Telefax: 214-550-0495
Dan Flaherty, Vice President
   Christmas Products   Halloween Novelties

GG ENTERPRISES, INC.
7010 South 400 West
Midvale, UT 84047
Telephone: 801-255-9292   Telefax: 801-562-9200
Laura Bichler, Senior Sales Associate
>   Athletic Products   Backyard Play Equipment
>   Books-Coloring   Educational Toys & Games
>   Games, Action & Skill   Games, Adventure
>   Games, Board & Card
>   Pre-School Toys & Playsets

GORDY INTERNATIONAL
900 North Avenue, P.O. Box 2769
Plainfield, NJ 07062
Telephone: 908-755-9660   Telefax: 908-755-9670
Richard Glassman, Vice President, Marketing
>   Action Figures & Accessories   Bubbles & Sets
>   Cars & Trucks   Chalk & Chalkboards
>   Character Products   Clocks & Watches
>   Crafts, Kits & Supplies   Crayons & Markers
>   Games, Action & Skill   Kites & Windsocks
>   Magic Sets   Novelties
>   Paint Sets   Play Cosmetics & Make-up
>   Premiums & Promotional Items   Pre-School Toys & Playsets
>   Stickers   Stuffed Toys

GREAT AMERICAN FUN CORP.
3656 Paragon Drive
Columbus, OH 43228
Telephone: 614-771-1544   Telefax: 614-771-1599
Morton Rosenberg, Executive Vice President
>   Battery Operated Toys   Christmas Products
>   Halloween Novelties   Mechanical Toys
>   Robots   Stuffed Toys

GREAT AMERICAN PUZZLE FACTORY, INC.
16 South Main Street
South Norwalk, CT 06854
Telephone: 203-838-4240   Telefax: 203-838-2065
Pat Duncan, President
>   Educational Toys & Games   Games, Board & Card
>   Puzzles

HAPPINESS EXPRESS, INC.
50 West 23rd Street, 6th Floor
New York, NY 10023
Telephone: 212-675-0461   Telefax: 212-675-9271
Ms. Gina Sirard, Vice President, Marketing

Action Figures & Accessories	Animals & Figures (Hard)
Athletic Products	Balls
Battery Operated Toys	Bubbles & Sets
Crafts, Kits & Supplies	Crayons & Markers
Dolls, Fashion	Electronic Toys
Halloween Novelties	Infant Toys
Inflatable Toys	Mechanical Toys
Novelties	Premiums & Promotional Items
Pre-School Toys & Playsets	Puppets
Remote Control Toys	Stickers
Stuffed Toys	Trains

HARMONY TOY LTD.
570 Taxter Road
Elmsford, NY 10523
Telephone: 914-592-2266   Telefax: 914-592-7404
Bruce Baum, Sales Manager

Halloween Novelties	Magic Sets

HOWLAND ASSOCIATES, INC.
156 Fifth Avenue, #230
New York, NY 10010
Telephone: 212-929-1120   Telefax: 212-463-0571
Michael G. Antunes, President

Action Figures & Accessories	Battery Operated Toys
Bicycles	Cars & Trucks
Character Products	Construction Toys & Sets
Dolls, Fashion	Doll Accessories
Electronic Toys	Infant Toys
Inflatable Toys	Mechanical Toys
Musical Toys & Instruments	Novelties
Pre-School Toys & Playsets	Remote Control Toys
Riding Vehicles	Road Racing Sets
Robots	Roller Skates & Blades

HUGG-A-PLANET
224 Rockingstone Avenue
Larchmont, NY 10538
Telephone: 914-833-0200
Patricia Howard, VP Marketing Director

Doll Accessories	Educational Toys & Games
Infant Toys	Stuffed Toys

IDEAL
1400 N.W. 93rd Avenue
Miami, FL 33172
Telephone: 305-593-6016   Telefax: 305-477-1807
Marcia Cooper, Administrative Manager

Cars & Trucks	Premiums & Promotional Items
Pre-School Toys & Playsets	Road Racing Sets

IMAGI-TOY GROUP
805 Camino La Posada
Camarillo, CA 93010
Kevin Kenny, V.P., Product Development

Action Figures & Accessories	Animals & Figures (Hard)
Battery Operated Toys	Character Products
Educational Toys & Games	Electronic Toys
Halloween Novelties	Mechanical Toys
Novelties	Premiums & Promotional Items
Stuffed Toys	

INFANTINO INC.
650 Arizona Street
Chula Vista, CA 91911
Telephone: 619-420-1221   Telefax: 619-420-0836
Michael Silberstein, President

Crafts, Kits & Supplies	Educational Toys & Games
Furniture, Juvenile	Infant Toys
Pre-School Toys & Playsets	Stuffed Toys

INFINITE POTENTIAL
44-11 Skillman Avenue
Sunnyside, NY 11104
Telephone: 718-472-5825   Telefax: 718-392-5453
Bridgid Infante, Partner

Construction Toys & Sets	Educational Toys & Games
Furniture, Juvenile	Pre-School Toys & Playsets
Wooden Toys	

INTEGRA TOYS, INC.
1225 S. Downing
Denver, CO 80210
Telephone: 303-777-1236
Craig Shillingburg, Chief Playmaster

Educational Toys & Games	Games, Board & Card
Premiums & Promotional Items	Road Racing Sets

INTERNATIONAL BON-TON TOYS
182 Rte. 522 Suite "I"
Dayton, NJ 08810
Telephone: 908-274-1144   Telefax: 908-274-1090
Louis Preanselaar, Vice-President
  Stuffed Toys

INTOYS, INC.
433 South Salem Drive
Schaumburg, IL 60193
Telephone: 708-351-6334   Telefax: 708-924-8257
R.M. Rounyak, President
  Athletic Products   Backyard Play Equipment

JACK RUSSELL (USA) COMPANY, INC.
465 Riverside Drive
Stuart, FL 34994
Telephone: 407-287-1377   Telefax: 407-288-4969
Alan Griffiths, Marketing
  Premiums & Promotional Items   Yo-yos

JAMES IND. INC.
P.O. Box 467
Hollidaysburg, PA 16648
Telephone: 814-695-5681
Mrs. Betty M. James, President
  Construction Toys & Sets   Novelties
  Pre-School Toys & Playsets

JANEX/DIVISION OF MJL MARKETING
615 Hope Road, Bldg. #1, Floor 1, Victoria Plaza
Eatontown, NJ 07724
Telephone: 908-935-0555   Telefax: 908-935-0825
Dan Lesnick, VP Marketing
  Battery Operated Toys   Character Products
  Clocks & Watches   Musical Toys & Instruments
  Novelties

JOHN WILEY & SONS PUBLISHERS
605 Third Avenue
New York, NY 10158-0012
Telephone: 212-850-6037
Kate Bradford, Editor
  Books, Word/Picture

JTG OF NASHVILLE
1024 C 18th Avenue South
Nashville, TN 37215
Telephone: 615-329-4028
Neil Peters, VP, Product Development

Balloons	Balls
Books & Cassettes	Books, Coloring
Books, Word/Picture	Construction Toys & Sets
Crafts, Kits & Supplies	Dolls, Fashion
Educational Toys & Games	Musical Toys & Instruments
Pre-School Toys & Playsets	Puzzles
Stuffed Toys	Musical Instruments

K-NEX CONNECTOR SET TOY COMPANY
P.O. Box 700
Hatfield, PA 19440

KAZOOCO, A DIVISION OF BRIMMS, INC.
425 Fillmore Avenue
Tonawanda, NY 14150
Telephone: 716-694-7100   Telefax: 716-694-8652
Tony Dinatale, Division Manager

Construction Toys & Sets	Educational Toys & Games
Musical Toys & Instruments	Pre-School Toys & Playsets

KIDPOWER, INC.
8005 Church Street
Brentwood, TN 37027
Telephone: 615-371-1954   Telefax: 615-371-1846
J. Mac Brown, Marketing-New Products

Airplanes & Accessories	Athletic Products
Backyard Play Equipment	Balls
Battery-Operated Toys	Cars & Trucks
Guns	Mechanical Toys
Riding Vehicles	Wading Pools & Summer Toys

KLEIN INTERNATIONAL, LTD.
7970 SW Cirrus Drive, #13
Beaverton, OR 97005
Telephone: 503-626-7582   Telefax: 503-626-7620
Barry Klein, VP Sales

Christmas Products	Halloween Novelties

KLING MAGNETICS INC.
Route 23B
Hudson, NY 12534
Telephone: 518-828-2808   Telefax: 518-828-2809
Scott Wolfe, Director Marketing/Sales

Books, Coloring	Books, Word/Picture
Character Products	Crafts, Kits & Supplies
Educational Toys & Games	Games, Board & Card
Premiums & Promotional Items	Puzzles
Stickers	Magnetic Materials

KOPLOW GAMES
369 Congress Street
Boston, MA 02210
Telephone: 617-482-4011   Telefax: 617-482-3423

LEARNING RESOURCES
675 Heathrow Drive
Lincolnshire, IL 60069
Telephone: 708-793-4500   Telefax: 708-793-4510
Lisa Hoffman, Marketing Manager

Educational Toys & Games	Science Kits

LEGO SYSTEMS, INC.
555 Taylor Road
Enfield, CT 06082
Telephone: 203-749-2291   Telefax: 203-749-9096

LEWIS EDUCATIONAL GAMES
2221 Inwood Road
Wilmington, DE 19810
Telephone: 302-695-4564   Telefax: 302-695-2747
Richard W. Lewis, President

Educational Toys & Games	Games, Board & Card

LIBBY LEE TOYS, INC.
7650 School Road
Cincinnati, OH 45249
Telephone: 513-489-8080   Telefax: 513-489-5668
Susan Walker, Director of Product Development

Crafts, Kits & Supplies	Crayons & Markers
Educational Toys & Games	Housekeeping & Cooking Toys
Play Cosmetics & Make-Up	

LIFESTORIES, INC.
701 Decatur Avenue, North, Ste. 104
Golden Valley, MN 55427
Telephone: 612-544-0438   Telefax: 612-541-9779
Dean Fitch, President
 Games, Board & Card

LITTLE HARBOR CORP.
634 West Bethel Road
Bethel, ME 04217
Telephone: 207-836-3080   Telefax: 207-836-2708
Arthur McEvoy, Vice President/Owner
 Books-Coloring   Educational Toys & Games
 Games, Board & Card   Mazes
 Puzzles   Wooden Toys

LITTLE KIDS, INC.
2757 Pawtucket Avenue
East Providence, RI 02914
Telephone: 401-435-4120   Telefax: 401-435-0665
Keith Patterson, Executive Vice President R&D
 Athletic Products   Beach Toys
 Bubbles & Sets   Children Feeding Products
 Infant Toys   Novelties

LIVING & LEARNING (CAMBRIDGE) LTD.
Abbeygate House, East Road
Cambridge, CR1 1DB, England
Telephone: 01223 357788   Telefax: 01223 460557
Anne Hosmer, Product Development Secretary
 Crafts, Kits & Supplies   Educational Toys & Games
 Games, Board & Card   Science Kits

M & D INDUSTRIES INTERNATIONAL, INC.
711 Grove Street
Manteno, IL 60950
Telephone: 815-468-2500   Telefax: 815-468-2522
Mark Van Dyke, Vice President, Creative/Marketing
 Balloons

MANTUA INDUST./COSOM SPORTING GOODS
Grandview Avenue/P.O. Box 10
Woodbury Heights, NJ 08097
Telephone: 609-853-0300   Telefax: 609-384-108
C. Thomas Swartz, President
 Athletic Products   Backyard Games
 Balls

MARCHON, INC.
555 Corporate Woods Parkway
Vernon Hills, IL 60061
Telephone: 708-634-7733   Telefax: 708-634-7744
Harvey Katz or/Marvin Smollar; Senior VP, Marketing/President

Airplanes & Accessories	Animals & Figures (Hard)
Athletic Products	Battery Operated Toys
Cars & Trucks	Construction Toys & Sets
Crafts, Kits & Supplies	Girls' Collectibles
Road Racing Sets	Wading Pools & Summer Toys

MARX TOYS
1130 NW 159th Drive
Miami, FL 33169
Telephone: 305-625-9000   Telefax: 305-621-9063
Joel Wildman, General Manager

Action Figures & Accessories	Battery Operated Toys
Cars & Trucks	Character Products
Dolls, Collector	Playsets

MAUI TOYS, INC.
116 Linden Avenue
Youngstown, OH 44505
Telephone: 216-747-4333   Telefax: 216-747-1134
Jeff Sooper, Director of Sales & Marketing

Action Figures & Accessories	Athletic Products
Balls	Beach Toys
Bubbles & Sets	Character Products
Construction Toys & Sets	Educational Toys & Games
Games, Action & Skill	Games, Adventure

MAXSON IMPORT
55 Triangle Blvd.
Carlstadt, NJ 07072
Telephone: 201-939-9695   Telefax: 201-939-2660
Connie Wang

Balls	Bubbles & Sets
Cars & Trucks	Christmas Products
Electronic Toys	Halloween Novelties
Novelties	Stickers

MAYFAIR GAMES INC.
5641 Howard Street
Niles, IL 60714
Telephone: 708-647-9650   Telefax: 708-647-0939
Faith Price, Manager of Corporate Communications
    Games, Action & Skill   Games, Adventure
    Games, Board & Card   Games, Trivia

MICKI USA, INC.
500 Weston Avenue
Lake Forest, IL 60045
Telephone: 708-295-0359   Telefax: 708-295-0373
Egil C. Wigert, President
    Construction Toys & Sets   Dolls, Collector
    Dolls, Fashion   Educational Toys & Games
    Trains, Wood   Wooden Toys

MICRO GAMES OF AMERICA
16730 Schoenborn Street
N. Hills, CA 91343
Telephone: 818-894-2525
Larry Bernstein, Executive Vice President
    Battery-operated Toys   Electronic Toys
    Games, Electronic & Video

MIGHTY STAR INC.
925 Amboy Avenue
Perth Amboy, NJ 08861
Telephone: 908-826-5200   Telefax: 908-826-7370
Marvin H. Young, Vice President, Marketing
    Stuffed Toys & Dolls

MIKE MOSS ASSOCIATES
2125 Center Avenue
Fort Lee, NJ 07024
Telephone: 201-461-0206   Telefax: 201-461-0765
Jeanine Careri, Director of New Products
    Character Products   Crafts, Kits & Supplies
    Pogs   Stickers

MINAMI INTERNATIONAL CORPORATION
4 Executive Plaza
Yonkers, NY 10701
Telephone: 914-969-7555   Telefax: 914-965-3461
Nori Juba, Product Manager
    Christmas Products   Halloween Novelties
    Novelties

MUSEUM PIECES CORPORATION
121 East 2nd Street
Mineola, NY 11501
Telephone: 516-759-3940   Telefax: 516-759-4179
Stephen Bernhardt
    Dolls, Collector   Doll Accessories

MUSEUM PRODUCTS COMPANY
84 Route 27
Mystic, CT 06355
Telephone: 203-536-6433   Telefax: 203-572-9589
John Bannister, President
    Books-Coloring   Crafts, Kits & Supplies
    Educational Toys & Games   Games, Board & Card
    Kites and Windsocks   Magic Sets
    Model Kits   Puzzles
    Science Kits

NATIONAL LATEX PROD. CO.
246 E. 4th Street
Ashland, OH 44805
Telephone: 419-289-3300   Telefax: 419-289-1889
Ross Gill, President
    Backyard Play Equipment   Balloons
    Balls   Crafts, Kits & Supplies
    Novelties   Premiums & Promotional Items

NEW TECH SPORTS
7208 McNeil Drive #207
Austin, TX 78729
Telephone: 512-250-0485   Telefax: 512-250-7127
Tim Miller, Sales Manager
    Kites & Windsocks

NYLINT TOY CORP.
1800 16th Avenue
Rockford, IL 61104
Telephone: 815-397-2880   Telefax: 815-397-7845
Mark McCall, Design Director
    Airplanes & Accessories   Animals & Figures (Hard)
    Battery-Operated Toys   Cars & Trucks
    Character Products   Construction Toys & Sets
    Educational Toys & Games   Electronic Toys
    Magic Sets   Mechanical Toys
    Model Kits   Science Kits
    Wooden Toys

OHIO ART COMPANY, THE
1 Toy Street
Bryan, OH 43506
Telephone: 419-636-3141   Telefax: 419-636-7614
Danielle Childs/Chet Dahl, Product Manager/Vice President,
Marketing

Athletic Products	Balloons
Balls	Battery-Operated Toys
Bubbles & Sets	Chalk & Chalkboards
Character Products	Computer Software
Construction Toys & Sets	Creative Activities
Electronic Toys	Musical Toys & Instruments
Paint Sets	Rubber Stamps
Sports Toys	Stickers

OLMEC TOYS, INC.
2408 Ownby Lane
Richmond, VA 10010
Telephone: 800-677-6966
Joanne Hansen, General Manager

Action Figures & Accessories	Books-Coloring
Books-Word/Picture	Character Products
Construction Toys & Sets	Crafts, Kits & Supplies
Dolls, Collector	Dolls, Fashion
Doll Accessories	Educational Toys & Games
Games, Board & Card	Games, Electronic & Video
Infant Toys	Mechanical Toys
Play Cosmetics & Make-up	Premiums & Promotional Items
Pre-School Toys & Playsets	Puzzles

ONTEX ELECTRONICS LTD.
9211 Beatty Drive
Sacramento, CA 95826
Telephone: 916-368-0206   Telefax: 916-368-0277
Benny Kwong   R/D Manager

Battery Operated Toys	Clocks and Watches
Construction Toys & Sets	Educational Toys & Games
Electronic Toys	Games, Action & Skill
Games, Adventure	Games, Board & Card
Games, Electronic & Video	Infant Toys
Mechanical Toys	Musical Toys & Instruments
Pre-School Toys & Playsets	Puzzles
Remote Control Toys	Science Kits
Stuffed Toys	Wooden Toys

246

OWI INC.
1160 Mahalo Place
Compton, CA 90220
Telephone: 310-638-4732   Telefax: 310-638-8347
Craig Merck, Vice President, Marketing

Battery Operated Toys	Construction Toys & Sets
Crafts, Kits & Supplies	Educational Toys & Games
Electronic Toys	Mechanical Toys
Model Kits	Remote Control Toys
Robots	Science Kits

OZ INTERNATIONAL
1601 -A Dover Highway, P.O. Box 637
Sandpoint, ID 83864
Telephone: 208-263-7756   Telefax: 208-263-7757

PACE DESIGNS
P.O. Box 162
Skokie, IL 60076
Telephone: 708-675-3656   Telefax: 708-625-8508
Sherwin Katz, President

Books, Coloring	Books, Word/Picture
Character Products	Christmas Products
Crafts, Kits & Supplies	Crayons & Markers
Stickers	

PARADE STREET MARIONETTES
3800 San Rafael Avenue
Los Angeles, CA 90065-3225
Telephone: 213-221-1377   Telefax: 213-221-4123
Donald Battjes, Division Vice President
    Puppets & Marionettes

PARKER BROTHERS GAMES
50 Dunham Road
Beverly, MA 01915
Telephone: 508-921-3182   Telefax: 508-921-3066
Thomas Dusenberry, VP-Business Development
    Bubbles & Sets

PATCH PRODUCTS, INC.
2944 Graybill Drive
Beloit, WI 53511
Telephone: 608-362-6896
    Puzzles

PECK GANDRE
3453 South West Temple
Salt Lake City, UT 84115
Telephone: 801-467-6400   Telefax: 801-467-6477
Linda Peck, President

Books & Cassettes	Books, Coloring
Books, Word/Picture	Crayons & Markers
Dolls, Collector	Dolls, Fashion
Doll Accessories	Educational Toys & Games
Games, Board & Card	Paint Sets
Puzzles	Stickers

PETRICK'S SALES, INC.
1116 Honey Court, P.O. Box 477
De Pere, WI 54115
Telephone: 414-337-9773   Telefax: 414-337-6619
Joe Kastenmeier, Sales Manager

Animals & Figures (Hard)	Athletic Products
Backyard Play Equipment	Balls
Construction Toys & Sets	Crafts, Kits & Supplies
Educational Toys & Games	Games, Action & Skill
Novelties	Premiums & Promotional Items
Wading Pools & Summer Toys	

PLAY IT SMART PRODUCTS (PUFFIN CORP.)
12221 Sam Furr Road
Huntersville, NC 28078
Telephone: 704-892-4263   Telefax: 704-892-4263
Alan Cone, President

Educational Toys & Games	Games, Action & Skill
Games, Adventure	Games, Board & Card
Games, Trivia	

PLAY VISIONS
1137 N. 96th
Seattle, WA 98103
Telephone: 206-524-2774   Telefax: 206-524-2766
President

Airplanes & Accessories	Animals & Figures (Hard)
Balls	Battery-Operated Toys
Crafts, Kits & Supplies	Educational Toys & Games
Electronic Toys	Games, Action & Skill
Horses, Hobby, Rocking	Novelties
Premiums & Promotional Items	Puzzles
Science Kits	

PLAYING MANTIS
805 Wolfe
Cassopolis, MI 49031
Telephone: 616-445-2413   Telefax: 616-445-8772
Thomas E. Lowe, President

Action Figures & Accessories	Backyard Play Equipment
Balls	Battery Operated Toys
Cars & Trucks	Games, Action & Skill
Games, Adventure	Games, Board & Card
Model Kits	Puzzles
Remote Control Toys	

PLAYMATES TOYS, INC.
16200 Trojan Way
La Mirada, CA 90638
Telephone: 714-739-1929   Telefax: 714-739-2912
Sharon Bowman, Business Affairs

Action Figures & Accessories	Airplanes & Accessories
Animals & Figures (Hard)	Battery-Operated Toys
Cars & Trucks	Character Products
Computer Software	Costumes & Masks
Dolls, Fashion	Doll Accessories
Electronic Toys	Games, Action & Skill
Guns	Housekeeping & Cooking Toys
Mechanical Toys	Novelties
Play Cosmetics & Make-up	Remote Control Toys
Robots	Stuffed Toys

POCKETS OF LEARNING
31-G Union Avenue
Sudbury, MA 01776
Telephone: 800-635-2994   Telefax: 800-370-1580
Kyra Silva, Product Coordinator

Christmas Products	Dolls, Fashion
Educational Toys & Games	Infant Toys
Puppets	Stuffed Toys

POOF TOY PRODUCTS, INC.
45605 Helm Street, P.O. Box 701394
Plymouth, MI 48170-0964
Telephone: 313-454-9552   Telefax: 313-454-9540
Doug Ferner, Vice President

Airplanes & Accessories	Athletic Products
Balls	Battery-Operated Toys
Character Products	Christmas Products
Educational Toys & Games	Foam Toys
Novelties	Pre-School Toys & Playsets

PROCESSED PLASTIC COMPANY
1001 Aucutt Road
Montgomery, IL 60538
Telephone: 800-323-6165   Telefax: 708-892-6056
David Plotnick, Marketing Director

Airplanes & Accessories	Athletic Products
Backyard Play Equipment	Banks
Battery Operated Toys	Bubbles & Sets
Cars & Trucks	Construction Toys & Sets
Doll Accessories	Furniture, Juvenile
Horses, Hobby, Rocking etc.	Housekeeping & Cooking Toys
Infant Toys	Play Cosmetics & Make-up
Pre-School Toys & Playsets	Riding Vehicles
Wading Pools & Summer Toys	

PRODUCT RESOURCES & DEVELOPMENT, INC.
P.O. Box 3828
Albany, GA 31708
Telephone: 912-878-6112   Telefax: 912-878-6106
Wayne Rich, President

Athletic Products	Backyard Play Equipment
Construction Toys & Sets	Educational Toys & Games
Games, Action & Skill	

PUFFIN CORPORATION, THE
P.O. Box 2002
Huntersville, NC 28078
Telephone: 704-892-4263
A. Cone, President

Educational Toys & Games	Games, Action & Skill
Games, Adventure	Games, Board & Card

QUINCRAFTS CORPORATION
300 Granite Street
Braintree, MA 02184
Telephone: 617-356-1650   Telefax: 617-356-4641
Debbie Sugarman, Vice President

Crafts, Kits & Supplies	Model Kits
Paint Sets	

RADIO FLYER, INC.
6515 West Grand Avenue
Chicago, IL 60635-3495
Telephone: 312-637-7100
Mark Pasin, Marketing Manager

Bicycles	Doll Accessories
Riding Vehicles	Wooden Toys

RAINBOW MARKETING LTD.
795 Office Parkway, Suite 215
St. Louis, MO 63141
Telephone: 314-991-1440   Telefax: 314-991-4254
Steve Rosen, President
    Games, Adventure   Novelties
    Science Kits

RICH FROG INDUSTRIES
84 Howard Street
Burlington, VT 95401-4815
Telephone: 802-865-9225   Telefax: 802-865-2423

RITVIK TOYS INC.
5151 Thimens
Ville Saint-Laurent, Quebec H4R 2C8, Canada
Telephone: 514-333-5555   Telefax: 514-333-7853
Brahm G. Segal, Director of IP & Legal Affairs
    Cars & Trucks   Construction Toys & Sets
    Doll Accessories   Educational Toys & Games
    Infant Toys   Magic Sets
    Mechanical Toys   Pre-School Toys & Playsets
    Robots   Trains

RTOY INDUSTRIES
7740 Luane Trail
Colton, CA 92324
Telephone: 909-370-2295   Telefax: 909-370-2293
Richard H. Anderson, President
    All

RUBBER STAMPEDE
P.O. Box 246
Berkeley, CA 95401
Telephone: 510-420-6800   Telefax: 510-420-6888
Sam Ratzen, President
    Character Products   Christmas Products
    Crafts, Kits & Supplies   Crayons & Markers
    Educational Toys & Games Halloween Novelties
    Novelties   Paint Sets
    Play Cosmetics & Make-up Premiums & Promotional Items
    Puzzles   Rubber Stamps

SAFARI LTD.
Box 630685
Miami, FL 33163
Telephone: 305-621-1000   Telefax: 305-621-6894
Doug Rubel, Vice President
   Construction Toys & Sets   Puppets
   Puzzles   Science Kits

SANDY DOLLS, INC.
3389-A S. Scenic/P.O. Box 3222
Springfield, MO 65808
Telephone: 800-607-2639   Telefax: 417-887-7327
BJ Nocera, Vice President, Marketing

SANITOY, INC.
1 Nursery Lane, P.O. Box 2167
Fitchburg, MA 01420
Telephone: 508-345-7571   Telefax: 508-342-5887
Richard Boucher, V.P. of Product Development
   Furniture, Juvenile   Horses, Hobby, Rocking
   Infant Toys   Inflatable Toys
   Pre-School Toys & Playsets   Stuffed Toys

SCHYLLING
P.O. Box 667
Ipswich, MA 01938
Telephone: 508-356-1600   Telefax: 508-356-5929
Jack Schylling, Owner
   Character Products   Educational Toys & Games
   Mechanical Toys   Musical Toys & Instruments
   Novelties   Paint Sets
   Puzzles   Science Kits

SCIENTIFIC EXPLORER
2802 E. Madison Street, Suite 114
Seattle, WA 98112
Telephone: 206-322-7611   Telefax: 206-322-7610
Susan Rives, Product Development
   Crafts, Kits & Supplies (Science Theme) Puzzles (Science & Nature)
   Science Kits

SHELLY ADVENTURES, INC.
55 Mercer Street
New York, NY 10013
Telephone: 212-941-1905   Telefax: 212-226-3227
Shelly Meridith, President
Character Products
Computer Software
Costumes & Masks
Doll Accessories
Novelties
Stuffed Toys
Clocks & Watches
Construction Toys & Sets
Dolls, Fashion
Educational Toys & Games
Premiums & Promotional Items

SILER/SILER VENTURES
3328 Lakeview Blvd.
Lake Oswego, OR 97035
Telephone: 503-635-6333   Telefax: 503-697-7123
Buzz Siler, President
Computer Software Games
Games, Board
Games, Action & Skill

STEIFF USA
200 Fifth Avenue, #1205
New York, NY 10010
Telephone: 212-675-2727

STRAIGHT EDGE, THE
296 Court Street
Brooklyn, NY 11231
Telephone: 718-643-2794
Amy Epstein, President
Educational Toys & Games

STROMBECKER CORPORATION
600 N. Pulaski Road
Chicago, IL 60624
Telephone: 312-638-1000
Kevin Alexander, Vice President of Marketing
Action Figures & Accessories
Balls
Bubbles & Sets
Chalk & Chalkboards
Construction Toys & Sets
Electronic Toys
Novelties
Trains
Wooden Toys
Airplanes & Accessories
Battery Operated Toys
Cars & Trucks
Character Products
Educational Toys & Games
Guns
Pre-School Toys & Playsets
Wading Pools & Summer Toys

STUFFINS INC.
31674 Center Ridge Road, Suite 2
North Ridgeville, OH 44039
Telephone: 216-327-1900   Telefax: 216-327-9396
Tony Byrd, Vice President - Creative
    Novelties   Stuffed Toys

SUN-MATE CORP.
8223 Remmet Avenue
Canoga Park, CA 91304
Telephone: 818-883-7766   Telefax: 818-883-8171
Research & Development Vice President
    Action Figures & Accessories   Airplanes & Accessories
    Animals & Figures (Hard)   Battery Operated Toys
    Character Products   Construction Toys & Sets
    Crafts, Kits & Supplies   Educational Toys & Games
    Mechanical Toys   Model Kits
    Solar Toys

SUPERTOYS USA
2145 Jacqueline Avenue
North Bellmore, NY 11710
Telephone: 516-785-0846   Telefax: 516-781-6860
Leo Hoffman, VP Marketing & Sales
    Action Figures & Accessories   Backyard Play Equipment
    Battery Operated Toys   Bubbles & Sets
    Cars & Trucks   Construction Toys & Sets
    Educational Toys & Games   Electronic Toys
    Infant Toys   Mechanical Toys
    Premiums & Promotional Items   Pre-School Toys & Playsets
    Remote Control Toys   Road Racing Sets
    Robots   Trains

T-N-T INTERNATIONAL INC.
3208 Greenleaf Drive
Waco, TX 76710
Telephone: 817-776-7850   Telefax: 817-776-1640
David Kidwell, President
    Construction Toys & Sets   Educational Toys & Games
    Furniture, Juvenile   Pre-School Toys & Playsets
    Wooden Toys

TABLETOYS, INC.
2500 Cont. Parkway, Suite P
Houston, TX 77092
Telephone: 713-956-9900   Telefax: 713-956-9905
Bruce C. Gilman, Chief Operating Officer
  Backyard Play Equipment   Chalk & Chalkboards
  Construction Toys & Sets   Educational Toys & Games
  Furniture, Juvenile   Mechanical Toys
  Road Racing Sets   Wading Pools & Summer Toys

TAKARA
230 5th Avenue, Suite 1201
New York, NY 10001
Telephone: 212-689-1212   Telefax: 212-689-6889
Toshi Sugimoto, Director
  Action Figures & Accessories   Animals & Figures (Hard)
  Battery Operated Toys   Cars & Trucks
  Character Products   Christmas Products
  Clocks & Watches   Dolls, Fashion
  Doll Accessories   Educational Toys & Games
  Electronic Toys   Games, Action & Skill
  Games, Adventure   Games, Electronic & Video
  Housekeeping & Cooking Toys   Infant Toys
  Musical Toys & Instruments   Novelties
  Play Cosmetics & Make-Up   Pre-School Toys & Playsets
  Remote Control Toys   Robots
  Stuffed Toys

TALICOR, INC.
190 Gentry Street
Pomora, CA 91767
Telephone: 909-593-5877   Telefax: 909-596-6586
Lew Herndon, President
  Educational Toys & Games   Games, Action & Skill
  Games, Adventure   Games, Board & Card
  Games, Electronic & Video   Games, Trivia
  Puzzles

TARA TOY
40 Adams Avenue
Hauppauge, NY 11788
Telephone: 516-273-8697   Telefax: 516-273-8583
Kris Lynch, Senior Director Product Development/Marketing

Action Figures & Accessories	Balls
Battery Operated Toys	Bubbles & Sets
Cars & Trucks	Character Products
Clocks & Watches	Crafts, Kits & Supplies
Doll Accessories	Electronic Toys
Guns	Mechanical Toys
Play Cosmetics & Make-up	Puppets
Remote Control Toys	Robots
Rubber Stamps	Science Kits
Stuffed Toys	

TARKO DOLLCO
100 North Main Street
George, IA 51237
Telephone: 712-475-2821
Michael Bathke, Director of Marketing

Christmas Products	Costumes & Masks
Crafts, Kits & Supplies	Dolls, Collector
Dolls, Fashion	Doll Accessories
Novelties	Premiums & Promotional Items
Puppets	

TC TIMBER/HABERMAASS CORP.
P.O. Box 42
Skaneateles, NY 13152
Telephone: 315-685-6660   Telefax: 315-685-3792
Scott Wisner, General Manager

Educational Toys & Games	Pre-School Toys & Playsets
Trains	Wooden Toys

TEDCO, INC.
498 S. Washington Street
Hagerstown, IN 47346
Telephone: 317-489-4527   Telefax: 317-489-5752
Jane Shadle, Sales Director

Educational Toys & Games	Science Kits

THAT'S ALL SHE STAMPED
P.O. BOX 32098
Cocoa Beach, FL 32932-0398
Telephone: 407-784-4930   Telefax: 407-784-4963
Philip Kean, Owner
    Rubber Stamps

Tiger Electronics, Inc.
980 Woodlands Parkway
Vernon Hills, IL 60061
Telephone: 708-913-8100   Telefax: 708-913-8118
Liane Czirjak, Vice President, Inventor Relations
    Computer Software   Electronic Toys
    Games, Electronic & Video

TOI
4532 Telephone Road, Suite 115
Ventura, CA 93003
Telephone: 805-654-0070 ext. 16 Telefax: 805-654-0235
Rod Cameron, Director of Marketing and Advertising
    Books & Cassettes   Bubbles & Sets
    Puppets

TOP TOYS INC.
3200 Union Pacific Avenue
Los Angeles, CA 90023
Telephone: 213-267-1888   Telefax: 213-267-4427
Nelson Chu, President
    Halloween Novelties   Novelties
    Stickers   Stuffed Toys

TORPEDO INC.
52 Park Street
South Paris, ME 04281
Telephone: 207-743-6896   Telefax: 207-743-2530
Henry R. Morton, Vice President Sales
    Athletic Products   Backyard Play Equipment
    Furniture, Juvenile

TOTSY MANUFACTURING CO., INC.
One Bigelow Street
Holyoke, MA 01040
Telephone: 413-536-0510   Telefax: 413-532-9804
Patricia Boissonneault, Director of Design and Development
    Action Figures & Accessories   Character Products
    Dolls, Fashion   Doll Accessories

TOY DREAMS INC.
200 Fifth Avenue, Room 509
New York, NY 10010
Telephone: 212-924-4470
Ted Ang, President

Athletic Products	Backyard Play Equipment
Games, Action & Skill	Novelties

TRANSNATIONAL TRADE
10900 N.E. 8th St., Suite 900
Bellevue, WA 98004
Telephone: 206-462-5795   Telefax: 206-643-2360
Mrs. Vilma T. Shakabpa, Executive Vice President

Christmas Products	Dolls, Fashion
Doll Accessories	Educational Toys & Games
Infant Toys	Sleeping Bags
Stuffed Toys	

TWO HUNDRED TOY INC.
745 Silver Hill Road
Milford, MA 01757
Telephone: 508-478-5531   Telefax: 508-473-7609
Bill Devlin, President

Battery-Operated Toys	Cars & Trucks
Clocks & Watches	Housekeeping & Cooking Toys
Mechanical Toys	Musical Toys & Instruments
Pre-School Toys & Playsets	

TYCO PRESCHOOL
1107 Broadway
New York, NY 10010
Telephone: 212-741-7222   Telefax: 212-620-8336
Stan Clutton, V.P. Marketing

Balls	Bubbles & Sets
Chalk & Chalkboards	Character Products
Crafts, Kits & Supplies	Crayons & Markers
Educational Toys & Games	Electronic Toys
Infant Toys	Inflatable Toys
Mechanical Toys	Paint Sets
Pre-School Toys & Playsets	Puppets
Puzzles	Remote Control Toys
Rubber Stamps	Stuffed Toys

TYMARC, INC.
1090 Bristol Road
Mountainside, NJ 07092
Telephone: 908-317-9099   Telefax: 908-317-9096
Jeff Menin, Marketing Director
     Chalk & Chalkboards   Crafts, Kits & Supplies
     Furniture, Juvenile   Horses, Hobby, Rocking etc.
     Model Kits   Pre-School Toys & Playsets
     Wooden Toys

U.S. GAMES SYSTEMS, INC.
179 Ludlow Street
Stamford, CT 06902
Telephone: 203-353-8400   Telefax: 203-353-8431
Anna May Wegbreit, Assistant to the Chairman
     Games, Adventure   Games, Board & Card
     Playing Cards

ULTIMATE MANUFACTURING, INC.
2905 Lake City Highway
Lake City, TN 37769
Telephone: 615-426-4447   Telefax: 615-426-7960
Margaret L. Justice, Sales Manager
     Educational Toys & Games   Pre-School Toys & Playsets

UNCLE MILTON INDUSTRIES INC.
5717 Corsa Avenue
Westlake Village, CA 91362
Telephone: 818-707-0800   Telefax: 818-707-0878
Frank Adler, Director of Marketing
     Animals & Figures (Hard)   Bubbles & Sets
     Cars & Trucks   Chalk & Chalkboards
     Construction Toys & Sets   Crafts, Kits & Supplies
     Crayons & Markers   Educational Toys & Games
     Games, Action & Skill   Games, Adventure
     Games, Board & Card   Games, Electronic & Video
     Games, Trivia   Novelties
     Pain Sets   Premiums & Promotional Items
     Pre-School Toys & Playsets   Robots
     Rubber Stamps   Science Kits
     Stickers

W.J. FANTASY
955 Connecticut Avenue, Suite 1305
Bridgeport, CT 06607
Telephone: 203-333-5212   Telefax: 203-366-3826
Joan Chickvary Cavanaugh, Founder/C.E.O

Books & Cassettes	Books, Word/Picture
Christmas Products	Educational Toys & Games
Puzzles	Advent Calendars

WATER STREET MATHEMATICS
2874 Creed Road, Box 16
Yorklyn, DE 19736
Telephone: 800-866-8228   Telefax: 302-234-3440
Amy Sellars, Product Manager
    Educational Toys & Games

WEX INCORPORATED
P.O. Box 1076
Drexel Hill, PA 19026
Telephone: 215-259-2266
Jean Wechsler, Vice President
    Novelties

WHOLE SYSTEMS DESIGN, INC.
P.O. Box 308, 5224 Mallow Trail
Lorton, VA 22079
Telephone: 703-550-7565   Telefax: 703-339-5012
Peter J. Weyland, President

Athletic Products	Electronic Toys
Games, Action & Skill	Games, Adventure
Games, Board & Card	Games, Electronic & Video
Games, Trivia	Puzzles

WING IT INC.
599 Franklin Avenue
Nutley, NJ 07110
Telephone: 201-667-8903   Telefax: 201-667-8903
Louis Scerbo, President

Action Figures & Accessories	Athletic Products
Backyard Play Equipment	Balloons
Balls	Character Products

WIZARD TOYS INC.
329 South Greeno Road
Fairhope, AL 36532
Telephone: 334-990-6667
Russ Fullmer, National Sales Manager & Product Manager

Animals & Figures (Hard)
Christmas Products
Premiums & Promotional Items

Character Products
Halloween Novelties
Pre-School Toys & Playsets

WONDER WORKS
234 Hancox Avenue
Nutley, NJ 07110
Telephone: 201-661-0068   Telefax: 201-661-0105
Christine O'Connor, President/Owner

Books and Cassettes
Books-Word/Picture
Construction Toys & Sets
Furniture, Juvenile
Infant Toys
Puppets
Wooden Toys

Books-Coloring
Christmas Products
Educational Toys & Games
Housekeeping & Cooking Toys
Pre-School Toys & Playsets
Puzzles

WOOD 4 PLAY
HCR 1, Box 180
Sciata, PA 18354-9723
Telephone: 717-992-3360   Telefax: 717-992-9071
Karen Stewart, Owner

Cars & Trucks
Horses, Hobby, Rocking etc.
Riding Vehicles

Furniture, Juvenile
Infant Toys
Wooden Toys

WORLD RECORD PAPER AIRPLANES
1270 Clearmont Street, N.E.
Palm Bay, FL 32905
Telephone: 407-724-6700   Telefax: 407-724-4267
Jeff Lammers, New Product Coordinator

Airplanes & Accessories
Books, Word/Picture
Construction Toys & Sets
Educational Toys & Games
Model Kits
Premiums & Promotional Items
Science Kits

Books & Cassettes
Computer Software
Crafts, Kits & Supplies
Kites & Windsocks
Novelties
Robots

Index

U

Utility patents, 24

V

V.A.T., 118

Video game market, 7-8

W

Waiver agreements, 65,
182-184

Warranties, 57, 94-95

Western Publishing, 8, 109

Titles of Interest from Kent Press

A Copyright Guide for Authors
   by Robert E. Lee

The Essential Guide to Merchandising Forms
   by Gregory J. Battersby & Charles W. Grimes

Licensee Survival Guide
   by Jack Revoyr

The New Complete "How To" Guide to Collegiate Licensing
   by Jack Revoyr

A Primer on Licensing, Second Edition
   by Jack Revoyr

The Toy & Game Inventor's Guide
   by Gregory J. Battersby & Charles W. Grimes

The Licensing Journal
   a monthly publication on licensing issues

The IP Litigator
   a bi-monthly publication on intellectual property litigation
   and enforcement

Toy Development Seminars

Kent Press periodically sponsors Toy Development Seminars directed toward toy company executives, toy inventors and designers, attorneys and marketing professionals. To receive information about these seminars, fill out this form and return to the address below.

Name: _____

Firm: _____

Address: _____

City: _____ State: _____

Zip: _____ Telephone: _____

Kent Press • P.O. Box 1169 • Stamford, CT 06904-1169
Telephone: (203) 358-0848 • Telefax (203) 348-2720